THE
DUFFY-STITH
FAMILY

From Arkansas Cotton Fields to Global Investments

Bernice Duffy Johnson and Siblings

NEWMAN SPRINGS PUBLISHING
320 Broad Street
Red Bank, NJ 07701

First originally published by Newman Springs Publishing 2022

ISBN 978-1-68498-154-0 (Paperback)
ISBN 979-8-88763-221-6 (Digital)

Printed in the United States of America

The Duffy-Stith Family book is dedicated to the memory of the following family members: our parents, Mr. Octavris C. Duffy (1903–1991) and Mrs. Leona Stith Duffy (1911–2011); our sister Everlee, who died in infancy in 1950; and our brother Henry, who died in 2005.

This book is also dedicated to the memory of our deceased aunts, uncles, children, grandchildren, cousins, nieces, nephews, and in-laws.

Our strength to produce this work comes from those who went before us, and for this we are grateful.

Contents

Acknowledgments

---·•·•·○·•·•·---

First, we give thanks to the God of our parents and foreparents who led and guided us from the darkness of ignorance to the light of knowledge. We were blessed with parents who taught us the meaning of life and the difference between right and wrong. We were blessed with parents who loved us enough to cause us to imagine beyond where we were to where we could be with the right attitude and tools of life. They dreamed the impossible dream and paved the way for those dreams to be manifest in the lives we lead today.

I am thankful for the kindness, patience, and encouragement of my husband, Larry, who quietly supported my efforts, suggested titles, commented on my chapter, and prayed for the success of this manuscript. I acknowledge the talents of our two daughters: Fatima, who designed the front cover, and Selena, who labeled numerous pictures, organized them, and developed a directory that enabled the successful electronic submission of the manuscript.

This book would not have been possible without the kind cooperation of my ten siblings: Spencer, Marie, Cora, Edna, Leona, O.C. Jr., Edward, Nancy, Mary, and James. They unanimously agreed in February of 2020 to write their chapters, provide photographs, and I agreed to put it all together. Although there were distractions and anxiety along the way, we managed to get it done. We reported on our progress in our monthly Zoom meetings, and some soon learned not to say they had written when they had not. I appreciate their help in trying to determine the title for our book. They came through, and we are pleased with the title we chose: *The Duffy-Stith Family: From Arkansas Cotton Fields to Global Investments.*

I am especially grateful to our sisters Mary and Marie, who took time to search for and send me many pictures that have truly enhanced the appearance of the book. I am thankful to have artists in the family of in-laws, Barbara Duffy, sister-in-law, and Lionel English, my son-in-law, who were able to sketch pictures of our first four homes from recollected descriptions and pictures of similar houses; these homes have since been destroyed. Their work certainly adds beauty and completeness to our chapters.

We are thankful for the advice on the publishing process from brothers Edward and Spencer, who have published their own books. The two chapters about our parents are taken, with permission, from Spencer's book *The Chinaberry Hill: Tidbits of My Life*. Some revisions and additions were made.

I appreciate all the help of friends and family who read drafts and provided feedback to make corrections, add emphasis, and improve clarity. I thank my editor, Ayana Hernandez, and typist, Selina Mumford, who transformed our challenging work into a beautiful masterpiece.

Introduction

This book is a compilation of stories of the lives of twelve Duffy siblings born to Octavris C. and Leona S. Duffy. One sibling, Everlee, died in infancy. We grew up in two small rural towns: Augusta and Cavell, Arkansas. At the time of our upbringing, the population of Augusta reached a high of 2,217. Both towns are in Woodruff County, which is in the northeast corner of the state. Augusta is located on the banks of the White River, with a beautiful beach that most of us did not know existed until we had left home and were grown. We grew up surrounded by farmland with crops of cotton, corn, soybeans, rice, sorghum, watermelons, and muskmelons. Many trees populated the area, including the black walnut, black gum, chinaberry, elm, hackberry, hickory, holly, oak, spruce, sumac, sweet gum, sycamore, weeping willows, wild cherry, and all kinds of fruit trees. Blackberry bushes and muscadine vines were also prevalent.

We grew up in poverty and lived in houses without running water and indoor toilets until we moved to town in 1960. We pumped water outside and brought it inside in two- and five-gallon buckets. We heated water on top of a wood-burning stove in the living room or on the wood-burning stove in the kitchen. Water was heated for baths, and then it was poured into metal tubs in the living room or bedrooms where bathing took place. We worked and did homework by lanterns and candlelight until 1956 when our cousin Helen Williams and her husband, Theodore, worked with the city to bring electricity down the road to the house in which we lived. We had no heat in our bedrooms so aside from the body heat generated by three to four of us sleeping in one bed, there were Mama's thick handmade quilts and blankets to keep us warm.

We chopped cotton, picked cotton and strawberries, husked corn, thrashed peas, and harvested sweet and white potatoes and peanuts. We cared for farm animals and cultivated gardens and groves. Transportation was by foot or wagon, in neighbors' cars, or an occasional bus that ran between Cavell and Augusta. The last five siblings enjoyed the convenience of a car before they left home.

We played typical children's games, such as baseball, softball, catch ball, Chinese and regular checkers, bingo, hide-and-seek, jumping rope, jacks, swinging, rolling down hills in twenty-gallon barrels, and sing-alongs. The girls played with dolls, many homemade, and the boys liked BB guns, trucks, and toy airplanes. Some years, there were tricycles and bicycles to ride—one for the whole crew, not one for each child.

Although the twelve siblings were born to the same mother and father and we have some of our parents' features, we are distinctly different in skin tones, hair texture, body build, and speech. None of us came away with the Southern twang some Arkansans have. In fact, we have been told many times that we speak "too proper."

All of us attended the same all-black elementary and high school located on what resembled a college campus with five separate buildings; there were no middle or junior high schools at that time. Our youngest brother, James, was the only sibling to attend an integrated high school. Each sibling experienced different treatment at school depending on where we landed in the order of birth. The oldest sibling, Spencer, left a legacy of academic excellence having made all As and Bs in his classes and graduated valedictorian of his class. He set the bar high, which meant that all who followed had to measure up to him, or we may be scolded at home and at school.

As the middle child, I had the best of two worlds. I learned from my six older siblings and was able to use that information and knowledge to lead, guide, and teach my younger siblings. I lived in four of the five homes we inhabited and can remember activities and behaviors that went on in each. In most of the houses, we did not have running water so the reliance on pumps and outhouses were the order of the day. We read and studied by light from kerosene lamps, lanterns, and candles. I remember when we finally got electricity and compared that to the candle and lamp lights—what a revelation! We really saw the light.

Yes, we grew up in the same community, with the same mother and father, yet each of us established and maintained a different relationship with our parents and each other. Our parents were not outwardly affectionate toward us, but there was no doubt that they loved and cared dearly for each of us. They did all they could for our well-being and sacrificed much so we would have the necessities of life. They were nurturing and mentoring parents and great teachers. They wanted a better life for us than they had. Therefore, education was the number one goal for each of us. In other words, there was no dropping out of school and no remaining at home after graduating from high school. The choice was clear: go to college or get a job.

The older siblings helped the younger siblings to find their way after high school and all of us were high achievers. Five of the siblings were valedictorians of their high school classes. Nine siblings went to a state, four-year Historically Black College and University (HBCU)—Agricultural, Mechanical, and Normal College (AM&N College) in Pine Bluff, Arkansas (now the University of Arkansas at Pine Bluff). Eight siblings finished at AM&N College, one started there, but transferred to Southern University in Baton Rouge, Louisiana, to obtain a bachelor's degree. One sibling went to a private HBCU—Philander Smith College in Little Rock, Arkansas. Two other siblings attended community colleges in Los Angeles, California.

At AM&N College, our family's name recognition also became a concern because Spencer again set the bar high, so we were known before we even arrived at college. And there too, we had to measure up. This was helpful to some but frustrating to others who wanted to make and leave their own legacy. However, we were all successful. Today, one sibling is an ordained and licensed clergy minister. Nine siblings earned bachelor's degrees. Eight siblings earned master's degrees, two earned doctorates, and one holds two honorary doctorates.

Henry died of a heart attack in 2005. His story was written by several siblings, principally Marie, the oldest girl who took care of him when he left Augusta and went to the big city of Los Angeles. His son, Henry Jr., contributed information from a child's perspective.

Edward's information was invaluable as he shared life with Henry in St. Louis, Missouri and they also shared their military experiences. Edna shared information about special times with Henry and Maria. Bernice contributed as the middle sibling who had an opportunity to interact with all her siblings and was the object of many of Henry's inventions and experiments.

Our aim in this book is to present each sibling's story as they tell it. In reading the different sibling's accounts, you may notice different relationships and sides of the same story. The accounts may not be congruent because of the times and places in which they occur. We grew up in contrasting times and different places and therefore experienced relationships with our parents and each other in unique ways.

We now live in six different states: four in Arkansas, two in California, and one each in Florida, Indiana, Maryland, North Carolina, and Ohio.

We had an exciting time writing the Duffy-Stith family book, although some probably disliked me for a time when they were trying to get their chapter together with a deadline pending. Yet we gladly share our stories with the hope that others may be inspired and led to write their own.

This book is an account of the lives of twelve siblings. Each one wrote his or her own chapter. The chapters were edited by Bernice and put together by Bernice. Each sibling participated in the organization and content outline of the book.

Grandparents

Mr. Henry Stith. Only Spencer and Marie remember our paternal grandmother. We have no memory of our paternal grandfather or maternal grandmother. They were deceased before we were born.

All of us remember Grandfather Stith, Mama's father. He was small in stature with straight black hair with little gray hair even at his death just shy of one hundred years in 1966. He would visit us from his home in St. Louis, Missouri, once or twice a year before his health began to decline. He would tell us stories of his travels and some from books he read. Grandfather Stith was the son of a slave and had a college education at a time when Black folks barely received a third-grade education. He was a very smart man.

Grandpa Stith would sit on the front porch and shoot squirrels from electric wires running from the house and never hit the wire. He often bragged about the educational attainments of Lee's (our mom) children. He was proud to see ten of the twelve finish high school before he died.

Spencer and Eliza Duffy—paternal grandparents

Henry Stith—maternal grandfather

Our parents, Mr. Octavris C. Duffy Sr. and Mrs. Leona Stith Duffy

Chapter 1

· • ◦ • ·

Daddy

Daddy was a God-fearing and hardworking skilled carpenter and farmer. He was a religious man with strong convictions about the way one should live. He was politically astute, and oh, what I would give to hear his commentary on the political climate in our world today. He was a strict disciplinarian and took care of our family against great odds.

Daddy was a strict disciplinarian with a drill sergeant's attitude. In fact, I do believe if he had been called to the military, he would have made master sergeant—no sweat. He would have been called to serve in World War II, but he was exempted because he had too many children to support. He ruled our house with bold and unquestioned authority. He took no mess from us, particularly the oldest. Spencer was the first child and a boy, and I guess Dad chose him to make an example out of for those who would follow. Daddy was outspoken and did not bite his tongue about his opinions or feelings. Tact was not his strong suit, and Daddy had a temper. He had a red mule named Shorty. Daddy said he had mustang in him. After a weekend of rest, Shorty would run around the lot and be difficult to catch and harness. One Monday morning, Shorty was determined not to be caught. Every time Daddy would get near him, he would take off. When Daddy finally caught him, he took him inside the stable (feeding barn) and beat him mercilessly then took him to the field and worked him all day. That broke Shorty from being difficult to

1

catch. From then on, Daddy could walk into the barn lot and say to Shorty, "Whoa," and Shorty would stop in his tracks.

Daddy was a good man. He was strong physically and blessed with good judgement. Daddy could sing. He had a strong, clear, and beautiful baritone voice. Our church, Jackson Chapel CME, was too small to have a choir. Daddy was the song leader for the congregation. Many times at home after work, Daddy would gather us around him and we would have a song fest. These were special moments for us, for in singing, we could see Daddy's more gentle side. Daddy was a natural leader. He became district superintendent for the Sunday School. This task required him to travel across the region to the various churches to do business. There were several times when Mama would need wood cut for the fireplace and kitchen stove while Daddy was away. Spencer was too small at that time to help Mama cut wood, so Mama would manage to cut enough to cook our meals. Daddy was active in the community. He became president of the Men's Federation in Augusta and held that office for more than two decades. He was a member of the NAACP, the Masonic Lodge, where he became a thirty-third-degree Mason and the Farm Bureau.

As with other farmers, Daddy spent most of his time tending the farm. In addition to the field crops that included cotton, corn, hay, and sorghum, we raised hogs, cows, and chickens. We also had a large garden plot in which we grew most of our vegetables. During the off season from late fall to early winter, Daddy spent a lot of time in the woods, cutting down trees for firewood for the winter months. Mama would worry a lot when Daddy would go to the woods. You see, felling large trees in the woods is tricky and dangerous because wind shifts can cause the tree to fall in a different direction or lodge in another tree. If it lodged, the other tree would have to be cut down. This complicated the situation and increased the danger. There had been terrible accidents in the woods. Men would get crushed by falling trees or would accidentally wound themselves, sometimes fatally, while felling trees or splitting the logs. Daddy was an expert woodsman. He never injured himself or Spencer. He could look at a large tree and tell you where it was going to fall. He would begin the felling operation by sawing a distance into the trunk of the tree on the falling side. Then next, he would hew out a notch above the saw cut. He then moved to the operation side of the tree and began sawing at an angle parallel to the notch on the falling side. If it were a very large tree, he would use steel wedges to tilt the tree in the direction of the fall as he sawed.

When Spencer was ten years of age, he became Daddy's helper. He purchased a single-blade axe and a one-man saw for him (Daddy used a double-bladed axe) and off to the woods they would go. Spencer learned to chop wood like an experienced logger. Daddy would cut down a large tree, and Spencer would trim off the branches, pile the brush, and they would stack the logs to be picked up with the wagon later that day or the next day if they stayed in the woods until dark. Spencer recalled the wood-gathering experience as one of their most difficult chores. The woods were wet, the weather was usually cold (sometimes they had to break through ice to get to the trees), and the logs were heavy. They wore heavy rubber (gum) boots and heavy socks to keep their feet dry. Wood cutting kept the body warm, but their feet after a while felt like they were freezing. Before long, the pain left, and the feet felt like two blocks of ice. Spencer was proud to say that by the time he reached eighteen, he could cut wood as well as Daddy. The woodsman skills Daddy taught him served him very well during the twenty-five years that he owned and operated Duffy's Landscape Service in Washington, DC.

Except for work-related matters, Daddy talked very little with us children. Perhaps we were afraid to ask him questions about things because of the way we thought he might respond. We would confide in Mama any concerns we had, and she always took time to listen to us and give freely her wise counsel and advice. After we left home for college and would return home for the holidays or semester break, Daddy would sit with us on the front porch and talk a while. However, most of us never really developed a free and open line of communication with our daddy. An exception would be brother O.C. and sisters, Cora and Mary.

Daddy and our family left the farm in 1960. We had talked about the steady decline in sharecropping and how difficult it was to make it as a small farmer, particularly if you did not own your farm. During that time, mechanization was rapidly reducing the need for manual labor, and the large farms were buying out the small farmers to increase their acreage. Much to Mama's and our regret, Daddy never expressed interest in buying a farm. Mama tried several times to persuade Daddy to buy a small farm but to no avail. Shortly after Spencer entered the military, Daddy moved our family to town in Augusta. Being a single person, Spencer had no real need for his military pay, so he sent his allotment to Daddy to help pay for the house. By the time Spencer got out of the military, Daddy had paid for the house. It was a good house but needed a lot of repairs, and Daddy had good carpentry skills. He practically rebuilt the inside of the house and replaced major support beams for the foundation. He painted the exterior and put on a new roof.

Daddy did show signs of love and care for us in his own ways. I remember times when we were hired by other farmers to chop and pick in their cotton fields. Daddy would help us along so that we were all at about the same place or length on the rows of cotton. I was so afraid of chopping up all the cotton plants that I took too much time manicuring one stalk. I was never good at chopping cotton. I did much better with picking because you did not have the "keeping up with everyone" factor; you just had to fill up the cotton sack.

Daddy also showed compassion toward us during the winter months when the weather was extremely cold. We did not have heat in our bedrooms, and during the night when the temperature dropped below freezing, Dad would ease into our rooms and place large handmade quilts Mom had made on us to keep us warm.

He was proud to show us off in Sunday worship services. We would parade up to form the choir and recite speech after speech with clarity and presence, especially for Easter, Children's Day, Thanksgiving, Black History Month, Education Sunday, and Christmas.

Daddy made sure we did our homework, and there was no playing games or sports until all homework assignments were completed.

Daddy was wise in his counsel and would interpret words, phrases, and scenes on television shows which we were allowed to watch. These included the following: *Amos 'n' Andy*, *The Andy Griffith Show*, *Perry Mason*, *Gunsmoke*, *Bonanza*, *The Waltons*, *Little House on the Prairie*, *Hee Haw*, *Julia*, *To Tell the Truth*, Edward R. Morrow, and *60 Minutes*. His political views were publicly shared, and he had difficulty understanding why many people's views were so far left of his.

Daddy was a deeply religious man. But when he left the worship service and went to a business meeting of the church, his demeanor changed. He would call people out of their names, criticize the treasurer if the money count seemed off by his count or did not tally correctly, and get impatient with folks who talked a lot with little substance. He called one woman "goat headed" and another one "pitiful." Mama would be embarrassed and quietly say to Daddy, "Mr. Oct, you should be ashamed of yourself, you know better." Then she would try to comfort those whose feelings were hurt.

On other occasions, Daddy would sit on the front porch and watch people walk by. If someone walked by and did not speak to him or greet him in some way, he would say, "They don't have good sense. You see anybody who walks by another's house and don't speak is just stupid, with no home training." He was especially hard on teachers who happened to walk by on their way home from Carver High School. He called them "educated fools."

But overall Daddy's love for his family, friends, and the community could be summed up in his active work of helping widows and orphans and families. He gave wise counsel to young men in the community especially those who had lost their way in life. After Dad died and Mom was living alone, those young men protected her, and nobody bothered Mrs. Duffy. Daddy repaired homes, shared food, and single-handedly maintained the buildings and grounds of Jackson Chapel CME church. He always paid tithes and offerings regardless of hardships he often faced with failing crops and inclement weather conditions. Quite often, Daddy paid the church's utility bills and supplied wood for its wood burning stove.

He and Mom provided for the family and made sure we all took advantage of all educational opportunities available to us through Carver Elementary and High Schools and the Augusta community. At this writing, the homeplace has burned down and our brother O.C., who has a construction firm, is going to rebuild it for his daughter and her family. While in Augusta, Daddy worked for the city maintenance department. He later took a job as the groundkeeper for the Quiet Cemetery on the outskirts of Augusta.

He worked there until his health failed. Daddy lived to be eighty-eight years of age. He died in 1991 and is buried in the cemetery he so proudly kept for many years.

Our mother, Mrs. Leona Stith Duffy

Chapter 2

· • · ○ · • ·

Mama

Mama was a sweet, quiet, soft spoken, gentle, and bright woman. She was cool, calm, and collected with a quiet yet assertive demeanor when necessary. The love she had for her family was irrefutable.

Mama had a way of correcting us without scolding, chastising, without hostility, yet with enough firmness that we understood, she was not playing with us. She loved all of us unconditionally. Intellectually, we believed she was the brightest of us all. Although academically some of us attained the highest degree in education, our Mama could run circles around us in common knowledge of science and literature and the Bible. She could not remember when she learned to read but tells the story of how she just picked up one of her siblings' textbook one day and began reading it. They did not believe she was reading it but parroting what she had heard from them as they read their books aloud. They put her to the test: they got a book she has not seen, opened it near the middle, gave it to her, and said, "Now read." Mama took the book and read the full page. They were astonished. Mama finished the ninth grade, which was the highest grade at her school at the time. After she raised her family of thirteen children, she returned to high school under the senior's program and graduated as an A student at the tender age of sixty-four with two of her sons, O.C. Jr. and Edward.

Mama had a way with children, even the unruly ones. She connected with them in a unique way. She had a way of calming them by sitting them down and listening to them and speaking words of wisdom to them, words many carried with them during their lifetime.

After we moved back to Augusta after having lived on a farm for about eight years, Mama worked in a daycare center, and she did domestic work for several White families. One of the women she worked for, Mrs. Gregory, believed our family's story was so unusual that she called a journalist (Mr. Joseph A. Blank who at that time worked for *Reader's Digest*). Mr. Blank came to our 1976 family reunion, interviewed all the family members, wrote the story, and published it in the July 1977 issue of *Reader's Digest*. The article was titled "An American Family." We believe if Mama had been given the opportunity to pursue a professional teaching career, she would have been a master teacher in elementary and secondary education. She did a masterful job of teaching us the difference between right and wrong, social etiquette, history, ethics, philosophy, the Bible, the meaning of life, how to learn, and how to plan for a future career beyond the cotton fields of Augusta, Arkansas. Her teaching skills are manifested in the professional careers and homelife of her children. Eleven of whom are living at the writing of this manuscript. Out of the twelve children who lived to adulthood, seven—five girls and two boys—were/are professional educators. Three brothers are scientists, one a college professor; therefore, he is an educator also.

Although we paint Mama as sweet and easygoing, she could be tough. One time when Daddy was away on church business, she saw a man chasing our chickens. The man who looked like one of our neighbors had a rifle. Mama calmly went into the house, got Daddy's shotgun, and walked in plain view of the would-be chicken thief. When the man saw Mama with the shotgun, he quickly turned and headed into the woods as if he was merely hunting wild game.

We had never seen Mama fire a gun, but if the man had aimed his gun at one of the chickens, Mama would have at least fired over his head. Spencer recalled another time when Daddy was away, and we ran out of firewood for the stove in the kitchen, which was used for food preparation. Daddy usually had plenty of firewood cut to last in his absence since the children at home were too small to cut wood. He had left plenty of logs at the wood pile on the side of the yard. But none were cut and split into firewood and stove wood. So Mama, who at the time was five feet one inch tall and barely weighed one hundred pounds soaking wet, got Daddy's double-bladed axe and one-man saw, went to the woodpile, picked out a good-sized log, sawed it into stove length pieces, and split them into perfect stove wood. Spencer had never seen Mama use a saw or axe but was truly amazed and astonished at her strength. He helped her bring the wood into the house and sat down and watched her prepare the dinner meal.

In addition to keeping house, keeping us clean and under control, Mama found time to help us work in the field, even when pregnant. She would rise at dawn, fix breakfast for Daddy and us, (Daddy had a special breakfast which included foods we did not have), wash the dishes, and work with us in the field until a couple of hours before dinner (we now call this meal lunch). She would ring the bell to call us to dinner around noon. After washing the dinner dishes (this was before the girls were old enough to help with household chores), she would join us again in the field and work until about quitting time. We would all come home from the fields, but Mama did not rest. She went right to work and prepared a supper, which we now call dinner, which consisted of pork or chicken and plenty of vegetables from our garden.

She and Daddy would talk for a while, and if we kids did not have any homework, we would get ready for bed. Mama's health was excellent. Except for pregnancy, we do not recall her being sick until the time she was hit by a car while crossing the street after coming from a church meeting in town. She was taken to the hospital but came home that same night. We took care of her until she recovered. She also has an accident with a pressure cooker while cooking a hen. The pressure cooker was deep, and the hen had to be lifted out with a pair of large tongs. Somehow, while lifting the hen from the cooker, the tongs slipped and the hot pan with the chicken in it emptied onto Mama's foot. Her foot and ankle were severely burned. She dressed her foot and ankle with grease and leaves from a weed that grew in the fields. She did not go to the doctor who ran a clinic in town. Perhaps because she knew how to treat herself or because the clinic was segregated. At that time, the Black patients had to wait in a separate small room on one side of the clinic while White patients were being seen. If a White patient came in while a Black patient was being seen, the doctor would hastily finish with the Black patient and go to attend the White patient, although several Black patients would have already waited for a while. The nature or severity of your medical condition did not matter. Mama stayed in bed for a couple of days. There were just three of us then and our cousin Gloria Dean who lived with us was old enough to carry out the housekeeping chores while Mama rested. Before long, Mama was back at her post as full-time mother and wife.

Most of Mama's children had four or fewer children. We all marvel at how Mama was able to stay in good health, keep her sanity, and manage to keep all of us under control and getting along with each other for all those years. Mama was always at home during the time of the first five children. But we remember one time when she went away. It was when her brother Uncle Jimmy was shot in St Louis. Gloria Dean again took over the household chores. Those of us big enough to help pitched in and helped as best we could. Daddy, although appearing to be tough, seemed troubled and sad during Mama's brief absence. In a few days, Uncle Jimmy died, and Mama returned home. Uncle Jimmy was a kind and gentle man. He had visited us only a few times before his death. We were grief-stricken at his passing.

As the family increased, so did the work for Mama and Daddy. But by the time the oldest left home, the youngest was not yet born but would come a year later. Now Mom had seven girls old enough to assist with housework, and Daddy had three sons to help on the farm. The girls took turns with housecleaning and food preparation and working in the fields and Mama spent time teaching them the skills of food preparation and clothing construction and repair. She taught us how to can fruits, vegetables, and meats and to make jellies and jams. We learned to churn milk and make butter. Mother made homemade yeast rolls that would melt in your mouth and a desert called butter roll that none of her children came close to making.

Mama and women from the community made quilts for our family and others, and some of those quilts are still in use today.

Every one of us left home upon graduating from high school, so Mom and Dad were alone in the homeplace for several years. However, four siblings remained in Arkansas and were able to visit them frequently.

After Daddy died in 1991, Mama lived independently in the homeplace until she was well into her eighties. When home got to be too much for her, she moved into a senior citizen's apartment in Augusta, where she lived happily for several years. After she wandered away from home and could not find her way back, it was determined that she should no longer live by herself. That is when she went to live with our sister Cora in Little Rock, Arkansas. Cora took great care of Mom and traveled with her to her relatives across the state of Arkansas and those in St. Louis, Missouri. Cora made sure she attended church regularly. She started working crossword and other word puzzles which kept her mind sharp and engaged. As Cora's work became more demanding, requiring lots of in and out of state travel, Mama made her last move to Forrest City, Arkansas, to live with our sister Nancy. Mama continued to work puzzles and read her Bible daily. She had no substitute for God's word as recorded in the scriptures. When Mom was living alone in Augusta and when she was living with Cora and Nancy, the other siblings called her, wrote letters, sent cards, and visited her. Our brother Spencer wrote to her at least once a month and visited her every year on her birthday. Nancy hosted several birthday celebrations for Mom, including her one hundredth birthday where all siblings attended, and Mom received her letter from then President Barack Obama recognizing her milestone birthday as a centenarian.

We were blessed to have had our mother with us for one hundred years, to listen to her words of wisdom and seek her wise counsel. She taught us that we were no better than anyone else and no one else was any better than we were. She taught us to put God first in our lives, and we will not go wrong. She taught us to be courteous and kind to all people and to help those who were less fortunate than we and to respect our elders.

THE WHITE HOUSE
WASHINGTON

Happy 100th Birthday! We wish you the very best on this momentous occasion.

You have witnessed great milestones in our Nation's history, and your life represents an important part of the American story. As you reflect upon a century of memories, we hope that you are filled with tremendous pride and joy.

Congratulations on your birthday, and may you enjoy many more happy years as a centenarian.

Sincerely,

Michelle Obama

First house we lived in Augusta, Arkansas, which burned in 1952.
Artist, Barbara Duffy

The house we moved to after the first house burned
and stayed there for about one year.
Barbara Duffy

The third house we lived in for about two years
before we moved to the Red House.
Lionel A. English

The Red House we lived in from 1954 to 1960 in Cavell,
Arkansas, which is about seven miles from Augusta.
Barbara Duffy

Jackson Chapel, Christian Methodist Episcopal Church

Chapter 3

The First Child— Spencer Lee Duffy

Hello, everybody. I am Spencer Lee Duffy, firstborn of the late Octavris (O.C.) and Leona Stith Duffy. I came into this world early in the morning of October 25, 1934. My birthplace was a three-room shotgun house on the Jelks farm about ten miles northwest of Augusta, Arkansas. We moved from the Jelks Farm before I was three years old. From the Jelks Farm, we moved to the Clark Farm, about seven miles north of Augusta, Arkansas, on the banks of Cypress Creek. The Clark Farm was owned by an African American named Jim Clark. His name may have been James, but everybody called him Jim. The land on the Clark Farm was rich and crop yields were good. However, because it was low land, it sometimes flooded. This caused Daddy to struggle to get the cotton and corn crops planted in time for the fall harvest. What's more, the land was infected with snakes. In the spring when Daddy would list (plow) the ground in preparation for planting, he wore knee-high rubber (gum) boots to protect him from snake bites. He would stack the plowed-up snakes at the end of the turn row. Sometimes it would be a dozen or more snakes. My job, after coming home from school, was to gather the dead snakes and dump them into Cypress Creek.

Growing Up on the Farm

From the Clark Farm, we moved to the Deland Farm. It was larger than the Clark Farm and was located about a mile northeast of Augusta, Arkansas. The soil on the Deland Farm was sandy and rich. We raised cotton and corn. Yields were good, and we made enough money to carry us through the winter without borrowing from the company store. Success on the Deland Farm allowed Daddy to buy a new wagon and two draft horses (Maude and Bell). Also, from yields on the Deland Farm, I received a new Western Flyer bicycle for Christmas. This was one of the most joyous Christmases I remember.

Until I was about ten years old, I was Mama's shadow. I followed her wherever she went. I loved watching her wash our clothes, prepare our food, and keep our house clean. I did what I could to help. Mama appreciated my meager efforts, but I could tell my help was merely a token of appreciation rather than any meaningful assistance. Daddy would rise early in the morning to take care of the livestock and work the fields. He would return at dust dark. Mama and Daddy would talk a little while, and shortly, we were off to bed.

Mama is sweet, Mama is quiet
Mama is soft spoken, gentle and bright
Mama is cool, mama is meek
And her love is out of sight.

Mama has a way of correcting you without scolding, chastising you without anger, and loving you without condition. I sincerely believe Mama was the brightest one in our family, notwithstanding some of us have earned the highest degree in our chosen field of study.

Mama is sweet and easygoing, but Mama can be tough. I remember one time Daddy was away on church business (he was district superintendent for our church district), and we ran out of firewood for the kitchen stove. Daddy always had plenty of logs stacked in the yard, but this time, there were none cut up and split to fit the stove. I was too small to saw or split firewood. So Mama who weighed about one hundred pounds (soaking wet) calmly went and got Daddy's one man saw and his double blade axe, went to the wood pile, sawed several pieces, split them, brought them in the kitchen (I helped a little), and prepared our dinner. Now, I had never seen Mama pick up an axe or saw. I was astonished at her strength and skill.

Another time when Daddy was away, Mama saw a man in the field behind our house chasing our chickens (chicken thieves were common in farming areas at that time). Mama got Daddy's double-barreled twelve-gauge shotgun, which always stood in the front corner of our living room, walked out in plain sight of the would-be chicken thief. When he saw Mama with the shotgun, he quickly turned and ran deep into the woods. Now, I had never seen Mama handle or pick up a gun, but I honestly believe if the man had aimed at one of our chickens, Mama would have at least fired a warning shot over his head.

After our family moved from the farm to the city of Augusta (by this time, I was in college), Mama worked as a domestic assistant for several families in Augusta. While Mama was working for the Gregory family, Ms. Gregory started talking to Mama about our family. Ms. Gregory was so impressed by the things Mama said until she called her friend who was a journalist for *Reader's Digest*, Mr. Joseph A. Blank. Mr. Blank came down to Augusta from New York in the summer of 1976. He interviewed Daddy, Mama, and each sibling. He returned to New York and wrote our family story, and *Reader's Digest* published it in the July 1977 issue. It was entitled "An American Family."

Mama finished the ninth grade, which was the highest grade allowed for African Americans in Arkansas at that time. After raising thirteen children, Mama returned to Carver High School, adult education classes and graduated as an A student at the tender age of sixty-four with two of her sons O.C. Jr. and Edward.

School and Farming

By the time I reached the ninth grade, I decided I was going to college although I had no money to enter or pay for books and tuition. I was a serious student. I had a thirst for knowledge and enjoyed learning. My interest in courtship in high school was sparse. I had one girlfriend whom I met in the twelfth grade. I remember giving her my class ring upon graduation. By the time I graduated, I had made it to the top of my class. I graduated valedictorian for the Class of 1953 at Carver High School in Augusta, Arkansas.

Daddy had taught me everything I needed to know about farming. So I figured out a way to make money while carrying my responsibilities as Daddy's helper. I asked Daddy to give me a small plot of land to plant a garden. I would sell fresh vegetables from my garden to the town's people of Augusta. Surprisingly, he agreed but sternly warned me that I would be expected to carry out all my farming and household duties. So after I finished my chores, I would rush to weed and cultivate my garden until dark.

I was a member of the 4H Club, a youth group equivalent to the Boy Scouts for farm boys and girls. We worked on many projects in the 4H Club. Mr. Henry Smith, our USDA county extension agent, helped me construct a brooder (a small chicken house with a screened-in sun porch and a kerosene lamp for heat) designed for

18

growing broilers (frying-sized chickens). From the ninth through the twelfth grade, I raised broilers along with vegetables and sold them to the town's people of Augusta. I also sold the *Chicago Defender*, an African American weekly newspaper. My paper route covered a radius of about nine miles of dirt road. On Saturdays, after selling my vegetables and chickens, I would get on my bicycle and deliver the *Chicago Defender* to our neighbors. By the time I reached the twelfth grade, I had accumulated enough money to pay my college entrance fees at AM&N College (now the University of Arkansas at Pine Bluff). As fate would have it, about two weeks before graduation, our house burned to the ground, leaving me with only the clothes on my back. The money and all my earthly possessions went up in smoke. Although we lost everything, I was thankful that Mama, my cousin Gloria Dean, and the baby escaped without injury.

My Cousin James

During the summer when school turned out, my uncle Ishmael who lived in Chicago would sometimes bring his two children (James and Florida) to spend the summer with us. I would be so happy to see them. Although James Ellis was three years my junior, he was as big and as strong as me. Also, he was the only male near my age in our family. So I loved and treated him like a brother. He was curious about the country and farm animals. I took great pride in teaching him about the horses, cows, pigs, and chickens.

When we were not working in the fields, James and I would head to the woods, pick the tallest tree we could find, and climb our way to the top. I would shimmy my way to a strong limb. James would be right behind me. If we found a tree tall enough, when we reached the top, we could see the peaks of the Blue Ridge Mountains (a part of the Ozark Mountain Range). We thoroughly enjoyed the heights and sights. I taught James how to move from limb to limb and how to choose limbs that were not rotten and large enough to support his weight. Before long, we became expert climbers.

There was a peach tree in the cow pasture next to our yard. The tree was loaded with peaches. Some had fallen to the ground, and some hung low enough to be picked from the ground. As is commonly known, the best fruit is near the top of the tree. James fixed his eyes on several lush peaches near the top of the tree. I warned him about the small size of the limbs near the top of the tree, and if he chose a limb too small to support his weight, he would surely fall. I begged him to settle for some of the low-hanging fruit. He did not listen to me and proceeded to climb in hot pursuit of his prized peach. When he got in hand reach of the prized peach, he positioned himself in a standing position on a limb near the peach. I forgot to tell James that sometimes wasps made nests in fruit trees. Well, just as James reached for his prized peach, his head contacted a wasp nest. James began fighting the wasps with both hands while running on the limb like a squirrel. He turned around on the limb like a tight rope artist and headed toward the trunk of the tree. He almost made it but lost his footing and fell to the ground. James jumped up holding his head obviously in pain. I was laughing so hard, it was hard for me to gain enough composure to comfort him. When he got his breath, he shouted to me, "Why didn't you tell me there were bees in the tree." I told him that I did not know the bees were in the tree and that they were not bees but wasps that stung him.

James's head was beginning to swell. We forgot about the peaches and headed straight to Mama. I told her what happened. She just smiled, went and got some of Daddy's chewing tobacco, made a paste, and put it on James's head. Before long, the swelling began to go down. We went back to play but not near the peach tree. We had become excellent climbers. So we decided that trees near our home were not tall enough to satisfy our climbing skill. Now, White River Bridge is right outside of Augusta City Limits. So we decided to ride double on my bicycle to the foot of the White River Bridge and climb the superstructure to the top. Neither one of us could swim a lick, so I parked my bike at the guard rail of the bridge and began making my way to the superstructure. James was right behind me. I told James not to look down until we reached the top of the superstructure. White River Bridge is not a low bridge. The superstructure must tower one hundred feet above the river. We had almost reached the top railing when a tractor trailer, loaded with logs, came barreling across the bridge. I yelled to James to hold on and not to look down. The minute it took for the log truck to cross the bridge seemed like a lifetime. The superstructure convulsed and shook as if it was going to fall. After the log truck passed, I took a deep breath and told James to start descending down slowly. We forgot about the Blue Ridge Mountains and the scenery we hoped to see. We managed to get down to my bicycle safely. For the rest of the summer, we settled for climbing trees. I never told Daddy or Mama about our White River adventures, and I dared James to tell them or any of our siblings. It was our private secret, and it stuck.

Florida Mae, James' sister, spent most of her time playing. She and my siblings played and helped Mama with household chores. Sometimes she would watch with curiosity as James, and I went about our rough and tumble boyhood games. Florida Mae was a little girl with dimples. She was quiet and easygoing. She got along well with my younger siblings. It was always a sad day when Uncle Ishmael came to take them back to Chicago.

Enjoying Homelife and Chores

Sometimes during the growing season, it would rain, and we could not work the fields. So we would come home, go to our room, and play until suppertime. Daddy and Mama would be in the living/bedroom talking. Daddy was very strict about our behavior and decorum. When we got too loud, he would sternly warn us to calm down or he would come with his razor strap and whip us. So we would quiet down for a while, but soon, we would become noisy again. My being the oldest and a boy, Daddy expected me to set the example for obedience and behavior.

There were three girls born in sequence after me. As a result, there was always more girl toys than boy toys. So when I got tired of playing with my toys, I would gladly join my sisters and play with their toys.

As children of farmers, we all had chores. One of my chores was to stop by the mailbox and pick up the weekly *Kansas City Star* newspapers. The mailbox set on the side of Highway 33 about a half mile from our house. Sometimes we children would be laughing and playing, and I would forget to look in the mailbox on my way home. Most of the time, I would remember, turn back, and retrieve the paper. However, one time we were having so much fun, I forgot to turn back to get the paper. When Daddy got home that evening, he asked me if the *Kansas City Star* was in the mailbox. I replied, "No, sir." He looked at me strangely and said, "That's strange. The *Kansas City Star* always comes on Wednesday." For a moment, I really thought I had checked the mailbox on the way home. Wednesday night was the night for weekly prayer meetings at our church, which Daddy frequently attended. So on his way home from the prayer meeting, he looked in the mailbox, and behold there was within the *Kansas City Star*. Now, Daddy hated lies like God hates sin. If he caught you in a lie, you were severely punished. So that Wednesday night when Daddy got home from the prayer meeting, we were all in bed. I heard him open the door to our bedroom. My heart sunk. I knew he had looked in the mailbox and gotten the *Kansas City Star*. Without a word, Daddy pulled the cover back from my bed and began beating me unmercifully. He beat me until I fell off the bed onto the floor. As he left, he said, "Boy, don't you ever lie to me again"—and I didn't.

I remember the worst whipping I got. I was fifteen years old. Occasionally, we would have corn flakes for breakfast, usually on Sundays. Kellogg Corn Flakes Company had a special promotion. It consisted of a coupon placed in the box. When you accumulated enough coupons, with a few dollars you would mail them to Battle Creek, Michigan, and in return, you would receive a special ring that had a built-in compass on the top. I religiously saved coupons for several months until I accumulated enough to order my ring. I told no one about my plan or what I would receive. I wanted to surprise and excite my siblings. It took a long time for the ring to come. Finally, on the day it arrived, it rained, and we were at home. My siblings were busy playing when I walked in and asked them to gather around and see what I had received in the mail. They all were excited and filled with suspense. I carefully opened the box exposing my shiny silver ring with a glass bubble on the top under which was a compass which changed directions as you moved about.

So after I let them peek at my ring, I asked them to hold off a few minutes and let me enjoy the ring by myself. Well, one of my sisters could not wait. While I was savoring the beauty and utility of my beautiful ring, she grabbed my ring finger, tearing off the compass and destroying my ring. Instinctively, I recoiled and slapped her. She screamed as if I were murdering her. I heard Daddy get up and go for his razor strap. He came into the room, began beating me until I was prostrate on the floor, and left the room without uttering a word. When I gathered enough strength to get up, I said to myself, "Spencer, you must strive from now on to be at peace with your siblings and strive not to cross Daddy even if it meant taking the blame when I had been mistreated." From that day until I graduated, I was the coolest and most peaceful child in the family.

Leaving Home for College

Mr. Henry Smith, our county USDA extension agent, knew my circumstance and knew I was determined to go to college. So he asked me if I would be willing to work on the college campus over the summer to earn enough money to enter college in September. I replied without hesitation, "Yes, sir." Mr. Smith told me that he was going to the college that weekend and would talk to one of the professors in the Agriculture Department to see if I could be employed over the summer break. Summer jobs on campus were usually reserved for continuing students, so I realized my chances were small. Mr. Smith went to Pine Bluff and talked with Mr. O. R. Holiday, director of the Animal Husbandry Department. He told Mr. Holiday my condition and assured him if he hired me, I would be a good worker. I could not wait for Mr. Smith to return.

Finally, Mr. Smith returned and told me Mr. Holiday had agreed to hire me for the summer. I was simply overjoyed. I thanked him repeatedly and assured him I would work hard, obey my boss, and do a good job.

The next week, Mr. Smith came for me. I had my few belongings packed in a cardboard box. I had twenty-five dollars in my pocket. I said goodbye to Mama and my siblings (Daddy was not at home at the time), and we were off to Pine Bluff (about ninety miles from Augusta). Mr. Smith took me to the Agricultural Department to meet Mr. O. R. Holiday, the head of the Animal Husbandry Division. Mr. Holiday was a tall, dark, distinguished man. He greeted me warmly and asked me if I had any experience working with swine. I replied, "Yes, sir." I told him that I had worked with my father on the farm where we raised hogs, chickens, cows, and horses since I was ten years old. Mr. Holiday smiled and took me to the swine department complete with farrowing pens, feeding stations, storage sheds, and an abattoir (slaughterhouse). We returned to the campus. He showed me my room in the dormitory (other continuing students were staying there). I said goodbye to Mr. Smith and thanked him again for helping me. For the first time, I was on my own. It was hard to sleep the first night. I could not wait to start my first summer job. By the opening of college in September, I had saved enough money to pay my dormitory fees, tuition, and buy my textbooks. With exceeding joy, I entered my first-year class.

I worked part time while college was in session and full time during the summer break. After working for Mr. Holiday for about a month, I decided to organize the swine department. I did not tell Mr. Holiday my plan. First, I named all the adult hogs including the boar. Then I gave each of them a control number. I kept a record of the sow's (female) breeding dates and the number of pigs born by each sow. Mr. Holiday was overly impressed with my ideas and work. In fact, he told me he had drawn up a similar plan to be effective the next summer. I was delighted to know we shared similar ideas.

During my first year, I met Mr. J. M. Cheatham, the professor of agricultural engineering. He was a heavyset, light-complexioned, jolly man. He seemed to have a way of simplifying complex problems. Many times, on weekends, I would go to his home or to his farm in Homer, Louisiana, to repair fences and do other farming chores. Sometimes his lovely wife would invite me to have dinner with them. I remember at one dinner meal; she served a meat dish that looked and tasted like steak. Mr. Cheatham watched me as I enjoyed eating what I thought was beef steak. Finally, he asked me if I knew what I was eating. I replied, "Beef steak, of course." He smiled and said, "You are eating venison." He told me that he, not his wife, had cooked it. I was surprised. I complimented him and said, "Well, it is my first time eating venison and it is just as good as beef steak."

One summer, I worked for the campus postmaster Mr. Stevens. Mr. Stevens was an extremely focused man. He gave clear and specific instructions. Each day, I would drive Mr. Stevens' car to the post office in downtown Pine Bluff and pick up the campus mail. I was instructed to drive his car only to the post office, pick up the mail, drop it off at the college post office, and park the car in the space reserved for him. One time, I violated Mr. Stevens's rules. After a dance in the Student Union Building, I took Mr. Stevens's car along with my girlfriend for a trip down lover's lane.

I also met and worked for Mr. Alexander Haley, professor of soil conservation and the grandfather of Alex Haley the author of *Roots*. Mr. Haley allowed me to use his pickup truck to run errands back and forth between the campus and the college farm. Mr. Haley was a soft-spoken, easygoing gentleman. I remember over steering one day as I entered the campus gate and put a dent in his right rear fender. I was frightened. I thought he would chastise and fire me. When I told him I had bent the fender on his truck, he asked me how bad it was. I said it was not bad enough to affect the drivability of the truck. He said, "Okay, give me the details, and I will file an accident report." He said, "Be careful and go back to work." I apologized for the accident and thanked him for not firing me.

My college days were some of the happiest days of my life. Once I got familiar with the campus (class buildings) and my class schedule, I had no problem. I stayed on top of my class work and consistently made the Dean's list. My part-time work during the time when college was in session and my class work seriously limited my social life. My first real courtship began my junior year. By the time I reached my senior year, I became involved in campus politics.

I ran for and was elected president of the Student Government. President Lawrence A. Davis invited me to his office, congratulated me on my winning the presidency. He told me he was very much involved with student affairs on campus, and he expected me to inform him of any issues the students had about campus life. He said his office was open to me, and all I would have to do was call. Dr. Davis was one of the most congenial and stately gentlemen I have ever met.

One of the hallmarks of my administration was to greet the students as they ate breakfast each morning in the cafeteria. The dietitian was kind enough to allow me to use the public address (PA) system to say good morning, give the weather forecast, and invite anyone to my office if he or she had any issues to discuss with me. One of the main achievements of my administration was the ending of mandatory attendance of Sunday evening vesper services. This was possible only with the cooperation and understanding of President Davis.

Sometimes on semester break, I would hitch a ride with a friend, Floyd Worsham whose father owned a car that Floyd would occasionally drive to the campus. Floyd was from a little town McCrory, about twelve miles east of Augusta. He would pick me up on campus, drop me off in Augusta, and pick me up on his way back to the campus.

I had only a few girlfriends while attending college. Most of my dating was casual. During my senior year, I met and courted Bobbie, the girl who would become my first wife. We were married three years after my discharge from the US Army.

Shortly after graduation from college, I left Arkansas to seek employment and to move my draft board from Augusta to Saint Louis. I did not want to be drafted from Arkansas. I had been deferred from the military service under a special program, which allowed college students to remain in school if they made good grades and maintained good behavior. I had earned a bachelor's degree and did not want to go to the infantry. In Arkansas, if you were Black, regardless of your educational background, you would be drafted into the infantry.

While in Saint Louis, I lived with my Aunt Clytis Mae and Uncle Bill. Aunt Mae was a plump and friendly lady, deeply religious. She was known in the community as a lay minister. Uncle Bill was a quiet, proud, and stately man who knew Saint Louis like a walk around his house. When I wanted to venture out into some unfamiliar part of the city, I would ask him for directions. He took pride in telling me which streets and avenues to take and which direction to turn. I was impressed with his knowledge and accuracy. His directions were as good as any road map or GPS.

During my college career, I gave little thought to the military, although I knew I would have to go. I had fundamental problems about military service. I asked myself, why should I defend a country that supported prejudice, racism, Jim Crowism, and contempt for Black people? How could I defend a country that had enslaved my people and slaughtered them by the thousands? How could I serve in a military that fought to win freedom for nations abroad when I could not enjoy that same freedom here at home?

Well, by the time I graduated, I had constructed a rationale that allowed me to be mentally at peace when I took the military oath which states, "I am an American fighting man. I serve in the forces that protect our freedom and our way of life and I am willing to give my life in their defense." I silently added my addendum by saying to myself, "I fight not for what my country is today but for the hope of what it will become someday in the future. For by its constitution and its form of government, one day it will by necessity grant to all its citizens the blessings of freedom, liberty, and justice regardless of race, creed, or color."

I stayed in Saint Louis three months, knowing I would soon be called. I decided to get ahead of my "Uncle Sam wants you" letter. So I asked Uncle Bill for directions to the nearest Army Recruiting Station. When I arrived at the station, the officer greeted me warmly and asked how could he help me. I told him I would soon be called to the military and having earned a college degree, I felt I could serve my country better outside of the infantry. Surprisingly, he agreed. However, he said the only way to avoid being drafted into the infantry was to agree to serve three years instead of two. I thought about it for a while and finally agreed. The officer gave me a series of tests. I scored high in mechanics and intelligence. I chose the intelligence area.

My Time with Uncle Sam

I entered the military in August 1957. I completed my basic training at Fort Leonard Wood (Little Korea). I breezed through basic training without a hitch. I was awarded best recruit for my company, and I scored expert (highest rank) rifleman on the firing range.

After basic training, I was shipped to Ayer, Massachusetts (a place of which I had never heard), by train. We had sleeper cars which made the trip very pleasant. We arrived in Massachusetts mid-November 1957. I remember the weather shock when I exited the train. The temperature was in the midsixties when we left Fort Leonard Wood. When we exited the train in Ayer, Massachusetts, the temperature was in the low twenties. I knew at once I was in for a new weather as well as a new military experience. During that winter, temperature fell to thirteen degrees below zero, and sometimes snow drifts were six feet deep.

I spent six months training to be an electronic intercept operator. I joined the forces of the military intercept operations worldwide. My job required a top-secret security clearance (TSC). This clearance required an exhaustive background investigation by the Federal Bureau of Investigation (FBI). I had no idea what such an investigation entailed. However, the training officer informed me that upon completion of this investigation, the army would know more about me than I knew about myself. (I found this hard to believe.) He also said I would be handling highly classified information vital to the security of the United States, and that if I violated the TSC, I would spend ten years in Federal Prison and be fined ten thousand dollars. Finally, he said after completing my active military duty, I would be confined to the United States for ten years.

While in training, the FBI paid a visit to my home in Augusta, Arkansas. Now Augusta is a small rural town of about two thousand people. It was most unusual to see FBI agents roaming around. My parents were frightened when they pulled up to our house, identified themselves, and said they wanted to talk to them. My parents surely thought that I had gotten into trouble. The agents assured them that I was okay, and the background investigation was needed for the kind of work I would be doing, the details of which they could not divulge. When I came home, before being deployed overseas, my parents asked me why did I not tell them the FBI would visit our home. I told them I did not know they were going to visit Augusta or interview them. I assured them that everything was okay and the visit from the FBI was a part of the requirements to handle classified information for the military.

Compared to college, my military training was easy. We were training to use a typewriter-like machine called a mill. It looked like a typewriter except for two extra rows of keys. The hardest part for me was to reach the thirty-five-word-per-minute typing speed. You see, typewriters were not common in homes or schools in Augusta except in the school's secretary's office. As a result, I had no typing skills at all. So I had to work awfully hard to meet the thirty-five-word requirement.

After finishing my training in Massachusetts, I was given two weeks leave before deployment overseas. I headed straight to Saint Louis to visit my girlfriend and relatives. Then I headed to Augusta to see my parents, siblings, and friends. I was allowed to wear my Class A Uniform while on leave. My family was excited to see me in uniform. I was at my peak of physical and mental fitness and felt I could handle whatever my overseas duties required. My siblings had many questions about the army and what I would be doing. I limited my response to my basic training. I could not tell them anything about my specific duties because they were highly classified.

My leave time passed, and before long, I was headed to Seattle, Washington, where the transport ship, USS *Mann* was waiting to transport me and my buddies to Okinawa. I arrived in Seattle the day before departure. I went out to look at the ship that would take me the farthest distance I had ever been from home. The USS *Mann* was a big ship "twin stacker," longer than a football field. I had a small hawk-eye box camera. I backed away from the ship as far as possible but not far enough to get a full-length picture of the ship. The USS *Mann* carried both military and civilian personnel. Upon boarding, I gave my military orders to the receiving sergeant. He, after carefully inspecting them, assigned me to my quarters and placed my name on the duty roster (work list for details I would perform while enroute to Okinawa). The first day out was almost like a vacation for me. There was an outdoor movie theatre and a recreation room on the deck. I chose to go up and watch the movie. Charleston Heston was starring in *The Ten Commandments*. I had not seen this movie and was excited to see it free. I thoroughly enjoyed the movie. So I stayed on the top deck a while after the show. It felt good to relax and enjoy the cool night breeze and the smooth sailing of the USS *Mann* on the clear calm waters of the Pacific Ocean.

By the time I got ready to go down to my quarters for bed, I was surprised to find that many of my buddies were suffering from acute sea sickness. Our quarters echoed with grunts and groans from sick and vomiting soldiers and reeked with all kinds of most unpleasant odors. So I returned to the upper deck, found a comfortable chair, and slept for the rest of the night. Fortunately, I never got seasick.

Every morning after breakfast, which consisted of potatoes, eggs, and navy beans, the sergeant would ask us to line up and call the names of those who would be pulling details (work) for the day. The rest of us were free to go back to our quarters or just wander around the ship. Three days passed, and the sergeant had not called my name. I began to think something was wrong. Some of my buddies began to ask me where I was working. I told them I was assigned care of quarters (CQ) duties.

After four days passed, I concluded that somehow, my name had been left off the duty roster. Because there were about two thousand passengers aboard the USS *Mann* and about half of them civilians, I figured, with a little bit of luck, I could make the seventeen-day journey to Okinawa without doing any work.

So I decided to play the work schedule game to the fullest. Every morning, I would get up, get dressed, and fall out (line up) with the rest of my buddies. I would position myself near the back of the pack. When the last name for duty was called, I would quickly go up to the upper deck where the civilians hung out. It was quite easy to mix with the civilian passengers because we did not wear our military uniform except when we were pulling details (on duty). By the time we reached Okinawa, all decks and inner parts of the ship had been painted. I was lucky the seventeen-day trip from Seattle, Washington, was like a vacation. I made the entire trip without working one day. I did not tell my buddies about my fortune until we reached Okinawa.

While enroute to Okinawa, we stopped overnight in Incheon, Korea. Our ship docked beside another military ship that was headed back to the United States from Korea. I was shocked and surprised to see one of my college classmates yelling and waving violently at me.

He called me and said, "You lucky dog, Korea is hell." I waved back without a word. Little did he know that I was not headed to Korea but to Okinawa. Two days later, we arrived in Okinawa. I was struck by the beauty but amazed that I saw no trees. I later learned that all the trees had been destroyed by artillery fire from the big guns of World War II.

After four months in Okinawa, I was deployed to Taiwan where I completed the rest of my military active duty.

Taiwan is a beautiful island off the coast of mainland China. The people are friendly and curious about America. I spent a lot of time in the USO (United States Oversees). I was pleasantly surprised to learn that the University of Maryland had a satellite campus in Taiwan. I managed to visit the campus numerous times while off duty. I was surprised to learn that their textbooks were in English, and most of the students spoke fluid English.

My compound (workstation) was mostly underground. It was located up in the mountain about fifteen miles from Taipei, the capital city of Taiwan. It operated twenty-four hours a day, seven days a week, and three hundred and sixty-five days a year. We had three eight-hour shifts—the day shift, the swing shift, and the night shift. I dreaded the night shift because I found it difficult to sleep during the day. My unit electronically collected intelligence data from around the world, with emphasis on the east.

Once a month, we would get three days off. I would rent a bicycle and ride out into the countryside. Although I spoke very little Chinese and the country folks spoke little English, we managed to communicate. I was surprised to learn that most of the young ladies spoke English.

I finished my overseas tour of duty in January 1960 and flew back to the United States. I would not take a million dollars for what I learned and my experiences while serving in the army. However, I would not give a dime to have that experience again.

Walking with the King

After two years in Saint Louis, I decided to come to Washington, DC, to earn an advanced degree in biological science at Howard

University. This was the height of the Civil Rights Monument. I missed two opportunities to see Dr. King when he spoke at Cramton Auditorium. Then came the March on Washington in August 1963. I arose early that morning, went over to Sergeant Road, NE, and picked up my friend, and we drove to within a few blocks of Constitution Avenue and parked. It was a beautiful summer day. We began walking toward the Lincoln Memorial. The crowd thickened exponentially as we walked. By the time we were in shouting distance of the Lincoln Memorial, I found myself in a sea of humanity. I could not move except in the direction the crowd was headed. For the first time in my adult life, I felt helpless. I had no choice but to go along with the crowd. We stopped about a block from the reflecting pool in front of the Lincoln Memorial. A sea of people filled the mall all the way from the Lincoln Memorial to the West Capitol steps. Some ambitious young men perched themselves in the trees along the way. Dr. King's strong end eloquent voice boomed over the speakers. The crowd fell uncommonly silent and listened intently to every word of his most noted speech, "I Have a Dream."

I realized I was experiencing history in the making and that neither I nor any of those in this March would ever be the same. It was reported that two hundred thousand people attended the March. It was completely peaceful and no violence occurred.

Love and Marriage

They say love and marriage go together like a horse and carriage. Well, I don't know about that, but I do know that love is the only thing that can keep the horse and carriage together.

I was a late bloomer. My first serious relationship was in my junior year. I met and courted the girl who would later become my first wife. She was a first-year student, and I was a senior. We got engaged shortly before I graduated and got married three years later after I completed my military duty. There was no shortage of love between us. However, there were some things on which we just could not see eye to eye. I was a man on fire, full of energy and ambition. I had set a goal for myself: to accumulate enough wealth so I could retire at age forty-five. I was twenty-nine, and she was twenty-six when we got married. She was a good wife and mother. She was quiet and somewhat an introvert. Many times, rather than communicating her feelings, she would become silent. By the time I realized our marriage was in trouble, it was too late. She had given up on me. I was working and attending graduate school at Howard University. She "felt neglected and I was suspected of making whoopee."

Six months after I graduated from Howard University, I was employed by the United States Department of Agriculture (USDA) research service (ARS) as a plant physiologist (I believe the first African American). I worked in the Pesticide Regulation Division. My job included testing agricultural pesticides for efficacy and safety. One day while at work, my property owner called me, very upset, and said a U-Haul truck was backed up to my front door, and my family was moving out. I was shocked. I thanked him for calling me and assured him that I was not moving out and that I was on my way home. He said he would meet me there. I arrived about twenty minutes later only to find my house empty, except for a small card table and a bunk bed. I assured my property owner that I was not running out on him and that I would continue to be a good tenant. Our two children were three and seven years old, respectively. The pain of losing my wife compounded by the thought of losing my children made this experience the coldest days of my life.

After about two months, I got a call from my wife. She was in Atlanta, Georgia. Shortly afterward, she called me and said she wanted to come home. I sent for her and the children. She wanted to bring back the furniture. I told her rather than spend money on shipping, we would get new furniture when she returned. We tried to make up, but somehow, we had lost that lovely feeling. Our relationship was strained. We could not see eye to eye for our future. After about a year, she left again. We communicated sparingly. I told her I wanted her back home and that I could not long endure her running away with our children. I told her I would give her one year to decide whether she wanted to be my wife. I said to her, "If you do not return within one year, I will file for divorce." One year passed, she did not call or return, so I filed for divorce. We were married for ten years.

Someone said, "You learn as much from your failures as you do from your successes." Well, I say, you learn more from your failures than you do from your successes. In your successes, your heart, mind, and strength are tested. In your failures, your heart, mind, strength, and soul are tested. Your failures really show you the stuff of which you are made. On the other side of failure, you will be stronger and wiser, and you are less likely to make that same mistake again.

Then along came Barbara. She was one among the number of women I dated during the five years after my divorce. I had bought the house in which I was living. I was well set in my career as a research scientist. I had opened my landscaping business and was doing well. You may say serendipity brought us together. I had taken voice lessons from a lady two years earlier before Barbara called me. My voice teacher liked to talk about her former students. Somehow, my name came up. She described me to Barbara and told her she believed it would be good if we met. I was sitting in my office, posting my ledger, when my phone rang.

I answered in the customary fashion, "Duffy's Landscape. Can I help you?" There was a brief pause on the line and then a very sweet girlish voice came on and said, "Hello my name is Barbara, and I am interested in some landscaping service." I said, "Very well. May I have your address?" She said, "I live at 10 Cedar Street, NW."

"Well," I said, "that is not far from here. My office is on Kennedy Street, NW." We talked a little while. I realized 10 Cedar Street was an apartment house. Before I could make an appointment, I thought that she may have been the owner of the apartment. However, as we continued to talk, I sensed that Barbara was as interested in the landscaper as she was in the landscape. I asked her for her phone number and followed up with a call the next evening. Her daughter answered the phone and said, "Mama is out of town. I will tell her you called when she returns." This went on for several months. I became extremely interested in meeting this woman. I did not ask her where she worked or the nature of her employment. I began thinking perhaps she is a traveling salesperson or had a government job that required a lot of travel. I finally gave up calling her.

I had experiments in the laboratory that required my visiting the laboratory some weekends. I would stop by 10 Cedar Street and knock on the door. Her beautiful pregnant daughter would answer the door and say, "Sorry, Mama is not here. I will tell her you stopped by when she returns." This went on for several weekends. So I said to myself, "I will stop by 10 Cedar Street one more time, and if Barbara is not there, I will give up and conclude that it was not meant for us to meet." So the next Sunday, after church, I headed to the laboratory to check on my experiments. I stopped at 10 Cedar Street, Northwest, took a deep breath, and knocked on the door. Behold, a petite, teasing, brown-skinned, very attractive young lady answered the door and said, "Hello, I am Barbara. Would you like to come in."

I said, "No, I am on my way to Beltsville, Maryland, to check on my laboratory experiments." We talked briefly. I reached out as if I were going to shake her hand, but before she could reach for my hand, I kissed her. She was stunned. Before she could recover, I said bye and was off to Beltsville.

We talked via phone for several weeks before her work schedule allowed us to get together. I was working full time and running my landscaping business. So my schedule also was tight. After several weeks, we finally got together. On our first date, I took Barbara to Arena Stage in Southwest, Washington, DC. I don't remember the name of the play, but it was not very good. Barbara had trouble staying awake.

After nodding off several times, she asked me if she could rest her head on my shoulder. I said without hesitation, "Sure." I apologized for the quality of the play and told her how it ended. I learned later that Barbara was working two jobs. This accounted for her being tired. I was very happy with our relationship but was not thinking of marriage. Before long, we settled into a serious relationship. I found myself falling deeply in love and changing my mind about marrying again. Before long, I started looking at engagement rings. I did not tell her my plans or how deeply I had fallen in love with her.

Our family reunion was to be held the next year in Los Angeles, California. I asked Barbara to go with me. I wanted the family to meet her, and I wanted to surprise her. We have a talent show as a regular part of our reunion activities. When my turn came to take the stage, I recited verses of my original poetry, sang a song, and invited Barbara to join me. She was very surprised because she did not know why I asked her to join me. She came to the stage. I took her hand, presented her to the family, announced our engagement, and presented to her a half-carat blue diamond engagement ring. While her eyes were still beaming with joy, I kissed her, and we exited stage left with thunderous applause. We got married the following year, October 25, my birthday. Our wedding was at Mount Zion Baptist Church, at Fourteenth and Gallatin Streets, NW, Washington, DC. Ironically, my church is Saint Paul AME Church at Fourteenth and Emerson Streets, NW, Washington, DC. Little did we know that we had been worshiping in churches two blocks away many years before we met.

A songwriter once wrote, "Love is better the second time around." Well, I am a living witness of that truth. Barbara and I have been married forty beautiful years without any serious domestic issues. Between us, we have four lovely adult children who are solid citizens making their mark in society. Every now and then, Barbara will say or do something that tells me the best is yet to come.

Spencer and Barbara at home in Maryland.

WHO IS SHE

Who is she who snaps my head as she walks by
Who is she who makes me think that I can fly
Who is she who makes me think I own the world
My dearest, my darling, my girl
Who is she who takes me by the hand
Who is she who leads me to a wonderland

Who is she who loves me 'til I sweat
My sweetheart, my lady, my pet
Who is she whose love will never die
Who is she who knows but asks not why
Who is she who rules my fragile life
My friend, my lover, my wife.

My Career with the Federal Government

I worked for the federal government for thirty years (twenty-seven as a civilian and three years in the military). Twenty years for the USDA, seven years for the Environmental Protection Agency. Three years with Uncle Sam. While working at the Beltsville Laboratory, I became a journeyman research plant physiologist. I published ten-plus research papers in several scientific agricultural journals. My colleagues were graduates of Auburn University, Georgetown University, and the University of Maryland. They looked surprised to see an African American research plant physiologist. The day I reported to the laboratory, the director looked at me strangely and asked if I were sure I was reporting to the right place. This took me by surprise. So without a word, I simply reached into my pocket and handed him my personnel orders to report to the Beltsville Pesticide Laboratory for work. He took a long look and said, "Okay, I will show you the laboratory."

The laboratory was a short distance from the administrative office. My colleagues greeted me politely, but I sensed they were skeptical of my skills as a research scientist. It was amusing to me. I was very confident of my training at Howard University and my skills in the laboratory. So I enjoyed the challenge. We worked mostly independently on various research projects relative to the effectiveness of and the effects on plants from the application of pesticides. If our findings were good enough, they would be published in various national and international journals of plant science.

I recall one project required a device that would apply accurately a very small amount of liquid to a plant surface. I searched the universe of plant literature for such a device. Finding none, I asked one of my colleagues to join me in fabricating such a device. He agreed, and within six months, we had invented a device that could accurately apply from one to one thousand milliliters of liquid to a given surface.

Our findings were published later that year in the Journal of Weed Science. Now had we been in private industry, this device could have been patented. At that time, any invention or discovery by an employee of the federal government became property of the government. Today this rule no longer exists. Private industry picked out our publication and manufactured a prototype of our device, patented it, and as of this writing, is in garden stores all over the US.

My research career was cut short by the deregulation policies established by the Reagan Administration. As a result, the Pesticides Regulations Laboratory in Beltsville was closed, and I, with great sorrow, was involuntarily transferred to the Environmental Protection Agency (a brand-new agency) in Arlington, Virginia. My job in Arlington was supervising a team of scientists who reviewed and approved scientific data from manufacturers wishing to market pesticides.

The last ten years of my career with government was difficult because I felt Uncle Sam had betrayed me. I felt I did not spend four years beyond high school and two years in graduate school studying plant science only to end up supervising a team of scientists who reviewed the scientific work like what I had done in the laboratory. However, thanks to my first supervisor and her secretary who encouraged me to look on the bright side and take advantage of the opportunities presented by being part of a new Federal Agency (EPA), I listened to them and settled down for a desk job at headquarters EPA.

Three years after being transferred to EPA Headquarters, I decided to open my own part-time landscaping business. Because the work at headquarters EPA was much easier than the work at the laboratory, I felt I could run a part-time landscaping business evenings and weekends. My agricultural background and my working with landscaping companies while in college gave me a good technical background for a landscaping business. However, I felt the need for some business training. So I enrolled in Howard University's evening small business class. After finishing Howard's small business class, I took a course in landscape architecture from the USDA Graduate School. After which, I applied for a small business loan from the Small Business Administration (SBA). My application was rejected. So I decided to finance my business from my personal savings (much to the consternation of my wife). I assured her that I would put the money back into our savings account within three years. This I did.

Duffy's Landscape Company opened the spring of 1968 and became a successful business serving the Washington Metropolitan Area. It specialized in landscape design and landscape construction for new homes. Duffy's Landscape Service also became a significant source of income for our family. It paid a major part of our youngest daughter's college education. Duffy's Landscape Service with the help of my son Andre and a friend became a highly successful business.

After twenty-five years of serving citizens of the Washington, DC, metropolitan area, Duffy's Landscape Service closed. I had hoped to turn the business over to my son and my friend, but neither showed any interest in owning a landscaping business. Fortunately, both found their calling in other less labor-intensive fields of endeavor.

After closing my landscaping business, I became fully retired. I picked out and purchased a lot adjacent to the USDA Agricultural Research Center. I always wanted a custom-built house. From a catalogue of custom-house blueprints, I selected my dream house. I carried the blueprints around with me for twenty years. Unfortunately, the company that issued the catalogue was based in Pennsylvania and its building license extended no further than Baltimore. A friend and former coworker suggested a local company that built custom homes. I contacted this company and showed them my blueprint. The manager looked at the blueprints and said his company did not build that style of house. He invited me to look at his catalogue of blueprints and see if I could find a blueprint like the ones I had. I looked and found one close enough. However, the floor plan for my blueprints called for a Rambler-style (single story) house whereas the blueprints from his catalogue called for a bilevel type of construction.

I took the plans to Barbara for her opinion. Fortunately, Barbara liked the plans. I was off to the county office to get a permit to build my house. There was a problem. The lot I purchased was pie shaped. The narrow point (ten feet) came out to Ellington Drive. The county zoning ordinance required a seventy-foot frontage. I petitioned the zoning board to grant me a variance based on two facts about my lots.

(1) There was an existing house on the lot at the time I bought it.
(2) The area of my lot was one acre, and my house could be set back off Ellington Drive far enough to accommodate the seventy-foot frontage requirement.

After meeting with the county zoning board several times and after it sent out a petition to the neighborhood asking its opinion, I was granted a zoning variance with one condition. My house would have to be set back 150 feet off Ellington Drive. This put my house offline with my neighbors' homes and on the highest point of the lot. Barbara liked the requirements of zoning variance. Barbara told me after construction began that she always wanted to live in a house on the hill. So by default, she got her wishes. Our home was built in 1990. It is a good house. We have had no major structural problems. Barbara likes the house and the way it is positioned on our lot. She takes care of the inside, and I take care of the outside. We enjoy our custom home and take pride in knowing it was built just for us.

I thought I would be restless after retirement. However, I quickly learned that if you have a house, a car, a wife, and a dog (dog optional), you always have something to do. Barbara and I are singers, so between singing and taking care of our home, we stay busy. Also, friends, relatives, and neighbors who know you are retired are eager to ask for your assistance. Lest you become too busy, you must learn to politely say no.

Retirement, once called the golden years, is a wonderful time of life. I find four words to describe it: "how sweet it is." However, let me hasten to say, you should start planning for retirement when you land your first permanent job. You should take full advantage of your employer's retirement plan. If you work for the Federal Government, you should join the Thrift Saving Plan (TSP). In addition, you should have your own Individual Retirement Account (IRA) and invest in a long-term health insurance plan. You should also have a good health insurance plan. Above all, take good care of yourself. Eat right, sleep right, do the right things, and develop an exercise program that you can practice for the rest of your life.

Commentary on Life

When I consider all the books that have been written, all the history that has been recorded, and all the science humankind has produced, the beginning and the ending of our life and the life of

the universe are a mystery. I believe all life is a part of an intercon-
nected whole. The universe is a dynamic, self-sustaining, self-recy-
cling, self-generating everlasting system. It is controlled and directed
by a mighty force that humankind has called by many names. Some
even call it God.

If humankind properly regards itself considering the scope,
power, and complexity of the universe, it is but a minor blimp on
the universe's radar. I believe that long after humankind has vanished
from this earth or anywhere, it may journey in space, the universe will
go merrily on as if it never existed. The order, power, and harmony
that exist in the universe did not occur by accident. The power and
purpose that caused it to be are far beyond human's ability to phan-
tom. Humankind is a part of the universe and cannot escape from it.
Therefore, any attempt to find the answer to life or the meaning or
purpose of the universe will be inherently flawed because it will lack
the objectivity and intelligence necessary to find the truth.

Therefore, I believe we should not waste a lot of time trying to
figure out how we got here or what will happen to us when we leave
this veil of tears. Rather, we can better spend our time striving to live
together in peace and enjoy this beautiful planet called earth that has
so freely been given to us. We should be sensitive to the suffering of
our fellow humans, develop our God-given talents, and use them to
make this world a better place.

Finally, we should strive to love one another and in the words of
the famous Poet, William Cullen Bryant:

> So live, that when thy summons comes to join
> the innumerable caravan which moves
> to that mysterious realm. Where each shall take
> his chamber in the silent halls of death.
> Thou go not like the quarry-slave at night,
> scourged to his dungeon, but, sustained and
> soothed,
> by an unfaltering trust. Approach thy grave,
> like one who wraps the draperies of his couch
> about him and lies down to pleasant dreams.

LIFE
(Spencer L. Duffy 2014)

I don't know what this life's about
This life's too short to sort it out
And so, I live from day to day
So, in the end my soul can say
I walked this journey sometimes alone
But always moving toward my home
Where darkness rules the day and night
And time and space are infinite
Where bits of ash and dust disperse
To wander through the Universe
And through the force of sun and rain
Condense, reform and live again.

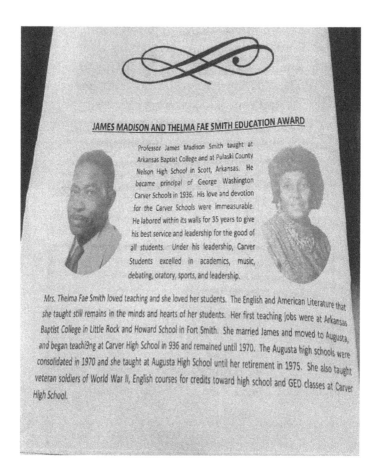

JAMES MADISON AND THELMA FAE SMITH EDUCATION AWARD

Professor James Madison Smith taught at Arkansas Baptist College and at Pulaski County Nelson High School in Scott, Arkansas. He became principal of George Washington Carver Schools in 1936. His love and devotion for the Carver Schools were immeasurable. He labored within its walls for 35 years to give his best service and leadership for the good of all students. Under his leadership, Carver Students excelled in academics, music, debating, oratory, sports, and leadership.

Mrs. Thelma Fae Smith loved teaching and she loved her students. The English and American Literature that she taught still remains in the minds and hearts of her students. Her first teaching jobs were at Arkansas Baptist College in Little Rock and Howard School in Fort Smith. She married James and moved to Augusta, and began teachi9ng at Carver High School in 936 and remained until 1970. The Augusta high schools were consolidated in 1970 and she taught at Augusta High School until her retirement in 1975. She also taught veteran soldiers of World War II, English courses for credits toward high school and GED classes at Carver High School.

George Washington Carver Schools

Today, the only remaining building at George Washington Carver School is the Home Economics/ 4th, 5th and 6th grades building. The Augusta School Board deeded the building to the Arkansas Chapter of the Augusta Club. Several alumni and interested donors have contributed monies, furniture, appliances and building materials to its renovation. The building is still being renovated and will house a museum of Carver and community artifacts.

REFLECTING ON THE PAST

Oh Carver

Oh Carver, we'll always live,
To boost and praise your name,
Our school, we love we'll always fight,
For Carver and her aims.
Oh Carver, we pledge to Thee
A world of loyalty,
To keep Thee ever in our hearts,
A school of memory.

Professor James Madison Smitvh was principal of the elementary and secondary school the Duffy children attended. His wife, Ms. Thelma Faye Smith, was an excellent English and literature teacher who assisted in preparing us for acting roles in plays we wrote for the literature classes. She also assisted all valedictorians in writing their commencement speeches.

Chapter 4

The Second Child—Eliza Marie Duffy Bunzy

Eliza Marie Duffy Bunzy was born in Augusta, Arkansas, Woodruff County, on January 4, 1937, to the union of Mr. Octavris Duffy and Mrs. Leona Stith Duffy, the second of thirteen children and the first girl. Marie accepted Christ at age thirteen in a revival at Wards Chapel AME Church. The revival started on Sunday night, and the preacher asked all the guests to come to the front bench that was known as the Mourner's Bench. Mama looked back for me and my sister to come to the front. I acted as if I didn't see her. On that Monday night, the preacher gave the same invitation, so I thought I would try it again without looking when Mama beckoned us to come to the front seat. My Mama, who was short at five feet tall, marched to the back of that church and ushered us up to the front seat.

"Well," I said to myself, "Mom made me come up here."

But the revival will be over on Friday night, and I'm going to still be sitting here. But when that old preacher came out of that pulpit and came in front of that mourner's bench, I forgot about my little school friends being there and did not want them to see me shout. But before I knew anything, I was shouting all over that church, so I can surely say, I went to the church that night and my heart wasn't right but something got a hold of me. It was on a Monday night, and I never shall forget that experience as I went in doubting but came up shouting, "Praise be to God!"

In the summer, we would chop cotton. It would be so hot that you could see little stars before your eyes. I would sometimes fall asleep chopping cotton and would chop up the cotton instead of the weeds. My daddy would fuss at me and say I was just lazy. They decided to take me to see the doctor. The doctor told my dad I could not help from falling asleep because I had a sluggish liver. Dad felt bad, but now he understood what my problem was.

During my early childhood, I grew up on a farm. We had to pick and chop cotton, which I hated. My back would be hurting so bad when I picked cotton. But my daddy would say, "You don't have no back. You only have a gristle." I would say to myself, "Well, whatever it is, it hurts when I'm bent over all day picking cotton." Sometimes when we would pick cotton, it would be so cold that you could see ice spurring up out of the ground. My feet would be so cold that they would be numb.

To help earn money, I would join my parents and siblings picking and chopping cotton for other farmers. We worked from sunup to sundown for a few dollars. Even so, our parents never complained.

Mama told us, "What counts is what's on the inside, not what you are wearing on the outside."

I learned how to pray at an early age. I would pray that it would rain so I would not have to go to the field.

School Days—High School and College

I attended School at Carver High School, a school for Black students only. Schools were segregated then so White and Black students did not go to the same school. I completed my elementary and high school education there and graduated valedictorian of my high school class with high grades of mostly As and Bs. I led the class academically but was the shortest one in stature, so I also always ended up on the front row in pictures. My sisters still tease me about being short, especially Leona and Mary.

I was looking forward to going to my high school prom. Helen, my cousin, had sent me a beautiful black and lime color formal to wear to the prom, and I was so excited. On prom night, I was going to spend the night with my Aunt Dora, my dad's sister who lived in town across from the school. Dad had been downtown where he and all the men could be found sitting on the gossip bench talking to each other. One of the men said to Dad, "You know it's going to be a dance at that school tonight, don't you?" When Dad came home, I was getting ready to go to Aunt Dora's house. He told me I was not going anywhere. That really did hurt me because my prom date was so fine! I had told Dad that I was going to be in a play as I was always in plays. Dad did not allow us to go to dances, at least not when I was at home. I think the younger siblings got away with murder. I guess Dad had gotten tired by the time they were born. Remember, I'm the second of thirteen children.

I told my mother the day after I finished school, "I'm going to leave here," and so I did. I left and went to St Louis, Missouri, and spent summer with my mom's sister, Aunt Clytis Mae. When fall came, I went back to Arkansas and enrolled in Philander Smith College in Little Rock, Arkansas. I'm the only one of the thirteen children that went to a religious college. I received a scholarship from

Ward's Chapel AME Church where Mom had her church membership. We went to church with Mom until we were able to care for ourselves and pay attention in church. Shortly after, we went to church with our father. During my college years, I lived on campus and attended a CME Church in Little Rock, Arkansas. On Sunday mornings, I went to Sunday School on campus. In the evening, I attended Vesper services in the campus auditorium where the college choir would sing.

Even though I received a scholarship to attend Philander Smith, I worked in the dining hall to help pay my way through college. After studying some nights until well past midnight, I would get up at dawn to help prepare breakfast at the cafeteria, and then it was off to classes and, later, back to the cafeteria to assist with other meals. Challenging work for me was always a pleasure except for work in the cotton fields of Arkansas.

One of my roommates at Philander Smith College was Melba McHenry who later became the sister-in-law of my sister Cora, who married her brother, Henry (HL). I met my college sweetheart Jessie in my first year. But when he went back to college for his junior year, I was not there. When school was out, I stayed in Little Rock to work. On Sundays, I attended church, which is where I met Reverend James Robins. I heard him sing and preach and held on to every word and note. He must have noticed me too because he asked me if he could take me to dinner, I said yes. Big mistake! After that first dinner date, we started seeing each other regularly, especially on Sunday evenings. Then he decided he was going to leave Arkansas and go to California to sing with the group the Soul Revivers. He was going to be leaving next week, and he wanted me to go with him. I told him he would have to take me to Cavell, Arkansas, and ask my father and mother if he could marry me before he could take me to California.

He had a meeting with Reverend Joe Mays in Memphis, Tennessee, so we left Little Rock, Arkansas, and went to Memphis. He met with Reverend Mays that evening and from there to my parents' house in Cavell.

Married Life

James asked Dad and Mom if he could marry me and take me to California. My dad said, "Yes, but if you can't treat her right, bring her back home." Daddy gave him a good lesson. Then we left that night to go to Texas to his mother's house to give her the news. We left his mother's house and went to California with the Soul Revivers. James joined that group. They sang from church to church. I remember on one occasion the group had an evening service, and they were singing. The background singers didn't have their parts right. James stopped and said, "You all sit down. I don't need you anyway. I'll do it myself." So he sang, and he sang. People were shouting all over the church; he was just that good. We separated, and he went to Chicago; my heart was broken but I had to deal with it. I did not have any relatives in California. I was a little country girl from Arkansas. I had to figure out life for me and my child. I worked two jobs to support my child and was determined that she would not be brought up on welfare and never feel less than anyone else. So with God's help, I was able to make it. I would send clothes home to my younger sisters and brothers. Mom would ask me, "How you can do this and take care of your child?" But I did it.

Two years later, I went to a nightclub called the 5-4 Ballroom to hear Johnny Guitar Watson, and I heard someone say, "Eliza Duffy." I turned and looked, and it was Jesse Carter, the guy I went to college with whom was in service and stationed at Camp Pendleton in San Diego, California. He asked me for my phone number, and we started dating again. On weekends, he would come down to see me. That relationship did not last. Then some years later, Mr. Robins called me and said he would be coming home to his family and asked me to pick him up at the airport. Reluctantly, I did with hopes that our family life together would last.

He came back and started pastoring a church on Central Avenue called Deliverance Missionary Baptist Church. Things were going well. We were buying a lot with two houses on it. We even broadcasted worship services on Sunday nights. Then James decided to go into the entertainment field singing in night clubs. That was not my lifestyle so that tore our family apart again. He stayed in California a while, and then he left and moved to New York.

Then while working for the bank, I met a young man named Joseph, and we dated for a while, then that relationship ended. I went to a funeral and saw Mr. Willie Bunzy. We had not seen each other in over thirteen years. He got my phone number from a friend of his. We talked on the phone about three months before we went to dinner together. Then things got serious, and we ended up getting married.

We were married at Silver Bell Wedding Chapel in Las Vegas, Nevada, on August 9,1975. We had been married for thirty-six years when the Lord called him home in 2011. He was a wonderful husband and a wonderful father to our children. We had a good life together. We would go home to Arkansas for our vacations. Sometimes we would drive and stop at night, get a hotel room, then get up the next morning, and start again. We would also go to Jackson, Mississippi, to visit his family. They showed me so much love and keep in touch with me, including his Aunt Marie. We would leave Mississippi and drive to my sister Nancy's home in Forrest City, Arkansas. Willie and Nancy's husband, Sam, would have fun. Sam took him as his brother that he never had. We would go to Las Vegas to visit his friends there, and we had an enjoyable time.

One year, my sister Nancy and her husband Sam, Willie, and I celebrated our wedding anniversaries together in Memphis, Tennessee. We rode in a white carriage with white horses pulling it and with a white driver. We rode all the way downtown and down Beale Street, we had lots of fun that night.

Willie and I also attended one of Edna's concerts in Cleveland, Ohio. We really enjoyed it. I attended many of my sister Edna's concerts and had the opportunity to sing in the Duffy Liturgical Ensemble. I appeared in "Let's Go There" at the Ohio Theatre and "The Front Porch," "Songs of Life" at the Intercontinental Convention Center in Cleveland, Ohio. Edna performed at numerous venues in Los Angeles, and sometimes, I shared the stage with her. I was also one of the lead singers on the CD of the Duffy Ensemble titled "Witnessing for Christ" with two of my sisters, Leona and Nancy. I also sang with my cousins Hazel and the Prunty Brothers. We formed a quartet and would go to the Men's Federation with Dad and sing on their program.

I have traveled to twelve different states in the United States. I've also been to London and Paris, inside the Windsor Palace, saw the queen's palace in London, and even had a glimpse of the queen. I saw the changing of the guards and were those guys good looking. One of the most memorable experiences I had was to attend the second inauguration of the forty-forth president of the United States, President Barack Obama. It was a wonderful experience.

Willie and I had four children, one preceded Willie in death, our baby son Joseph Ray. Joseph was an aspiring police officer and had just passed the exam for Beverly Hills Police Department when he was killed at the age of thirty-one years as he walked in Blockbuster to return a video during an armed robbery. He left behind a fiancée and three young children.

Joseph Paul

I am blessed now to be surrounded by my children, Dwight Ledell and his wife, Janet; Ferroll Marie; Leonard Benjamin and his wife, Michelle; and Joseph's fiancée, Trina. I also am blessed with ten grandchildren: Kingi Santiel, Porsha Lewis, Shannon Cromer, Jasmin Davis, Camille Jones, Adrian Jones, Alyssa Jones, Jordan Paul,

Jala Ranisha Paul, and Harmony Turner. I round out my family circle with ten great-grandchildren.

Marie and children—Janet, Dwight, Marie, Ferroll, and Leonard

Work Experience

My first work experience was at the S&H KRESS store, where I worked as a cashier for ten years. Next, I worked as a loan officer and assistant manager for Bank of America for twenty-five years. My last secular work experience was with my daughter, Ferroll's Loved Ones Victims Service, a nonprofit that works to counsel and provide comforting and healing services to families of persons who lose their lives to gun violence and other forms of violence in our society. I served as the Victim's Advocate and Outreach Coordinator.

Reflection of My Dad

As I think about my dad, there are so many things I could say but since I only have one chapter, I will have to condense it. Dad was a strong man, not wavery. He said what he meant and meant what he said. I had him the longest as Dad, except for my brother Spencer. Dad was not a big man, but he had a big voice. He had a melodious bass voice in singing and talking. I used to love to hear him sing and walk the floor at the Men's Federation. He would sing "I'll Fly Away." When he sang that song, the church would be filled with the Spirit. Dad was a man of integrity and dedication; he was a Christian man. He served as superintendent of the Sunday School for over sixty years.

Here are some of my dad's sayings:

1. You see that young man across the street, he's not worth the salt and soda that it takes to make his bread.
2. He would say we have people dying that never died before. And then he would just laugh.
3. You all are some of the greenest people in the world to know everything.
4. He would ask us, "Why did you do that?" Then he would say, "For the lack of knowledge." I wanted to say, "If you know why we did it, why did you ask?" But if I had said that, I would not have been here to write this chapter.
5. None of my children are lazy; they just hate to work.
6. One day he was looking for his hammer and asked, "Has anyone seen my hammer?" You know how you may have seen something but can't remember where you saw it. Well, my little mom said, "I can just see that hammer now," and my dad said, "Shit, if you see it get up and get it."
7. One Sunday we were getting ready to go to church, Mom said, "Oh, I have a run in my stocking." Dad said, "That's okay. If anyone's looking at your leg that hard, they are looking too close."

Now about my dear mom. My mother was a Christian woman, very soft spoken and very quiet. She was one of the greatest mothers one could have. She loved her children, but not only her children, but all children. She never had a bad word to say about anyone. The people that others looked down on were the people Mom would try to help. She would always say, "It's some good in everyone." Mother was president of the Missionary Society. She sang in the missionary choir, helped with Communion, and made the bread for Communion.

My mom and dad were genuinely concerned about their children getting an education and about our spiritual growth and development. My dad said, "If your last name is Duffy, you do not bring no Ds home on your report card and no more than two Cs." So we had to strive for excellence. They told us to aim for the moon and "if you fall among the stars, people will still have to look up to see you." My mother was very good with her hands. She could look at a dress in a catalogue, make a pattern from newspapers and make us dresses sewn by hand because she did not have a sewing machine and you could not see a stitch. She was better than the Singer sewing machine.

Here are some of Mom's sayings:

1. I'll stump a mudhole in you and wade it dry.
2. If I have to whip you, I'm going to knock you through that front door and bring you back through the back door.
3. When we would pass the cemetery, Mom would ask, "How many dead people do you think are in that cemetery?" We would start counting. After we counted a while, she would say smiling, "All of them."

My Life Now

I am a licensed, ordained minister of the gospel and serve on the ministerial staff of the Holy Mount Calvary Missionary Baptist Church in Los Angeles, California. I hold several positions and am currently president of the sisterhood, vice president of mission, treasurer of Sunday School, chaplain of senior choir, secretary of Pastor's Guild, on the Sick and Bereavement Committee, and one of the pastor's armor bearers. I am a proud member of Holy Mount Calvary Missionary Baptist Church located at 11102 South Main Street Los

Angeles, California, 90061 (323) 779-5340. Dr. Leonard E. White is my pastor and members of my family call him their Los Angeles pastor. As you read this chapter, may God's blessings rest upon you.

Pastor Leonard and Mrs. White with their daughter

BR: Leona, Marie, Mary
FR: Willie and Mom

Chapter 5

The Third Child—Cora Cornelius Duffy McHenry

Growing Up in Augusta and Cavell

I, Cora Cornelius Duffy McHenry, am the third child of thirteen children born to Mr. Octavris C. and Mrs. Leona S. Duffy. I am the second girl child. I grew up in rural Arkansas, the towns of Augusta and Cavell. I was a quiet and easygoing child, committed to doing my chores at home and studying at home and school to be successful in my elementary and high school classes.

We all grew up in Jackson Chapel CME and Ward's Chapel AME Churches in Augusta, Arkansas. We sang in the church choir, where our family made up just about the entire choir and Sunday School. I tutored my younger sisters and brothers and took piano lessons so I could play for the choir. I played well enough to get through familiar hymns for the choir. We read scriptures and recited poems and speeches from memory for Easter, Children's Day, and Christmas worship services. Some of my siblings believed I was Mom's and Dad's favorite because my skin was lighter and hair requires little work to make it look good, and I was petite. I also resembled my dad's sister, Aunt Dora. I put no stock in that because I was required to do all the chores that my older sister Eliza (Marie) also performed. I picked cotton and chopped cotton as everyone else did. I did, however, get some opportunities to stay home and care for younger sisters and brothers, perform housework, and prepare food for the family, when Mom needed a break from the children and housework.

I developed a love for history and literature and could easily commit poems, stories, fairy tales, and historical documents to memory. I used these skills to do storytelling to my younger siblings when I stayed home with them.

In our family, the oldest sibling became the leader of the younger ones when Mom and Dad were away in town, at a church meeting, or visiting relatives. I used this time with my siblings to demonstrate my leadership skills early on. It was my belief that kindness, caring, and shared leadership would work with sisters and brothers. As a leader at home, I did not cherish punishing my siblings or snitching on them so Mom and Dad would punish them. Instead, I would organize them to assist with household chores, tell stories, read stories, play games with them, and listen to their concerns and needs. I would tell them stories of faraway places in Africa, Europe, and Asia. Even though we had a wooden stove in the kitchen, Mama would often hang a big black iron pot over the fireplace to cook dinner, pinto beans, or black-eyed peas in winter. So there was always a hook that hung over the fireplace. Late at night when we believed Mama and Daddy to be asleep, Edna and I would tip into the kitchen and sneak/steal two eggs and a giant sweet potato. Our house was heated by what is now a luxury—a fireplace in our bedroom. We would take the black iron tea kettle, fill it with water, and slip the eggs into it. We would then hang the teakettle over the flaming coals in the fireplace waiting for the water to boil. When the flames died down, we would rake back the simmering coals in the fireplace, dig a pocket in the ashes, and hide the sweet potato underneath, covering it with hot coals piled upon the ashes so that there was plenty of heat to bake but not burn the hidden potato.

When both the eggs and the potato were done, we giggled as we ate the eggs and potato. And oh boy, was that some good eating! When we finished eating, we went off to bed and slept soundly until morning when we giggled some more believing we had a big secret.

Much later in life, we realized that Mama would immediately have realized that two eggs had vanished during the night. And since we were naïve enough to take the biggest potato from the pile of potatoes that she was saving to use in making sweet potato pies for Sunday dinner, she would certainly miss the potato too. It was years later that we found out that she and Daddy knew all along what was going on in our thin-walled house. They were snuggling and laughing as they listened to every move we made!

For some reason, I wanted to be the first to the door when relatives and friends came to visit. When the car pulled into our driveway, I would run to the door. Of course, Dad would gently push me aside and get to the door first. I liked cooking and making things look pretty and working in Mom's flower garden where I adored the zinnias and tulips planted there.

One of the household chores I learned early was food preparation. Cooking turnip and mustard greens became a specialty, and the cooking of cabbage came in as a close second. My cheese rice was not bad either. I perfected making Kool-Aid with just enough sugar and water to make it tasty.

I enjoyed helping Mom can fruits and vegetables from our own garden and orchards. Sometimes we did such an excellent job that Mom encouraged Eliza and me to join the 4H Club. The 4H Club is an organization that many farm boys and girls belonged to. The 4H Club emphasized the importance of the *head, heart, hands,* and *health*, hence the four Hs. The pledge for the 4H Club is still relevant today, and I remember it. "I pledge my head to clearer thinking, my heart to greater loyalty, my hands to greater service, and my health to better living, for my club, my community, my country, and my world." Mom would allow Eliza and me to do some canning on our own (with her supervision, of course), which we entered into competition at the Woodruff County Fair and won first-, second-, and third-place ribbons.

I did not like working in the cotton and strawberry fields nor milking cows and feeding livestock. However, I did not mind collecting eggs from the hens' nests. Besides, the outdoor environment did not agree with me, and I would develop health problems of nose bleeds and coughs because of being in the hot sun or cold damp weather.

School Days

With an older sister and brother preceding me at Carver Elementary and High School, I knew I had to measure up to what had been set as the Duffy legacy. I always loved reading and writing and was blessed with great penmanship. My writing resembled calligraphy, and I received many comments on it in high school and college. Learning was easy for me, and I liked all my subjects and spent ample time studying to be successful on assignments and tests. I liked my teachers and got along well with them. Because I was small in stature, I was overprotected by teachers but sometimes picked on by larger students and older students.

I remember one incident in a mathematics class. A couple of students were scheming about how they would cheat on the test. They would wait until I had completed my test and then reach over my shoulder, take my test, and copy my answers. Well, when one of them reached over my shoulder to take my test, I turned and struck her hard enough to knock her out of her seat, turn over a few chairs, and cause a bit of confusion during a test. I was sent to the principal's office. Principal S asked me what happened. I told him what happened. He said, "Uhm, young lady, you have two choices: you can sit here all day, or I will send you home." Now it is in the middle of the day and my dad was most likely working and would not want to be interrupted. Also, my dad and Principal S did not see eye to eye on most things and certainly not when it came to his daughters. So I knew I would not be sent home, and I was not.

At home, I did my chores, my homework, and looked forward to going to school every day. I did not engage in fights with my older sister and brother, and it was unthought of that I would engage in fighting a younger sibling. I served as a guide to visitors to Carver High School with duties to show them the unique campus and introduce them to teachers and students as they walked across the school grounds. Sometimes I would be called on to respond to guest speakers and international visitors after they gave remarks in assemblies and other programs. This was a start in developing my public speaking skills.

I was a very competitive debater in high school and took my debating skills to college and the floor of the Arkansas Legislature as I lobbied for the rights and protection of teachers and staff in the Arkansas Public School system.

College Days

My college days were spent as my high school days with great attention to my studies and preparation for my future. I attended Arkansas AM&N College (now the University of Arkansas at Pine Bluff) and graduated from Southern University in Baton Rouge, Louisiana, with a bachelor's degree in secondary education and English. In 1996, I was awarded an honorary doctorate of Humane Letters from Shorter College in North Little Rock, Arkansas, and the honorary doctor of laws degree from the University of Arkansas at Fayetteville.

In college, I continued to excel in my course of studies, following the example of my oldest brother Spencer who had made a name for himself by excelling in his studies and in becoming president of the Student Government Association. To enhance my knowledge of and skills in foreign languages, I studied foreign languages at several institutions, including the University of Arkansas at Fayetteville, Arkansas State University; Hamilton College in Clinton, New York; and Stillman College in Tuscaloosa, Alabama. I loved traveling to foreign countries in both English and American literature courses and was able to relate the historical context of literature to the realities in world and United States history. College life afforded me the opportunity to find my place in a society that was rapidly changing before my eyes.

HL and Cora's daughter, Stephanie McHenry

Life in Camden, Arkansas

Bernice came to spend a summer with HL and me in 1962. She would be a senior when school started back in October after the cotton crops were harvested. I had just given birth to our daughter, Stephanie, and the Camden school system was conducting its summer school. HL and I were both teaching summer school. Bernice babysat for us while I worked. She also helped with the household chores and some cooking. Camden was in the Southeast part of Arkansas where most of HL's family resided. When my family members visited, there were opportunities to visit my in-laws who welcomed them with open arms.

Henry L. McHenry and Cora at home in Little Rock

My church in Camden was a part of the Southeast Arkansas Conference. We were to enter in a competition with youth from all over the district. We put on the drama "Thirty Pieces of Silver." It was a dramatization of Judas's betrayal of Jesus as told in the Gospel of John in the New Testament of the Bible. I remember the first lines well: "Thirty pieces of silver and its mine, all mine, and to think. I was only offered twenty-six. Ah Judas, you were clever." At the end of the drama, Judas throws the thirty pieces of silver across the floor in a mad rage, as he realized what he had done. The drama received outstanding reviews.

Although I did not flaunt my success, my siblings did look up to me. I was happily married. We owned our home. Both HL and I were successful professionals, beginning as teachers in the same school and then going on to become successful in business, governmental, and educational professions in the state and the national government. HL was friendly, down to earth, and fitted right in with the family. He also grew up on a farm and had several siblings. He taught biology and other science courses. I taught English and French in the Camden Public Schools System for ten years. Later, I was on staff at Ouachita Baptist University in Arkadelphia as a teacher in the Upward Bound Program.

I continued to have my hair styled by the hair stylist who styled my hair while I was in college, and therefore, I visited Pine Bluff regularly. On one visit there, I stopped by AM&N College to visit my brother Edward. When I got there, he was carrying a packed suitcase. I asked him where he was going. He said he had not kept his grades up and lost his financial aid, and unless he could come up with $300, he would have to go home. Well, I knew that going home was not the answer, so without further conversation, I wrote a check for the amount he owed, walked him to the financial aid office, cleared the account, and made sure he was all set for his classes. He did well in his studies after that and graduated in four years.

In Camden, HL and I enjoyed life with our professional peers. We entertained at our home and were great hosts. I became popular at the high school in Camden and my reputation spread across the state as I worked to create a sense of fairness and due process in the ways teachers were treated in the public schools of Arkansas.

Move to Little Rock-The Big City

We moved to Little Rock, Arkansas, in 1970. It was here that we really enjoyed the interactions with the family, especially Mom and Dad. We spent a lot of time with them and were privy to a lot of our family history and stories.

We were happy to host the Duffy-Stith Family Reunions, which began in 1973, again in 1976, 1979, and the last one we hosted was in 1991, the year our father died. These reunions paved the way of making sure family members kept in touch with each other. We rotated the sites for the reunions among the family members who lived in cities across the United States. We worked to make reunions special when we hosted them. While most family members stayed in designated hotels for the reunion, HL and I opened our home to many family members. Sometimes we would host as many as thirty-five to forty-five children, youth, and adults at the Duffy-Stith Family Reunions for weekends of reflections, worship, recreation, education, and good food and fun. HL would chauffeur family members back and forth to the airports and bus stations with a friendly smile and a willing spirit.

I was remarkably close to our mom and dad especially after most of my sisters and brothers finished high school and moved away from Arkansas. I would see to Mom and Dad's personal needs, especially transportation since our parents owned no automobile, and Mom did not drive anyway. When HL, Stephanie, and I moved to Little Rock, we visited them often and would take them shopping, to church, doctor's office, and wherever they needed to go. During these visits, we talked about their childhood and what they wanted for their family, my siblings and me. They talked about wanting to see all of us grown up with our own families and making a life of our own. They said that they could die in peace knowing they had raised us to be responsible and useful citizens in the communities in which we lived.

Their living siblings lived out of state and had visited Mom and Dad when they were younger, and now Mom and Dad wanted to visit them in their homes. I enjoyed taking them on these trips and they enjoyed conversations with their siblings. They reminisced about old times growing up together and the mischief they got into as children.

As Mom and Dad got into their seventies and eighties, they enjoyed trips to the towns in which they were born. On the way we would visit state parks, caves, and other historic sites. One of their favorites was the Hot Springs of Hot Springs, Arkansas.

In addition to caring and supporting Mom and Dad, I supported my siblings by celebrating special occasions and accomplishments with them. I attended and took part in the wedding ceremonies for Edna, Bernice, and Mary. I also made it possible for Mom and Dad to visit their children and participate with them on memorable occasions. One of our trips to visit my siblings included the commencement ceremonies when Bernice received her PhD degree. They were so proud. Other trips included staying with Edna in Cleveland as she recovered from major surgery and being with O.C. Jr. as he went through several surgeries and recovery following a head-on car collision. So Mom and Dad traveled with me to visit my siblings for the birth of their grandchildren, graduations, and just fun visits.

Professional Life

I became associated with the all-White AEA with the merger of the all-Black Arkansas Teachers Association in 1969. I was one of four members from the ATA to assume a position on the Board of the reconstituted AEA. In 1970, I joined the staff of the Arkansas Education Association as the Assistant Director for Instruction and Human Relations.

My work with the Arkansas Education Association landed me into positions where I worked alongside senators, governors, and presidential nominees. So in 1974–1975, I took a leave of absence to become an education aide to Senator Dale Bumpers during his last year as governor and first year as US senator from Arkansas. In 1983 and 1984, I represented the AEA as a member of the state's high-profile Education Standards Committee, a group appointed by then Governor William Jefferson Clinton to upgrade state school standards.

Through the contacts with senators and governors, and the work with the Arkansas Education Association, I became a voice for the teachers and other educators in the state of Arkansas. In 1985, I became the executive director of the Arkansas Education Association, one of five females' executive directors of state associations in the United States and the first Black female ever to head an NEA State Association. During my tenure as executive director of the association, major changes were made to improve and raise educational standards for students and improve working conditions for teachers including regular salary increases.

President of Shorter College

Shorter College is a two-year private religious school in Little Rock, Arkansas. After my retirement as executive director of the Arkansas Education Association, the Shorter College Board of Trustees elected me in 2002 to take on the mantle of president of that institution. I was serving as acting presidents at the time. The college was in a crisis with low enrollment, loss of accreditation, and financial ruin. With my several years of executive and management experience, I was able to work with the Board of Trustees and college personnel in carrying out the two-phase program of revitalization and implementation of the newly adopted strategic plan.

Under my leadership from 2002 to 2004, three buildings that had been closed due to poor physical condition were returned to full service. A financial aid program with a student work-study component was instituted. A major indebtedness to the internal Revenue Service was satisfied and payment agreements were reached with several major local creditors and state agencies. The number of degree offerings grew from three to ten areas and a strong database of available properly credentialed faculty was established. The two goals which I worked smartly to achieve, and which resulted in turning the College around were (1) to ensure that the college begins each academic year with an increased student population and (2) to complete the process of accreditation by the Commission on Higher Learning of the North Central Association of Colleges and Schools and to seek accreditation by the Transactional Association of Christian Colleges and Schools. And in 2007, Shorter College, under my leadership, awarded the associate of arts degree in general studies to the graduating class of 2007 for the first time since losing its NCA Accreditation in 1998. My work at Shorter College was both gratifying and energy draining. I enjoyed the opportunity to interact with church and government leaders across the state as well as all the innocent yet visionary students who matriculated there during my presidency.

Community and Volunteer Service

Work in the church remained important to me throughout my life, and it served as the ground of my hope and the source of strength in times of crisis and challenges in my career and personal life. I have served faithfully as a member of Bethel AME Church for more than forty years. During this time, I served on the Stewardess Board, finance committee, and I also taught Sunday School. Other community service involvement included service on the Board of Directors for the Winthrop Rockefeller Foundation and Peace Links and the Southern Coalition for Education Equity. For several years, because of my work and passion for education, I was named one of the top 100 Women in Arkansas and listed in Horizons of Arkansas Women. I was the first female and first minority to serve as a member of the Board of Trustees of Arkansas Technical University in Russellville, Arkansas. The Cora McHenry Excellence in Teaching Scholarship was established in my honor at Arkansas Technical University to encourage minority students to enter the teaching profession. Several boards and agencies I served on contributed to raising awareness of critical needs related to access to education and successful educational attainment. These include the National Conference for Community and Justice, Arkansas Friends for better Schools, Art Porter Sr. Music Education Foundation, Inc., Arkansas Business and Education Alliance, and the Arkansas Academy for Leadership Training and School-Based Management.

70

My husband Henry died in November of 2019 after fifty-seven years of marriage. I am striving to live my life as a widow and am so grateful to my daughter Stephanie and my ten siblings for all the love and encouragement given and prayers prayed for my comfort, peace, and strength for life's continued journey.

Chapter 6

The Fourth Child—Edna Mae Duffy Murphy

Episodes

It was my first competition, and I won! Each year near the end of the summer, we looked forward to attending the county fair. On the Friday night of the fair, there was always a talent show. It was a competition. When I was in tenth grade, I entered the competition.

I won first place. I sang a solo. Nat King Cole had a popular song out at that time the song was titled "Answer Me My Love." And I sang it.

Now you need to realize that ours was a strictly religious family. My father ran a taut ship when it came to restricting the music we were allowed to listen to and to sing. We were only allowed to sing sacred, religious songs. The radio stations that we were allowed to listen to that played secular music were those that played popular music, most of the time by White artists. On CBS, the station our dark-brown battery-operated radio stayed tuned in to, there was a program included where often music sung by Nat King Cole was played. On that same station, there was even more often a duet performed by Louis Armstrong and Bing Crosby as the closing number for the Wednesday night weekly *The Bing Crosby Show*. I would try to get all my homework done so that I could just listen when the duet came on.

I was scared to tell my parents that I was entering the contest. I entered and won first prize without telling them. At breakfast on Saturday morning after the contest, I decided to tell them before someone from the community told them under the guise of congratulations.

My parents knew that I had gone to the fair because I had to ask for permission to go with my boyfriend, a handsome six-foot tall, very light-skinned African American young man with hazel eyes. We went in his green pickup truck with the three holes in a row, the insignia that was on the fender of the truck. I gathered courage and spoke. It took courage because in addition to being known for his good looks and his strong Christian character, my daddy was also known as a strict disciplinarian.

"I won first place in the talent show last night," I blurted out between bites of food. I will never forget the broad smile on my daddy's face. He had tons of questions for me. With his whole face beaming and through his smile, he asked first, "What? How much was the prize?"

"Fifteen dollars," I answered. His smile broadened, and he was almost beaming, leading up to the second question. "What did you sing?" he asked. I took a deep swallow of fresh cow's milk and replied almost inaudibly, "Answer Me My Love." He took a moment and then answered slowly. "Oh well," he said, "I guess there is a time and place for everything!" My smile met his, and we ate breakfast happily and smiling.

My music teacher, Mr. Buckner, was a short, round bottomed, yet handsome African American man. He played the piano as if he were Beethoven, and when he sat at the piano, his bottom completely covered the piano stool. His music classes were always packed with eager students. He was delighted that I had won first place in the state fair competition and proceeded to favor me in the social studies class that he taught and even more in choir. He even gave me private vocal lessons twice a week. There was no charge. Even at a youthful age, I decided that there should be some compensation for his time and instruction. So I invited him to our house for dinner one weekend. I was afraid to tell Mama until the last minute. She was not happy because I think perhaps she was ashamed of our sparse hand-me-down furniture. She gathered her wits about her and said okay but "You will have to do all the cleaning in preparation for his visit."

As a child, I did not know how to be embarrassed by our home. I cleaned! Mr. C. came and we all enjoyed a wonderful dinner of fried chicken, mashed potatoes, English peas, homemade biscuits, and butter roll for dessert with Kool Aid, milk, and buttermilk to drink.

Sunday Dinners at Aunt Dora's House

There was a white bungalow with red shutters. It had a lamp in the window. There was a yellow shade on the lamp. A White family lived there. They had a dog, a beautiful brown and white Collie. He barked viscously at us every Sunday when we passed by on our way to church. Not one family member ever came out to quiet the dog. We could see them peering out the window behind the slightly worn curtain. This always interrupted my imagination that because the light in the window glowed warmly, I always imagined that a loving family lived there.

We were afraid that the dog would bite us. My father assured us that the dog was all bark and no bite. Despite his words, I always dreaded having to pass that house on our way to and from church. Despite the dog, I grew to love that house, and when I was married and we bought our first home, it was a bungalow with a bay window. I placed a large warm lamp in front of that window.

My sister Cora had built a beautiful house in Camden, Arkansas, where she and her husband were teachers in the public school system there. On college break, I would go and visit them. I admired her red-and-white striped kitchen shades. I bought yellow-and-white striped shades for the kitchen in my bungalow.

Our Sundays were spent in Sunday School, Sunday worship service, and Epworth League (youth bible study group). For Sunday School each week, we had to learn and recite from memory a Bible verse. Then we would read our Sunday School lesson from a denominational published booklet. We would read aloud and discuss the lesson as a group.

On Sundays after church, we would go home with Aunt Dora, my father's oldest sister. I never knew my fraternal grandparents. Both died years before my birth. Aunt Dora filled that void. She was a lean, fair-skinned, five foot eight inches tall African American lady with long straight black hair which she wore in two knots (buns) in the back of her head. After dinner, I would help her do the dishes, and she would talk to me about men and boys. Her favorite quote that she repeated to me every Sunday as I was drying the dishes and putting them away, she would say, "Men love the dark because their deeds are evil." As if that was not enough to scare me away from men and boys, my mother added flame to the fire by telling me that if any of her girls became pregnant out of wedlock, she would tie them to a chair and whip them. She would beat only their legs and arms so as not to hurt the baby, she said. So I grew up thinking that men were evil and only interested in women for sexual satisfaction. There was an uncle who proved Aunt Dora right every chance he got when left alone with little girls.

When I went off to college, I found that there was even more evidence that Aunt Dora's warning about men was in many respects true. When I was a first-year student in college, a wonderful family wanted to adopt me. They were an upper middle class family who had helped make sure that my oldest brother was prepared to go to college by helping him learn ways to earn and save money so that he would have enough to at least get him in the door. One day Mr. B, the husband, came to campus and invited me to go to dinner with him the next day. Mr. B was a tall good-looking Black man who dressed impeccably in stylish suits and brown wingtip shoes. Mr. B had gotten permission from the dorm mother to pick me up at the dormitory with permission granted to return after the 9:00 p.m. curfew. Mr. B came to the dorm. He waited in the lobby. The dorm mother called my name over the PA as was the custom when one had a visitor. "Edna Duffy, you have a visitor. Please come to the lobby." I hid and never went down. At the time I did not realize that Mr. B. wanted to know how I felt about him and his wife adopting me. This would have helped my family tremendously because that would have been one less mouth to feed and one less child to worry about trying to get money to put them through college. He knew that there were twelve children in the family, and he and his wife had no children, and they wanted to adopt an older child. I found this out years later, and I felt so embarrassed. I had thought Mr. B may be interested in me sexually and would try to touch my breasts or rub against my leg inappropriately as my uncle had done whenever he invited me, whom he called "bright eyes," into his workshop or that Mr. B would make the same sexual advances I had experienced from two of my freshmen college professors.

Life on the Farm

Just before I was to enter high school, we moved to a farm, which I loved. There were fruit trees, grape vines, and a little red house with a pump over a sink in the kitchen. There was a long road leading from the highway, Highway 64, to the front porch of the house. The path ended with a beautiful white gate that remained closed. We, the children, often ran down to the gate to greet Daddy on Saturdays when he came home from town with the groceries.

There was a Greyhound Bus that would pass daily down the highway that ran past our homeplace. We would often stand on the porch and watch as it passed by. We wondered if we would ever get to ride that big blue and gray bus. One day to our surprise we did.

It was a Greyhound Bus, and we were quite excited about at last being scheduled to catch the bus to go to town. My father, my siblings, and I waited down by the white gate where the bus would stop to pick us up. The bus came, and we got on the bus. There were several empty seats near the front of the bus behind the driver. While Daddy kept walking past the empty seats, we stopped and sat in the first two empty seats we saw. As Daddy prepared to sit down, he glanced back and saw us sitting up front while the driver glared at us through the rearview mirror. Daddy calmly said, "You all come on back here. Come back here with me." That night I heard him recount the incident to Mama saying, "They did not know. The children didn't know." They never put into words what it was that we did not know, but in the pit of my stomach, I felt it could not be something good.

Quotes from Grandpa

My maternal Grandfather, Grandpa Stith, could out walk all of us. During our walks, Grandpa would talk to us about life. He would quote philosophers, poets, and authors. Robert Frost and Burns were often quoted. The quote that I remember that he quoted the most was from an anonymous source: "He who knows not and knows that he knows not is a child. Teach him. He who knows and knows not that he knows is asleep. Awake him. He who knows not and knows not that he knows not is a fool, shun him. He who knows and knows that he knows is wise. Follow him!"

The Lynching

When I was in the sixth grade, our house burned down. After the fire, we moved to a house that was too far away to walk to school, so we took the school bus to school from then on. Sue Ellen, a tall slender, wiry built girl with long sandy hair, which she wore in long braids, became my best friend. We would sit together on the bus. I got on first and so I would save her a seat. It was strange to me and then normal, a new kind of friendship, where we fought one day and the next day were holding hands as we walked to class together.

Sue Ellen had a big sister and a grownup brother whom I had never met. I had heard about her brother's misadventures while drinking and cavorting with White men. One night, I heard Mama and Daddy talking about him. It was not a happy conversation. My daddy was speaking softly and sadly, and my mama was crying. It seemed that the night before, something bad and an unforgivable act had occurred in our small town of Augusta, Arkansas. The White men with whom Sue Ellen's brother had hung around had decided to have a party at the expense, the life, of Sue Ellen's brother. They beat him to a pulp! They tied him to the back of their truck, legs spread apart, and dragged him down the street out into a dirt road and left him to die in the middle of the night.

My Daddy's sad tone turned to anger, and he said, "Well, that's what he gets for hanging around with those pecker woods. He should have known they were up to no good." When I went to school the next day, everyone was whispering about it. I chimed in. Remembering what I had overheard my daddy say, I said this: "Well, he got what he deserved for hanging around with those men." Sue Ellen's big sister was standing in the hallway and heard me. She walked over to me slowly and said, "If you had seen him, his face was all swollen so that he was unrecognizable. His body was bruised and broken. His legs were torn apart from his body, and his eyes were gouged out. If you had seen that, would you still say he got what he deserved?" She waited for a moment as we all stood in stark silence. Then she turned and walked away. I will never forget that day. The lesson that I learned will never ease the memory of that day and the memory of my life experience of a lynching that took place well into the twentieth century. A lynching that was as brutal as the song by Billie Holiday "Strange Fruit" hanging from a tree.

Singing and Dancing

My first church job was as a paid choir member at a Presbyterian church. I was one of three African American singers in the predominantly Caucasian choir. I loved the music we performed old traditional hymns, classic and classical anthems, and a bit of folk music and an occasional Negro spiritual. From time to time, I was assigned a solo. It was during the Civil Rights turmoil in the United States of America. The senior minister was Caucasian. He was a Civil Rights activist. He marched, and he wrote editorials that were published in the local newspaper and seemingly tried to live the Christian life. His best friend was the minister that had been run over by a bulldozer and killed as he protested the construction of a segregated school in Cleveland, Ohio, in 1964. This happened in advance of my coming to the city of Cleveland, but its mark in my mind can never be erased just from hearing about it. My minister gave powerful, passionate, heart-rending sermons on social justice issues. He was a good man, and I had been there about ten years before he left. The church and the city cried. It was a sadness that enveloped the city and left a lasting veil over the face of social justice in the Greater Cleveland community.

The Black Church Experience

Edna Duffy Murphy dances at the 2017 Duffy-Stith Family Reunion

I had already started my liturgical dance company when I met Mr. Lavert Stuart, an exceptional organist/pianist. At that time, he was the organist at a United Church of Christ (UCC) church. He heard me sing at a community concert and invited me to visit his church in the summer when I would have a break from the Presbyterian church where I was now a paid/soloist. By this time, I had begun to feel a bit uncomfortable soloing in a church where when I looked out into the congregation, I saw only a few faces that looked like me. Even when I looked around in the choir, the black faces had dwindled to two, including me.

When I finally got a Sunday off, I went to visit the UCC Church. The congregation was all African American, except one White couple. The choir was all Black and the organist, whom I had met, was also black.

The music was exceptional, both in choice of music and in deliverance. I was overjoyed to be in that congregation that Sunday. After service, I talked to the organist. He invited me to sing with his choir when he would be presenting Handel's Messiah, the fourth Sunday in December for their Christmas concert. I accepted the invitation, arranged my schedule to attend all the rehearsals and met a new group of African American musicians.

After the Christmas concert, the organist approached me. He thanked me for my service and shocked me by asking me, "Are you a paid soloist at a church now?" I said "Yes," and he said, "I would like for you to be a soloist here."

"Our soloists are not paid," he noted. "You have a vocal ensemble that performs as a part of your dance company. I will accompany you and your group for free if you come and be a soloist in my choir. Can we barter like this?" he asked.

I accepted and began my tenure at the UCC Church where I remained for twelve years, the last two years while there I served as choir director and received $12,000 a year in this paid position. The twelve years there taught me a lot about the dynamics of being a member of a large wealthy African American Church in the twentieth century.

Life in Cleveland

Many years have passed since I left Arkansas and made my home in Cleveland, Ohio. The beautiful snow in winter, the gorgeous fall season as tons of leaves fall covering the lawn, and the long days of summer make the city a beautiful place to live. Additionally, the lovely northern magnolias that blossom in my neighbor's front yard with branches hanging over my driveway in the spring contributes to the attractiveness of the city. The high quality and diversity of the arts here makes it even more appealing to me!

I live in a Cleveland Suburb with my husband of twenty-eight years, John Michael Murphy who is CEO of John Murphy and Associates Consulting Firm. I met John at a session which he led as consultant to Shaker Heights City School System where I taught AP French and first year Spanish at the high school.

I continue to teach French, dance, and vocal music at my studio, Duffy Liturgical Dance Studio located in University Circle, voted one of the best neighborhoods in the United States. I also serve as director of liturgical dance at University Circle United Methodist Church.

John and I enjoy traveling, reading, and visiting our favorite local restaurants for sumptuous meals on weekends.

Chapter 7

Fifth Child—Henry Ezzard Charles Duffy

Homelife

Henry Ezzard Charles Duffy was born June 22, 1942, during World War II. He was reared in Augusta, Arkansas. He was the fifth of thirteen children and the second male child born to Octavris C. and Leona Stith Duffy. He arrived on the scene eight years after the oldest child, Spencer, who was born in 1934. Henry was an unusual child and youth. You could say he was the outlier in the family. He did not spend a lot of time concentrating on schoolwork but liked to play tricks on others and tell jokes. He worked extremely hard in the garden and fields of cotton, corn, peas, and sorghum. It was known early that Henry did not like working in the fields for our own farm or being hired out by other farmers.

He liked to sing and formed a singing group in high school with three other young men and went around singing at each other's homes. Of course, Daddy would not allow any of us to frequent bars, clubs, or other establishments which sold or served alcoholic drinks and people used language not becoming a Duffy. So his talent was not seen by many to give him the chance to make it in the music world. But Henry really wanted to sing and had a beautiful bass voice, so he continued singing with the group throughout high school. They usually practiced at school because Daddy would not allow Henry to visit other young men and was not particularly fond of them coming to our house.

I remember one of the young men in his group was named Napoleon Bonaparte, and he got teased a lot because of his name. The young men would dress up in their best clothes, because on that day, you were expected to look the part when performing in public. These guys went so far as to "process" their hair to make it look slick like the Temptations, the Impressions, and the Platters—Black male musical groups popular during that era. I do believe they used the axle grease on their hair that Daddy used to grease the wheels of the family wagon. Yes, we had a wagon and used it regularly up until 1960, when we left the farm and moved to the big city of Augusta, Arkansas, some seven miles away.

The Duffy family went to church worship services regularly, Sunday School, morning worship at home or at the church house, youth fellowship on Sunday afternoon, and Wednesday night Bible study and prayer meetings. On the first and third Sunday's afternoons, we attended the Men and Women's Federation Services. There were special Sunday night services, special musical concerts, weeklong revivals, and services where we would be invited to other churches in and around Augusta. Well, Henry was one to speak his mind about things he did not like and usually he was smart enough to speak when Mom and Daddy were not around. Well, this time Henry had had it. He screamed, "Church, church, church, I am just sick of church!" Mother was nearby and heard him. Well, he got a sermon. None of us knew Mom could preach. She went from Genesis to Revelation and then back, in a soft yet stern and demanding and intentional tone. Henry never complained aloud about church again in the presence of either of our parents.

Henry led the family children in much mischief during his time as the oldest in the family at home. This role meant you were in charge of the younger sisters and brothers. By the time he was the oldest at home, there were six younger siblings for him to boss around. He liked that part but did not want any part of taking responsibility for what the younger children did while he was in charge. Now the rule was if the younger siblings in your charge got in trouble, you had the authority to discipline them with some restrictions. You could not kill anybody!

One day, Henry and younger brothers O.C. and Edward thought they would teach Leona and Bernice how to ride the mares, large female horses. Oh, by the way, with no saddle. Bernice and Leona were about nine and eleven, respectively. The brothers put the girls on the mares, hit the mares' behind, and off the girls went on the mares with no saddle. The mares took off fast at first, scaring the girls half-crazy. and then because of the mares' size, slowed the speed a bit and enabled the brothers to get control of the mares and the girls jumped off and ran in the house and didn't breathe a word of this to Mom and Dad. Because first, no one messed with Daddy's mares, Maud and Belle, they were work animals. Secondly, we had been told repeatedly, the mares were not to be ridden. Yes, that was a well-kept secret because we were afraid we would be beaten to shreds if the news reached Mom and Dad.

Henry also led two other ridiculous episodes in the family, Mary and the barn top story. Our sister Mary was put in a tin number 2 tub and pushed down a steep tin roof with a flat landing. Mary was saved by a bunch of peanuts Dad had drying out on top of that barn. Just think of what could have happened if that tub had gone off that roof! Then it was Bernice and Leona again. They were led to get in a canoe. The boys pushed it onto the lake, and none of us could swim. Henry and the neighbor's boy, Buddy, then turned the boat over in the lake. The girls were saved by the neighbor boy's mother who gave the boys a big scolding as she cleaned the girls up and sent them home. Mom and Dad never learned about that either.

High School

In school, Henry did not like sitting in the front of the class, although all the Duffy children did because the teachers in those days used alphabetical seating in all classes. Well, somehow one day, he ended up sitting in the back of the room, where he was sent because of getting in trouble. On that day, the teacher was teaching an English lesson, and Henry was bored and fidgeting in the back of the room and said quite loudly, "Give me liberty or give me death." The teacher asked, "Who said that?" Henry replied, "Patrick Henry." The teacher had to laugh because she was so surprised that Henry knew the author of the famous sayings.

Military Service

After high school graduation, Henry was drafted into the United States Army and served his two-year term. He looked quite handsome in his army uniform, and we were very proud of him. We do not know how he made it through those years because he did not like to take orders from anyone. He was not stationed overseas, just stateside. I am sure there were stories to tell of that part of his life. Unfortunately, we were not able to capture any of them before his death in 2005.

Henry was inducted into military service during the time of the draft July of 1960 and sent to Fort Lenningwood, Missouri, for basic training. He really wanted to go into military service and requested to be sent to Vietnam. Instead, he was sent to Washington, DC, to become an honor guard for six months. Henry hated being in the honor guard and was transferred to Fort Riley, Kansas, where he became military police and spent the rest of his tour of duty at Fort Riley.

It is interesting that Edward who also was drafted into military service in 1965, requested being an honor guard and military police and received neither. He was sent to Vietnam, which is where Henry wanted to go. Edward and Henry both ended their tour of duty at Fort Riley, Kansas.

Life in St. Louis

Henry worked as a grocery delivery man in St Louis. Edward also spent time in St. Louis after military service. He recalls occasions when he would be off work and would accompany Henry on his delivery route. One day as they were delivering groceries, Henry struck out a tune of the famed song "Rescue Me." And he danced to it up to the customer's door. Henry and Edward were greeted at the door by the famous Fontella Bass, who began singing and dancing with Henry. Of course, Fontella Bass was the recording artist who wrote and first recorded the song in 1965. She was so impressed with Henry's singing and dancing to her song that she said she had two tickets to a show on Friday night and invited them to the show. Of course, Henry and Edward quickly replied yes. She gave them the tickets and said, "I'll see you Friday night."

When Friday night came, Henry and Edward made it to Fontella's Show. She called Henry up on the stage and he sang and danced and sang and danced until Henry just about fell out from being tired. He sat for a while to cool off but was called back on stage for an encore performance. So Henry finally had his chance to perform before a large live audience. After the show, Fontella invited Henry and Edward to her dressing room where they chatted and just had a lovely time talking about songs and music.

While Henry and Edward were in St. Louis together, Edward worked at a job in Barnes Hospital which was located at a distance, so Edward rode a bus to and from work. The bus stop was located in an area where some youngsters who did not work preyed on those who did by jumping them and taking their money when they got off the bus. One day when Edward got off the bus, a young man came up to him and told him, "I know you work at the hospital and have a good-paying job, so when you get paid on Friday, we are going to be waiting for you, and we will take all your money." Edward told Henry what the man said, and Henry told Edward not to worry about it. Edward had no idea what Henry was planning. On the Friday when Edward got paid and was getting off the bus, he did not see the young man or his friends, but Henry was there packing a large butcher knife to stave off anyone who tried to take Edward's hard-earned wages. From that Friday on, Henry would meet Edward at that bus stop with his butcher knife.

In another job, Edward was a dishwasher. One day the boss called him into her office. He was wondering why he was called to the office. He had not done anything wrong on the job. He went to her office, and she asked him to have a seat. She then proceeded to (in an off-handed way) compliment him. She said she and others had seen how great a job he was doing washing dishes and that the chief dishwasher would soon retire, and she wanted Edward to become the chief dishwasher. In fact, she went on to say, in about five years, you will be an excellent dishwasher. Edward was not looking to wash dishes all his life and shared the boss's conversation with Henry.

Henry encouraged Edward to leave St. Louis and go back south and go to college and get a degree. Edward had interviewed once for other jobs with an aircraft company which paid good wages and was waiting for a second interview. Henry's words were so encouraging and convincing that Edward did in fact leave St. Louis and enrolled in college at AM&N College in Pine Bluff, Arkansas. Edward says Henry is the main reason he went to college.

Life in Los Angeles

After being discharged from the army, Henry spent a period in St. Louis Missouri. He lived with his Aunt Armentha Noble, Mom's sister. He later married Diane and they had a son, Leslie. Several years later, Henry and Diane were divorced.

After spending several years in St. Louis, working odd jobs and moving from house to house, Henry moved to Los Angeles, California, and stayed with his sister Marie until he was able to get his own apartment and make it on his own. Henry worked for Standard Brand Paint Co. for twelve years as warehouse supervisor. His last job was with Phonemate as a shipping and receiving supervisor. Henry was more like Marie's son than brother because whenever he was in need, he would call on her, and she was always there for him and his family. This held true through the good times and the troubled times.

Henry was a very jolly person who loved to have fun. He would go to the racetrack and play the horses. Marie would get on him about spending money at the racetrack. He would tell her, "I can stand to hear a baby cry for milk, but I can't stand to hear a horse holler for hay." Marie would get so angry with him, but he would just laugh and continue to chew gum. We would sometimes have family gatherings, and Henry would not come. His sister Marie would ask him, "Why didn't he come?" He would say, "You know I'm just a loner." Marie would say to him, "Crazy boy I'm your sister, you should come to my house." Sometimes when he came over, he teased our sister Leona. He would tell her he was going down on skid row and get one of those GR guys so she could clean him up and he would make her a good husband. Leona would get angry and leave the room. He meant no harm. He just liked to have fun.

Then Henry would put on a show for the family. He would get on the floor and start dancing, and he would act like he was out of his head and would be holding his hands in a crazy way, and acting like he was cripple, he would have everyone laughing. After his "playing the horses" days were over, Henry became a member of Harbor Christian Center where he served faithfully as usher, member of the choir, and was featured in many plays. He was very dedicated to his church. The pastor and members loved him and encouraged and supported him on his Christian journey.

One day, he went to his sister Marie's house with her husband's ex-girlfriend. Marie's husband became angry and raised his hand to hit Henry. Marie went to the kitchen, got a knife, and when her husband's hand went up to hit her brother, she cut his hand. She had to take him to emergency and told him he had better not tell them that she cut him. She told him, "Don't you ever raise your hand to hit my brother."

While in California, Henry met, courted, and married Maria Doctoler. To this union, three sons were born: Robert, Eric, and Henry Jr. Henry already had one son, Leslie, when he married Maria.

Henry and Maria loved children. Maria would babysit for people, and when Henry came home from work, he would play with the children and did not want the children to go home. Sometimes they would keep the children over the weekend.

Henry was a very healthy person, rarely sick. His death was such a shock to us. Maria called Marie at 5:00 a.m., asking her to come and take her to the hospital because they had taken Henry there. Marie said she jumped out of bed dressed and hit the freeway doing seventy to eighty miles an hour to get her there. When they got there, the doctor met them at the door and told them the news that Henry had passed. Maria was uncontrollably in tears. Marie was holding back her tears as she tried to console Maria.

Maria and Marie stayed in touch with each other long after Henry's death. They would go shopping, have lunch together, and enjoy each other's company until Maria left and moved to New York. They kept in touch by phone while Maria was in New York until her death.

Two of Henry's sons have joined him in death. Henry has two sons who are living. Marie keeps in touch with Henry Jr. He says she's the only mother he has now.

Chapter 8

The Sixth Child—Leona Marzetta Duffy

Leona Marzetta Duffy was born on June 14, 1943, the sixth child of Mr. Octavris C. and Mrs. Leona Stith Duffy. She is named after her mother and has many features of her mother, including her skin color and build. She says she never had hand-me-down clothing because she was so small. Mama said in her book that she fainted two times—the day Leona was born and lost her speaking ability for one day. The doctor and those around him thought Mom would die giving birth, so much so that my brother Spencer, who was just nine years old, asked that the baby be named Leona, so the family would have someone to remember Mama by.

Life at Home

I came along with an older brother, Henry, and a younger sister, Bernice. Even though I grew up with Bernice and Henry who were closest to me age wise, I tended to interact with Nancy more.

One Easter, all the girls had beautiful dresses and on the day after Easter, the girls wanted to wear their Easter dresses to school, and Mama told them not to because they could get dirty or torn. Some of the girls wore their Easter dresses to school, but I did not. I did not want to get punished by disobeying Mama. That is the day our house burned, and my Easter dress was burned along with all the other clothes. After the fire destroyed the Easter dresses, Mama told me, "Maybe you should have worn yours too."

Nancy and I used to fight once a day about something. I would give her 25 cents to wash dishes for me. The older girls alternated dishwashing so that Bernice and I washed dishes every other day. Nancy was not in the rotation yet, so I would give her 25 cents to wash dishes for me. Nancy would take the money but would not wash the dishes. So she and I fought all through the house on my day to wash dishes. I could not tell Mama because I would have been punished for trying to get Nancy to do my work.

One time Aunt Nancy came to visit us, and Mama was making teacakes. I was standing by the stove, and my aunt was facing me, but she could not see Nancy. Nancy came up behind me and took some teacakes off the plate. When Mama asked what happened to the missing teacakes, Aunt Nancy told Mama I was stealing the cookies. I tried to tell Mama that it was not me. It was Nancy. Mama said to me, "You are calling your aunt a liar." I was punished for something that I did not do, but Nancy did. In our family, the older child was punished if we did something to the younger ones or if we did something that got the younger one in trouble.

On another occasion when Nancy and I were fighting, I got really upset with her antics, and when the fighting became fierce,

Nancy threw a book at me. The fight was occurring in front of a large glass door. I ducked and the book went through that glass door and shattered it. Seeing this, all were shocked and scared. That door probably cost several days' worth of picking cotton. We all knew somebody was going to get a good whipping. We cleaned up the broken glass from the porch, and we tried to make up a story about how the glass door was broken to spare a life. Daddy and Mama had gone to town for a church meeting and would not be back until later that night. We kept framing our story to get the most plausible one. We even put a curtain over the door trying to keep the shattered glass hidden.

When Daddy and Mama came home, part of the curtain was flying out of the broken glass, and of course, Daddy knew that should not be. Upon close examination, he saw the huge hole and cracks in that glass door. We were so quiet you could hear a pin drop. We waited for Daddy's reactions.

Then it came. "What happened here?" We knew not to tell a lie, so I confessed, "Nancy threw a book at me, and I ducked, and the book went through the glass door and broke and shattered it." Nancy chimed in that I was fighting her, and that was why she threw the book at me. I don't remember much after that except I got punished again for something Nancy did.

One summer I was ironing, and it was extremely hot. The ironing board was directly under a light which got very hot on my head. I took the light bulb out and continued ironing. Daddy came in and asked who took the bulb out? I went to get the light bulb to put it back in. Daddy asked me why I did not answer him. So he hit me in my back so hard I went all the way to the back porch.

On another day, I got up on a chair to get some thread to sew a doll's dress. Bernice reached up to get my attention and accidentally tore the pocket on my dress. When Mama came home and asked me what happened, and I told her Bernice accidently tore it. Mama called me a tattletale.

We lived on the farm in the red house in Cavell. Edna and Henry were courting and we, the younger kids and I, would spy on them. We especially got a thrill and embarrassment to see them kiss their boyfriend or girlfriend.

One of the chores that most of us had on the farm was milking the cow. I was afraid of the cow, so when I went to grab the teats to milk the cow and she moved, I would get up and run to the house with only about a cup of milk in a two-gallon bucket. Mama would say, "I don't know why the milk always spoils when you milk the cows." I added a little water to make the milk appear to be more. I guess I really invented the 2 percent milk, and now I want my royalty. Ha!

We picked and chopped cotton and picked strawberries. Cotton picking paid 5 to 10 cents a pound, cotton chopping paid $2 to $3 per day per person, and for strawberries we were paid 10 cents per pint. It would be so cold picking cotton that ice would be on the ground. Our feet would be so cold that they felt like a block of ice. I could really pick a lot of cotton. One time I picked three hundred pounds in one day. I was so tired that day that when I kneeled to say my nighttime prayer, I went to sleep and stayed on my knees all night. One time I played sick so I would not have to go and pick cotton. Daddy gave me castor oil, and it had an awful taste. I wanted to go pick cotton the next day, but Daddy made me stay home two more days, taking castor oil. I never pretended to be sick to avoid going to the fields again.

Mama liked to make pickles. She would make the brine solution and put the solution and cucumbers in glass jars. I stayed hungry a lot, so Mama fed me the pickles.

One day Henry, Edward, and I were in the smokehouse in the backyard of the red house, smoking cotton leaves. When I had enough, I went into the house and told Daddy they were out there smoking cotton leaves. Daddy went out to the smokehouse, caught them in action, and gave them a whipping. Henry and Edward had it in for me. I would go to mission meetings with Mama, prayer meetings, and any other kind of meeting to avoid Edward and Henry. Mama would say to the others, "I wish all of you would like to go to church like Leona." She did not know. I was going to church to avoid Henry and Edward.

School Days

The teachers tried to hold me back in school because they thought I was too small to take care of myself. But I proved I could protect myself quite well. I did not incite trouble in school, but if someone bothered me, they soon learned that I could respond appropriately.

In high school, I told the physical education teacher that I could not be out in the direct sunlight without something on my head because my nose would bleed badly. The teacher did not listen to me, and I went out in the sun with my class with nothing on my head. I had a bad nosebleed and was sent to the nurse's station to lie down until my nose stopped bleeding. The teacher apologized later for making me go out in the hot sun. Overall, I had a blessed childhood growing up despite the many times I got in trouble because of other siblings and my own trouble making.

I did not have many friends in school. The only time I would have friends was when they wanted to copy off my tests. One time Mr. Alcorn marked my paper down because he said I let other people copy off my paper. Before I finished high school, Ida Nell came to stay with her grandparents and attended the same school and became my best friend.

Life in Los Angeles

After high school, I moved to Los Angeles, California, to attend college. I lived with my oldest sister Eliza Marie. She had two children, Ferroll Marie and Leonard. Joseph was born after I moved out and got married.

I attended Los Angeles City College and worked on my associate degree. I went on to do further study and earned certificates in banking from the American Institute of Banking. I attended night classes to further prepare myself for good-paying jobs in banking. I married Sylvester Harris in 1963 and two sons were born to that union. Michael was born in 1964 and Sylvester III in 1967. Our youngest son, Sylvester III, was killed in a car accident in Jacksonville, North Carolina, in 2005.

1984. Michael is in a convalescent center in Los Angeles after suffering a stroke in 2015.

Sister Marie, Lashaunda Duffy, Henry Duffy Jr., and Leona

I continued to attend church after moving to California and enjoyed singing in the choir at New Kingdom Baptist Church. It was here that I served as director of Christian Education, and the Baptist Training Union (BTU). I also taught Sunday School for children, and I really loved teaching the classes of children. I sang in the choir and served as financial secretary in churches in Los Angeles. The scripture spoke to me in a way that I could take comfort in who I was and am. At Shiloh Baptist Church, I served as assistant superintendent of the Sunday School, financial secretary, assistant to the board director, associate secretary of the association, and taught Sunday School for adults. It was at Shiloh that I was privileged to be the pastor's aide speaker and the speaker for the church's anniversary.

My first job in California was a cashier in the toy department with the S&H Kress Store. Other places of employment included J. J. Newberry's midtown store, United California Bank of Manchester Vermont, Security Pacific Bank–Wilsher Branch, and Hawthorne Savings and Loan. My jobs included bank teller, proof manager, vault teller, teller supervisor, management programmer, and assistant teller supervisor. I conducted workshops where I presented pertinent information to high school students who were interested in banking as a career choice. Students earned certificates for taking part in the workshops. When the Hawthorne Saving Bank changed names and became the Hawthorne Savings and Loans, we were required to take a test to keep our jobs. I was one point short of the passing score. The team suggested I talk to the manager to see if I would be able to keep my job. I asked to speak with her, and she said okay. But she kept putting me off, so I insisted she talk to me. At last, she agreed to talk, and I asked if I would be able to keep my job having missed the cut off score by just one point. The manager put her finger in my face and said, "I don't know what I am going to do." At that point, I knew I had to leave because I could not tolerate having her put her finger in my face. I would mop the floor with her behind and lose all the benefits I already had in the company. Since they were going to lay off some people anyway, and I knew I would be on that list, I left and went on unemployment for two years. I worked in banking for thirty-eight and a half years.

After working in banking for more than thirty-eight years, I went to work at May Company for two years and Chick-Fil-A for nearly two years.

Now, I work as a stock clerk at Smart-Final, and after two more years, I plan to retire.

Chapter 9

The Seventh Child—
Bernice Duffy Johnson

Growing Up in Augusta

I was born Bernice Duffy on August 10, 1945, the year World War II ended. You may say I was conceived during the war but greeted a world free of war. I was the seventh of thirteen children born to Octavris C. and Leona Stith Duffy in Augusta, Arkansas. My parents were sharecroppers for most of my homelife until we moved to the city in 1960. The seventh position placed me smack dab in the middle, with six older siblings and six younger siblings. Some called me Lucky Seven.

I started reading at the age of three years and remember reading from the Methodist hymnal "Hallelujah Thine the glory, Hallelujah Amen, Hallelujah Thine the Glory, Revive Us Again." While this may sound strange, it really isn't because as the seventh child, I used the resources of older siblings—their books, their speaking, listening to them read aloud to Mother—and looked intensely at words as Mom and my older siblings read me stories.

In the Duffy-Stith household, one had to learn early to walk, read, and work both in the home and on the farm. This was necessary so we would be out of the way of another sibling on the way soon after. Those who came after me came in 1946, 1947, 1948, and 1949. Two brothers first, then three sisters. It was two years between my older sister and me.

We were under strict discipline growing up. We experienced rich resourceful teaching from both parents, but most of the nurturing came from our mother. Dad did not show his feelings of love and caring well—it was the feelings of displeasure and disappointment that we noticed often. This was not to say he did not love his family, for he truly did. I can remember hearing Dad and Mom talking at night when the crops did not come in as anticipated. They were trying to figure out how they would manage with little money and such a large family. We were always put first with food and clothing, while both Mom and Dad made sacrifices. We had no central heat in the house. Therefore, bedrooms were not heated, the kitchen stove and the living room fireplace or stove provided heat for the house. On very cold subfreezing temperature nights, Dad would come in our rooms and put extra quilts on us to make sure we stayed warm enough during the night. Those quilts were so heavy. There was no need to try and turn over, even though that would be difficult anyway because there would be at least two people in a full-size bed, and sometimes three.

From the day we were born, our parents instilled in us the importance of being kind, courteous, patient, forgiving, respectful, hospitable, and generous. We learned early on that education was the way out of the cotton field. Our parents impressed upon each of us the importance of learning, knowledge, and education and how each of these components affected the other. To this end, we learned to memorize Bible verses, poems, quotations, songs, and plays. There were enough of us children to act out plays, play games of softball, and run track through the corn and cotton fields. Indoor activities for us included bingo, Chinese checkers, regular checkers, working puzzles, and putting puzzles together. We could not play any games that contained dice because that would have been sinful. Outside, I can remember building a playhouse in the woods, complete with an old stove, chair, and small table. We would go there in our rare spare time and pretend we were in a real house. It was fun.

A quite dangerous outdoor sport we enjoyed was ice skating with thin rubber boots on in a semi-frozen pond in the winter (unbeknown to our parents of course.) And then one time, my older brother and one younger one, along with a neighbor boy, took us out in a small floating boat and none of us could swim. Yes, they turned the boat over in the lake, and we were saved by the neighbor boy's mom who gave the older boys a good scolding for being reckless with the lives of the girls, my older sister and me.

Then there was the mealtime. Even though we were economically poor, we raised most of our foods, hogs and chicken for meat and eggs, cows for milk, a garden provided all sorts of vegetables and fruits and the grape, peach, apple, and pecans trees supplied fruits and nuts. So while we may not have always had what we wanted to eat, there was always enough food for us to eat.

Household chores for me included washing dishes (boys in the family did not wash dishes since they had major roles outside the house on the farm) sweeping and mopping floors, washing, rinsing clothes by hand, using a rubboard, and hanging clothes on an outside clothesline. Even in the cold of winter, I can remember seeing clothes frozen on the line and wishing for the sun to come and thaw the clothes.

I remember bringing wood from the yard and porch inside the house, pumping water for the livestock and chickens and bringing the calves back from the woods to get milk from their mother cows after we had milked the cows for family use. One of my chores was to milk the cow. After my first attempt produced less than a cup of milk, I was relieved of that chore. When the cow swished her tail to shoo away flies, it scared me so I could not sit under the cow and do any milking.

Picking fruits and vegetables and washing and preparing them for cooking were also chores for me. I remember thrashing peas and putting the peas in ten-gallon barrels for winter food. I enjoyed shucking and silking corn and storing it in barns as feed for the cows and hogs and the younger ears of corn for family meals.

School Days

We all attended Carver Elementary and High School in Augusta. The school was designed like a college campus with six buildings: a tall brick administration building stood in the center of the campus, and it contained the main offices, principal's and secretary's, classrooms, auditorium, and the library. Other buildings included a stand along cafeteria, a home economics building, agriculture building, elementary building, and a gymnasium.

It was on these hallowed grounds that I began my formal education that would later lead me to college, graduate school, and the position of provost and vice chancellor for Academic Affairs at NCCU in Durham, North Carolina. It was here that I gained basic knowledge in reading, social studies, writing, mathematics, and the other sciences. Already an avid reader when I started first grade at age five (there was no kindergarten in the school at that time and no head start), I excelled in all my classes, receiving all Ss in elementary school and mostly As in high school.

It was when I was in the second grade that I decided I wanted to become a teacher. This is what happened. There were no teacher aides during those days, so when a teacher needed to leave the room for personal reasons, a student was put in charge until he or she returned. Can you imagine that today!

Well, I was left in charge and proceeded to teach students to identify food and animals by pictures and pronounce and spell the name of the food or animal. I was unaware that Ms. B. Marshall had returned to the classroom and was observing me. She liked what she saw and said to me, "You are going to be a teacher." I agreed, and sixteen years later, I assumed my first teaching job in the public schools of Indianapolis, Indiana.

The only Cs I received in high school were in physical education because we were not allowed (by our father) to wear gym clothes, shorts were required to perform the exercises, and we could not wear shorts or any pants to school. After the first year, the PE teacher considered it unfair since I was not the one deciding not to dress out, it was made for me. So I performed other activities that could be done in a dress or skirt.

Because we all went to the same school, we had name recognition. I was the seventh child to attend and the siblings who preceded me were very smart. So I had a reputation to live up to from first grade on. I loved the challenge and did very well in school making mostly straight As on most assignments and tests. I loved school, loved studying, reading, and learning. I worked in the library during my high school years and read most of the classic novels of that time: *Silas Marner, Wuthering Heights, Les Misérables, Moby Dick, 2000 Leagues Under the Sea, Treasure Island, Gulliver's Travels, 12 Million Black Voices, The Autobiography of Frederick Douglass, George Washington Carver, Harriett Tubman, Sojourner Truth*, and *A Tale of Two Cities*. These classics related to the rich world literature and American literature classes we had with a remarkable teacher, Ms. T. F. Smith. She was the wife of the principal but was quite different from him. She loved teaching, and she loved her students and made sure we were prepared to meet the challenges of college and beyond. Her husband, the principal, seemed to be tired of the Duffys becoming valedictorian of their classes. There had been three before me, and he tried to make sure I would not make the fourth. After I earned the highest GPA and scored higher than any student in the Black school or White school in the whole county on a standardized scholastic test for two years, it was clear to everyone who had earned the title of valedictorian for the class of 1963.

During my teenage years I made friends with my cousin Julia and another girl named Ruby. Ruby would always ask me, "Bernice, Bernice, how much money you got?" I am not sure to this day why she always asked me that, because my answer was always the same. "I don't have any money today." Ruby and Julia were smart girls, and Ruby's parents were stricter with her than our parents because she was the only girl in her family. By the time I was eighth grade, we had moved from the farm to main street in Augusta, Arkansas. Julia and Ruby lived in the country. Sometimes Julia would spend the night with me, and I would spend the night with her. Ruby's parents did not allow any visitation either way. So we spent as much time together at school during recess and study halls to include her in our little circle.

Julia and I went to college together. Ruby went to a private religious school in Little Rock, Arkansas. Julia and I went to a state institution, AM&N College in Pine Bluff, Arkansas, about ninety miles from our hometown.

I only had one childhood fancy. His name was Lonnie, and we had one date at the house, corresponded shortly after we graduated high school, but then just stopped. To be truthful, I was not into boyfriends that much. My head and heart were set on getting a good education and getting out of the cotton fields of Augusta and Cavell, Arkansas. I did not want anything to stand in my way. So I devoted my time to the library and books.

Favorite Memories of Homelife

Memories include Mom and older siblings reading to me from Grimm's fairy tales, the Bible, and Sunday School books, singing hymns with Daddy leading them and playing games of Bingo and checkers. The family meals were special also. (Imagine ten to twelve people sitting at the table for breakfast, lunch, and dinner. There was always interesting discussion, and if anyone had gotten out of line in the fields, at school, at home, or sassed Mom, it would be discussed over meatloaf, turnip, mustard greens, black-eyed peas, cornbread, and buttermilk. We would have dessert for lunch and dinner, and sometimes the leftover dessert from lunch would be eaten at dinner time. Well, one day, Mom made her famous butter roll for lunch, and there was plenty left over for dinner, but some siblings, not me, decided to eat the leftover butter roll between lunch and dinner. After dinner, Daddy asked for the butter roll, and when Mom went to get it, the pan was empty. Daddy was in no way pleased. He asked, profoundly, who ate the butter roll, as if he expected someone to confess or someone to give them up. Everyone got so quiet, you could earnestly hear a pin drop. He asked again, a little stronger than the first time. This time, as if in concert, all heads turned toward the culprit, and Daddy called her out and gave her the sermon about stealing. Normally, that kind of action of eating the leftover butter roll would get you a good whipping with Daddy's strap, but I guess he was too tired and upset, he finished his mini sermon, then went and sat on the front porch and read the newspaper.

Although we, the girls, were not allowed to dance. I never learned to dance anyway. Daddy did escort me to the debutante's ball. I sang the song "Unchained Melody" and waltzed with my date, Lonnie. Daddy walked me into the gym with music playing and seemed to enjoy it and stayed through the entire ball.

For the last two years of high school, I worked at Spears' Grocery Store and saved some money for college. Mom and Dad were financially unable to assist me at that time.

In 1963, I graduated from Carver High School and was the valedictorian of my class. I remember the class motto, "The Past Cannot Be Changed. The Future Is Still in Our Hands." The opening line in my graduation address was, "Linger with me on the sentiments of our motto, the past cannot be changed, the future is still in our hands. Truly the past cannot be changed, but we can determine our future by using what we have learned and experienced at Carver High School to lead and guide us to that not so distant future." What a night that was? I believe President Lawrence A. Davis Sr., president of AM&N College, delivered our class's commencement address. As valedictorian, I received a $250 scholarship to attend AM&N College in Pine Bluff, Arkansas, which paid for my tuition, and I worked in the snack bar and received a loan to pay for fees, books, room, and board.

The College Years

After graduating high school, I worked at Spears' Grocery store during the summer and then went to summer school at AM&N and achieved a 3.0 GPA. An A average on the scale used then. My financial support from home was limited, so I used money from graduation gifts and money from older sisters and brothers to attend summer school. I did not have the advantage Cora and Edna had, which was using money from one day per week of our work picking cotton for others, to go for their education. However, both Edna and Cora were very supportive of me when I was in college. Cora paid for my hair appointments, the entire four years I was at AM&N. College and gave her brother-in-law, Carthell and me, cash when she visited us. Edna sent me money often while I was at AM&N College.

I had no driving license and had not learned to drive when I went off to college. I depended on neighbors and college friends to get to and from college which was ninety miles from Augusta, Arkansas. I could only come home from college when the residence halls were closed, which was at Thanksgiving and Christmas and between semesters. It was my first year in college when President John F. Kennedy was assassinated. I came to the residence hall from class about midafternoon, and the lounge was full of students sitting on chairs, the sofa, and on the floor, and our house mother, a strong and courageous woman, was in tears. I asked what was wrong and was told that President Kennedy had just been assassinated in Dallas, Texas. I immediately joined the group and wept with them. There was sadness on the campus for the next few weeks.

My major was home economics education with a minor in general science. I took several laboratory courses both in my major and in the sciences. I found myself explaining a lot, how science impacts home economics. The founder of the home economics profession, Ellen Richards, was a chemist and started the water purification system in the US Food Science and chemistry of textiles were real and I ended up with twenty-one science credits including courses in general chemistry, physical science, biology, anatomy and physiology, bacteriology, mathematics, and household physics. I enjoyed all of my classes and excelled in most.

My favorite faculty members included Ms. King, Ms. Sutton, Ms. Lamb, Ms. Godfrey, Father Hines, Dr. Fuller, Dr. Muzumda, Dr. Alexander, Dr. Lee, Dr. Greenhouse, and Dr. Hyman.

The management residence course was unique because four to six students lived in a house on campus for six weeks. The course was designed to simulate all normal duties of a household. Ms. King was the director and managed our activities in the home. We planned, shopped for food, prepared meals, including a guest meal and served them properly. We evaluated the meals for nutritional standards, taste, attractiveness, and other attributes of a well-planned and served meal. In addition to meal preparation, we performed functions of caring for the home, such as washing, cleaning floors and household appliances, reading electric meters, arranging furniture for special occasions, and doing laundry.

I recall being a first year student with mostly juniors and seniors in a social problems class taught by Dr. (Mrs.) Muzumda at 8:00 a.m. on Mondays and Wednesdays. I worked in the snack bar on campus, and a storm one night caused me to wait long hours for a delivery truck, which arrived at 7:15 a.m. on Wednesday. I could not leave the snack bar until the truck arrived. I had not brought my books with me that night because I was to get off work at 10:00 p.m. By the time I got back to my room, cleaned up a bit, and went to class, I had not read my homework. Wouldn't you know I was the first to be called on that morning, and I had to admit to the great doctor that I was not prepared. She ranted and went on to tell why she did not want first-year students in upper-level courses. And then she said to me, "Dr. Duffy, it gives me immense pleasure to give you an F for today." That taught me two lessons: never go to work without your schoolbooks and never go to Dr. M's class without having read your assignments and being prepared to answer questions about the assignments.

To redeem myself, I did much better on another assignment. I was to report on a chapter written by a priest whose last name was Duffy. I wrote to the priest, and he sent me a tape of one of his sessions related to the topic of antisocial behavior in children. So after I made my report, described the author, and played the tape, I was in Dr. M's good graces, but the upper classmates hated me. I made them look bad. That was okay. I only had a few more days in that class.

In a US history class, taught by the legendary Dr. Russell, again I was a sophomore in class with mostly juniors and seniors, many of whom were history majors. We were assigned various cabinet members in Lyndon B. Johnson's presidency. A senior history major and I were assigned to work independently on John Foster Dulles. I gave my report first and based it on a thorough review of the literature and research and then the male senior history major gave his report. It was obvious that the history major was ill prepared, and Dr. R. blasted him in front of the class and told him he was sorry that he was a history major. It was such a thrashing that I felt sorry for the history major. My intent was to present the best report I could, not to get a fellow classmate in trouble. This did not deter me from continuing to do my best on all reports. The upper-class students still said I was making them look bad.

In my major course of study, I did well, and there were several students who performed well in my major, so I did not get the push back I got when I performed well in subjects outside of my major. We had a family-like environment and got along well; I suppose this was because we saw each other regularly since we all took several of the same courses. The major courses helped set me on the course for my future career as a teacher in public schools. The student teaching part of the curriculum was a real highlight of my college career. This was done in Eldorado, Arkansas, with supervising teacher Ms. Lee. She taught me a lot, and I spent some afternoons at her house where she enjoyed the special cornbread I prepared from a special recipe adapted from that used at the House of Fine Foods in St. Louis, Missouri, where I spent two summers working.

In May of 1967, I graduated in the top 10 percent of a class of four hundred students. Mama and Daddy were able to attend and see me walk across the stage, the fourth of their thirteen children to receive a bachelor's degree, three from AM&N, and one from Southern University in Baton Rouge, Louisiana.

In April of 1967, I applied for and received a full scholarship to the Pennsylvania State University to study family economics and home management. I received a master of education degree in four quarter sessions from August 1967 to June 1968. The time at Penn State was filled with lots of sadness. In January of 1968, my brother O.C. Jr. was in a head-on car accident and lost his left leg. My sister's brother-in-law, Carthell, who graduated from AM &N with me was killed in Vietnam in the January 1968 TET Offensive, and one of my college roommates was killed in a head-on car collision in Little Rock, Arkansas, in February of 1968. As if that was not enough, on April 5, 1968, Dr. Martin Luther King Jr. was assassinated in Memphis, Tennessee. I returned from the library at about midnight and was in the bathroom washing my face when a White student who was washing her hands asked me how I was. I said fine, only tired from being in the library so long. She said, "You haven't heard, have you?" I said, "Heard what?" She said, "Dr. King has been shot." I asked about his condition. She said quietly, "He's dead." Shocked to hear the news, I dashed out of the restroom to find the other six Black students who lived in the graduate residence hall where I was staying. They could not be found. So I spent the night alone in sadness. I could not go home to be with my family through any of these times, so I managed to make it through by the grace of God.

I did not date much in college. There was one guy Cal who pestered me so much that I agreed to date him, and we did for about a year. Then I discovered he already had a girlfriend and wanted to use me for my brains to help him get through college. I was more interested in getting my college education because I could not return home to Augusta to a life of picking cotton and working in jobs with no future.

I spent the summer before my senior year of college in Chicago, Illinois, where I participated in a YM-YWCA sponsored Summer Program, SPECTRUM, which stands for Special Program on Evolving Cultural Trends and Race in an Urban Metropolis. The program included students from all over the US. We converged on

Chicago and worked to bring attention and solutions to discrim-ination in housing in the city and suburbs of Chicago. I worked as a Community Action Intern and lived with a Greek family in the suburbs of Chicago. Linda, my roommate, and I would take the EL train to Woodlawn YWCA and to the Illinois Institute of Technology where the other students were housed. Linda was from Chico, California. We worked with about fifty young children and youth on community projects at the Woodlawn YWCA. We assisted with stage props for plays, directing portions of the plays, teaching arts and crafts classes and meetings with parents and others from the Woodlawn community. One meeting of particular interest was when the director of the Woodlawn YWCA, Ms. Williams, invited Linda and me to a luncheon where we met Mrs. Coretta S. King and Dr. Dorothy Heights, at that time, a member of the National Council of Women, who later became its president. We were in awe of the significance of this experience and took away bits of information highlighting the unique roles of women in a changing society. They were both interested in our plans and wanted us to consider a career in the YWCA.

Love and Marriage

It was in the city of Chicago when I was working in the SPECTRUM program where I met my future husband Lawrence Edward Johnson. Everyone called him Larry, and that is how he was introduced to me. He was with another young man named Laquin when I met him. Laquin was trying to talk with me, and when I said I was from Arkansas, Larry took over and acted as if he had to take care of me "a shy little girl from a small town in Arkansas," now in the big city alone. At first, I wanted no part of any lasting relation-ship with Larry or anyone else. I was still on my career focus and did not want anyone or anything to get in the way of that goal. But Larry kept up with me, sheltering me from harm and danger.

Larry had completed his bachelor's degree at Wilberforce University in Ohio and was now a student at Garrett Theological Seminary in Evanston, Illinois. He had worked in Chicago and knew his way around. I had just finished my junior year at AM&N College and was looking forward to completing my senior year in 1966–1967. I was in the summer program to earn money to help finance my senior year in college. Larry was a research intern and lived on the campus of the Illinois Institute of Technology, where we met for our general meetings.

This was the summer of 1966 and the year Dr. King had decided to lead several marches in the suburbs of Chicago to protest discrimination in housing in Chicago and its suburbs. There were alternatives to actively participating in the marches. You could care for children of the marchers, prepare and serve refreshments for the marchers, or work in your usual community setting. It was here that Larry found out that I was not as shy as he thought. He told me instead of marching, I could help care for the children or prepare refreshments. Well, that did not sit well with me at all, and I said to myself, the audacity of this man! I was going to march and march I did through Gage and Hyde Park. We were scheduled to go to Cicero, but the authorities felt it was too dangerous. In Gage Park, we were walking on sidewalks through actual neighborhoods with neighborhood residents right in our faces. They were throwing bottles and rocks and jeering and spiting at and on us. Of course, it was a nonviolent protest, so we could not say anything or do anything but walk and look straight ahead. At one point in the march, a resident threw a rock that hit Dr. King on one side of his head, and he was bleeding. We were so concerned about him being hurt, but he was not. He turned around to the marchers and asked, "Is everyone all right?" We were all right but concerned that Dr. King was bleeding. He wiped his head and kept marching, and we did the same. Spit flew past Larry and me, and a bottle missed my head by about one inch. But we kept marching until the end, and we got back to our respective places safely.

Linda and I commuted to our work assignment using the EL Train that ran on Chicago's South Side. The south side was where the Black Stone Rangers and Rangerettes gangs were active. One day when we left work and were walking down Woodlawn Avenue to catch the El to return home, we encountered the Black Stone

Rangerettes. I tend to walk fast in public and as I was walking, I suddenly realized Linda was not beside me anymore. I looked around and the Rangerettes had accosted her and were saying terrible things to her and suggesting that she was in the wrong neighborhood. I just started praying that they would not harm Linda. It was five or six of them to our two. I was smart enough to know those odds were not good, yet I could not just stand there and do nothing. So I just said softly and probably trembling, "Linda, let's go," and she's with me, and we just want to catch the train and go home. They said a few choice words to me but backed away. Linda tried to keep up with me from then on, and I tried to make sure not to leave her behind again.

One night while returning from IIT on a city bus, I did not know which stop was right to get to the home where I was living. I was on the bus when the driver got to the end of his route, so he asked me where I was going. After I told him, he said I would need to remain on the bus, and he would make sure to let me know when to get off. I had to trust him because I had no idea of where I was and how to get to where I needed to get. So even after I got off at the right place, with my poor sense of directions, I was still lost. Finally, by God's grace, I found my way to the house where I lived that summer. Not a word of this to Linda or the family with which I lived. Then, later that evening, as we watched the news, we found out that Richard Speck killed eight nurses in their residence on Chicago's South Side. In my efforts to find my way home, I walked within three blocks of the residence where the eight nurses were killed. Whew, I still shudder to think of that night.

During the summer of 1966, I had an opportunity to meet Reverend Jesse Jackson, Andrew Young, Julian Bond, Reverend Ralph Abernathy, Reverend. C. T. Vivian, Richard Gregory, Mahalia Jackson, Joan Biaz, Harry Belafonte, and the group Sweet Honey in the Rock. I received an education not possible in the classroom that summer and was able to utilize knowledge and information gained there in my last year of college and into my graduate and postgraduate educational programs.

Yes, the summer of 1966 was quite a memorable one in my life. This was the summer I met my future husband.

Larry and I kept in contact with each other by phone calls and mail and developed a serious relationship. The summer of 1967, Larry came to meet my parents in Augusta, Arkansas. I was in the room next to the living room when Larry asked Daddy if he could marry me. After some lecturing about how to treat women, and his intentions and whether he could take care of a family, Daddy said we could be married, but told Larry, "If you find out you can't treat her right, bring her back where you found her."

A reunion for the program was held in December of that year in Chicago, and it was here that Larry proposed to me. We were at a restaurant with two White couples from the SPECTRUM program. We finished the meal's entrée and when the dessert was brought out, mine had a candle on it and a dollop of whipped cream. We had celebrated my twenty-first birthday the summer before in Chicago. So I knew it was not for my birthday. Everyone said at once-blow out the candle! I started to and then noticed something shining in the dessert. At that time, Larry stood up and said wait, then got on his knees, took my hand, and asked me to marry him. I was so shocked, "yes" just came out of my mouth. Then suddenly, one of the women got up and ran from the table. Everyone was shocked. I asked her date if I should follow her. He said yes, and I did. It turned out that she was expecting her date to propose to her and when it was me and not her, she was so disappointed. I felt badly for her, and we talked until she was calm enough to go back to the table where we finished our desserts. This was one of my first counseling lessons.

In December of 1967, Larry and I traveled by train to his home in Las Vegas, Nevada, where I met his parents. Mr. Harvey and Mrs. Alma Johnson. They were very hospitable to me. But Larry's dad wanted me to know I was better looking than the White girlfriend he brought to meet them a few years before. I remind Larry of that quote every now and then, just to get him stirred up. In spring of 1968, Larry met my sister Cora and brother-in-law Henry in Camden, Arkansas. We spent the night with them, and I cooked some pork chops with gravy. Larry still talks about how good the gravy was. Sister Cora and Henry approved of Larry, but Cora asked me if I had to get married. The answer of course was no.

The Wedding and Aftermaths

1968 Wedding of
Lawrence and Bernice

Larry and Bernice
in 2019

50th Wedding Anniversary 2018

On August 24, 1968, probably the hottest day ever in Augusta, Arkansas, Lawrence Edward Johnson, and Bernice Duffy were married in Jackson Chapel CME Church with no air-conditioning. Most of my siblings attended and participated. We were married by William (Bill) Carter who was to be Larry's best man, but the pastor of Jackson Chapel had a death in his family and could not perform the ceremony, so Bill did it, and Henry stood in as Larry's best man. Things just started to turn out wrong. When we got married, I had not seen Larry for several months, and he was clean shaven. He shows up a day before the wedding with a beard and sideburns, and I hated the look. Then I was making my wedding dress, and Mom's sewing machine broke, so I had to have a seamstress finish it. Brother O.C. suggested a baker for the cake that I was going to make myself. I had no wedding budget, and my parents could not afford to assist. When the baker brought me the cake the day of the wedding, I thought it was a sample. Well, it was not. It was a regular two-layer cake about four inches high. But that was my wedding cake. I am boiling over now.

The wedding went off smoothly despite all of this. But as if all the other things were not enough, when we got ready to leave for our honeymoon, Larry's car would not start. Larry had this habit of laughing at everything. This was not funny to me and several others. So my brothers and others worked on the car, and we were on our way, but only for about three miles, the car stopped again. This was repeated three times, fixing, starting, and stopping again. The last time, after my father-in-law said too many religious people were working on the car, I am told he cursed the car, and it started again. My brother Spencer volunteered to follow us to Memphis, eighty miles away, where we honeymooned. We made it that time! But wait, we are not done yet. Larry had a godmother who was blind, and she had come to our wedding. She accompanied us to Memphis and shared a room with us the first night of our honeymoon. She took a bus home the next day. Since the car was not working properly and because Larry needed to report to work the following week, we left early for Indianapolis, which would be our home for the next eleven years. Well, we still are not done.

Things were going well as we left Memphis, but just as we got to Lexington, Tennessee, about sixty miles out on our twelve-hour journey, the car stopped again along Interstate 40. That was the last ride for the White Rambler. Larry looked in a telephone directory and found the name and address of the closest United Methodist Church, the denominations of which we belong. He called and the minister of that church came and drove us to his home, where he and his wife hosted us for the night. The next day, we packed up gifts from the Rambler and other belongings and boarded a Greyhound bus headed for Indianapolis. The minister was to sell the Rambler, keep a 20 percent commission, and send the rest of the money to Larry. Well, to this day, we have not received any money nor heard whether the car was sold.

We arrived in Indy and took a cab to the parsonage that had been prepared for us. Larry carried me over the threshold, and we managed to get some needed rest after a long bus ride. We were able to continue some semblance of our short honeymoon.

I liked the new home, this would be our first home together, even though it was the church parsonage. By now, everyone should know I married a United Methodist minister. This was my first home since I left Augusta, Arkansas. I lived in residence halls for five years during the college and graduate school days and was anxious to put my signature touch on this home; however, the parsonage was already fully furnished. With added accents of interior design, we managed to get the Johnson customized touch.

The home was in the Southeast Section of Indianapolis, an area of changing socioeconomic statistics. Next door to us on one side was the church building, on the other was a very conservative thinking middle-aged White couple. Both were smokers. Whites who could were moving out, and urban renewal was evidenced. Businesses and churches had closed and left the area. There were few recreational opportunities for youth and children in the area. Larry's job was to revive a dying church and start a community center.

Teaching in Public Schools of Indianapolis, Indiana

I thought I would be able to rest for a couple of weeks, but Larry was insistent that I get a job. He took me to apply for a teaching position on a Tuesday. I was interviewed on Friday and reported to work on Tuesday of the following week. No rest for me. Forty-five years later, I would retire from teaching in junior high, middle school, high school, and the university.

I enjoyed teaching at every level of public education and developed innovations at each level. During my first year of teaching in a junior high school in Indy, I, along with twelve other teachers, was chosen to move with the sixth, seventh, and eighth grade students to a location south of the middle-income inner city of Indy to a White low-income area about fifteen miles away. Students who walked to school would now be bused. There was some resistance and some concern from the parents of students already in the area and those to be bused into the area.

We made it work through lots of negotiations, mediations, and reconciliation. We evaluated, planned, prepared, and established the first middle school in the Indianapolis Public School System and one of a few, at that time, in the Midwest. I worked there from 1969 to 1972 and spent long hours trying to make sure my students received the best education possible, and I was being the most effective teacher I could be. This was shaken a bit one Monday morning when I walked into my homeroom class to find a female student sitting there with a huge snake around her neck. Yes, I said snake. I ran out of the room screaming, "Come, come." The principal came out and tried to get from me what was wrong, all I could say was come. He did and he and the student found another place for the snake while she was in my homeroom.

My classroom/laboratory was partially below ground with high windows that you could not see out of. Indy is known for huge snowfalls. One day the custodian came into my room with a shovel. It was past 6:00 p.m. I asked him what he was doing with the shovel. He said he had cleaned snow off my car twice, and now I should leave because there was already three inches of snow on the ground, and he was leaving. I had no idea it was snowing. I thanked him and took his advice and left. Well, what usually takes fifteen minutes to get home took me one and a half hours. You can believe I started checking outside more frequently from that day hence.

In the summer of 1972, I was asked to take a teaching position at Broad Ripple High School in the inner city of Indy. My middle school principal, Mr. E, did not want me to leave the middle school and went all the way to the superintendent of the Indianapolis Public Schools to protest the Broad Ripple High School principal's audacity to ask me to leave his school. After all, I was instrumental in establishing that first middle school. Well, we made it through, and I did take the job of teaching at Broad Ripple High School.

At the time, I received the invitation to teach at Broad Ripple. I was about two months pregnant, so I felt the need tell my immediate supervisor, Mrs. R. She smiled and said, "Well, we should get along fine. I am too." I was twenty-six at the time, and she was in her forties. It would be the first pregnancy for both of us. We shared stories along the way. My pregnancy was uneventful, and most people didn't know I was pregnant until my eighth month. I stayed out six weeks after my daughter, Fatima, was born and was back in full swing teaching afterward. Ms. R. had a difficult pregnancy, and so the baby was quite sick when born. She also had a baby girl. Since she only taught one class, I was able to teach her class and manage the department chair duties as well while she was on childcare leave.

I really enjoyed teaching in high school. One of the highlights was establishing the first chapter of the Future Homemakers of America (FHA). In my role as chapter sponsor, I supervised the students to and from meeting away from the school, supervised the preparation students made for district and statewide competitions, and I corresponded with district and state chapter leaders. One contest was a formal dinner in which students planned, shopped, prepared, and served a formal dinner to a panel of judges. My student won, and she was featured in the local newspaper. I remember the menu was stuffed Cornish hens with wild rice and steamed carrots; the dessert was a raspberry sorbet.

I taught classes in food and nutrition, clothing, and textiles, family relationships and health education. My foods and nutrition classes entertained twenty-four principles of the IPS System. We had been studying international foods, and we prepared an international meal of Russian borscht, Greek baklava, coffee grog, red cabbage, doro wot, and scalloped potatoes. The principals came from varying backgrounds and two Russian and two Greek principals commented that the borscht and baklava tasted as authentic as those in the actual country. In fact, they came into the laboratory to get leftovers. We were so proud!

There was a food contest where my students won, and the prize was a side of pork. The pork packers came to school and cut the side of pork into the familiar cuts we find in the supermarkets and the students, and some faculty were able to see where steaks, hams, chops, hocks, and other cuts are located on the hog. Thank goodness I had a freezer to store all that pork. I had no need to purchase any pork for my food's laboratory classes for an entire year.

A young man in the food class seemed to have a problem sitting quietly and behaving in class. His reputation followed him to all his classes. His name was Jimmy, and he would come in and flit around like a butterfly from one student to another, bothering them and preventing them from doing their work. My observation of Jimmy was there was no reason he could not sit down as the other students were doing. I asked him to step into the hall with me, which he did, and we had a great talk. I asked him why he would not sit down and do his work. He replied, "Because I don't want to." When he realized, I was not going to tolerate his behavior, he attempted to get in step with the program.

In those days, we were able to call parents of students in our classes when there was a need. In my conversation with the mother, I learned that the family owned a bakery. Jimmy's lifetime goal was to become a baker and take over the family business and felt there was no need for him to be in school. With this information, I came up with a way to put Jimmy's energy to use. I asked him to come in early for class the next time the class met. He did, and I made him a laboratory assistant with responsibility for setting out supplies, utensils, and food items needed to conduct the lab. This gave him a sense of purpose and preparation for his future career. In addition to Jimmy, there were two other student assistants. Thus, Jimmy became good at doing this work and did his own lab work in record times and helped other students rather than pester them.

Some of the students in my class had been deemed unteachable by other teachers and administrators. In a family relationship class, one of the activities was to simulate a married couple with marital problems. I chose two of the more unlikely students to be spouses and gave them their parts to play. To help them work through the problem, I asked the school's guidance counselor to mediate their situation. These two students were brilliant in their portrayal of spouses and shocked the counselor, so she was hardly able to do her job. I too was shocked that they performed their roles so convincingly. Afterward, the counselor said to me, "Anybody who can get those two students to sit down together, let alone talk civilly to each other deserves a medal." As a teacher, my philosophy was simple: "All students can and want to learn and my job is to facilitate that happening by all means necessary."

During my fourth year at Broad Ripple High School, my sister Mary and our cousin Linda came to live with us until they could find work in the city and establish themselves. Both were a major help to Larry and me, and we found many ways they could be helpful to us. Sister Mary was a home economics major also. One of the teachers in my department at BR, Ms. M., was sick a lot and would be out for weeks at a time. So Ms. R., the department chair, asked Mary to substitute for Ms. M. Ms. M. said she would be out for six weeks in the Mayo clinic. We could not verify that she was at the clinic. However, Mary subbed for the six weeks and did such a terrific job, Ms. R. wanted to hire her permanently. Of course, Ms. M. could not be dismissed for being sick. Word got back to Ms. M. about Mary, and Ms. M never missed another day of work at Broad Ripple until she retired years later. Sister Mary soon found a wonderful job with the City Department of Social Services.

The Women's Division of the General Board of Global Ministries of the United Methodist Church

Larry was responsible for getting me started on a career in education and leadership which led to my advancement in the public schools, university, and the United Methodist Church.

About this time, I was active in the local, district, and conference level units of United Methodist Women. As dean of the annual school of mission, I secured space for classes and instructors for two sections of three classes. One of the instructors was impressed with the way I led and directed the activities of the school and submitted my name to become a director of the Women's Division. I was selected for this position in September of 1976 and served, finishing two terms in 1984. During the second four-year term, I was chosen to serve as vice president for Membership and Member Development of the organization with 1.5 million members and a budget of more than 5 million dollars. As one of three vice presidents, I presided over a body of seventy elected directors, from all fifty states and fifteen countries abroad, three times a year. My first born was three years old, I was still working full time and, during the last three years of my second term, was working on my doctoral degree. Other accomplishments included coauthoring a workbook with vice president, Marilyn Winters titled *Say Yes: A Self-Development Workbook for Women Leaders*. During my tenure as vice president, I was fortunate to have great enrichment opportunities with travels to Sierra Leone and Senegal, West Africa, Puerto Rico, Haiti, Dominican Republic, Aruba, Caracas, Venezuela, Barbados, Jamaica, Antigua, Trinidad, and Grenada.

Birth of First Daughter, Fatima

In March of 1973, Larry and I were blessed with a beautiful baby girl. We named her Fatima Ania. Fatima means "daughter of the prophet," and Ania means "born on Friday" in Swahili. Fatima was a happy baby and at first did not like to sleep. I was breastfeeding her at first, and the pediatrician told me she was not getting enough to eat, so I had to supplement with formula, Enfamil. We had to put her in her own room because every time she moved when in the room with Larry and me, I would get up and get her from the crib beside our bed. She had very delicate skin and could not tolerate wetness on her bottom, so we had to change from cloth to disposable diapers early on.

She was a smart child and loved books and stuffed animals and toys. Her favorite stuffed animal was Big Bird. She had one that was about as big as she was at the time. Her favorite story was "The Frog Prince." She loved strawberry shortcake curtains and bed sheets and spreads which adorned her room. Fatima went through grade school, middle, and high school with no difficulty. She was very likeable and sociable like her father, so she got along well with other students. At church, she was the little princess.

Fatima finished high school in 1991 and went to Howard University in Washington, DC. There she received a bachelor and master's degree in early childhood education. One teacher at Howard was so impressed with her class performance and work ethics, she hired her to work in her own Child Development Center. Later, Fatima would become the director of that center which served one hundred children. Her high school internship at Toddler's Academy in Durham, North Carolina, had paid off.

During the Howard University years, Fatima became a true leader and educator. She mastered training in a New Leaders program and later became an assistant principal and principal in four different elementary schools in DC. When her Kenilworth school closed in 2017, she became assistant principal at Patterson Elementary school where she works today.

Fatima was married to Cortez Avery in 2012. They have a beautiful eight-year-old daughter, Corlissa, who started reading before she was one-year-old and has not stopped. She is active in the Dance Dimensions Dance School and participates in many dance recitals where she performs: ballet, hip-hop, jazz, acrobatics, and tap, sings in the children's choir at her church, and takes part in girl scouts.

She illustrated her sharp educational attainment when we were on vacation in Las Vegas, Nevada, and eating at the Top of the World restaurant with a lady minister and her husband. The lady minister was just talking and talking. Corlissa said loudly (at age five), "You are exaggerating." We were stunned with our mouths open, but the lady minister said, "She's right. I was."

Second Born Selena Efia Johnson

Selena Efia Johnson, our second born, came to us in the cold of winter, on February 24, 1978. Larry and I were so sure she was a boy that we had not picked out any girl names. So when the doctor delivered her and placed her on my chest and asked, "What is her name?" Larry and I had to admit we had no name for her. So back to the book of names. She was "baby Johnson" for twenty-four hours, and then we agreed on Selena Efia. Selena means "daughter of wisdom" or "beautiful goddess." Her middle name Efia means "born on Friday." Yes, she and her sister Fatima were born on a Friday. When Selena found out the names, we had chosen for her had she been a boy, she was thrilled she was born a girl.

Selena was outgoing with a little fight in her but also shy at times and eager to help others. She loved food and early on had no problem asking for a certain amount of food. My oldest brother, Spencer, took her to eat breakfast with him and his wife, Barbara. He asked Selena how many eggs she wanted, and she said three. He said she ate all three eggs.

Selena was an excellent student excelling in all her courses. She would finish her class work early and then start talking. Some of her teachers attempted to take off points from her class work due to the talking. However, since there was also a conduct or deportment grade, Larry and I would not allow them to take away grades earned because she was talkative. We asked them to give her additional work or assignments to enrich her learning. Some teachers did; others did not. One third-grade teacher found out that I was giving Selena a big birthday party for her eighth birthday. She wanted to foil that party by sending home a negative conduct report on Selena the day before the party. Fortunately for Selena and the family, a close family friend was supervisor of the "before and after" school program at the school and had overheard the teacher's scheme to ruin the party for Selena. Selena had the most successful party.

Selena was a great test taker on course tests, statewide tests, and standardized tests. She scored highly on all of them. In one of her middle school Spanish classes, Selena took the test and said she had aced it. The teacher said she lost Selena's test, and therefore, Selena would receive the grade of F. Well, not so says this mom. I called the teacher at school to get an understanding of her rationale for the F grade. She hung up the phone. Within five minutes, I was walking into the school to confront the teacher, but she was in class. I waited outside her room;

some of the students saw me and told the teacher, "Selena's mom is out there." She then came to the door. Of course, she had no rationale for what she did. We agreed that Selena would take the same test, and that grade would stand. This was done, and Selena made a straight A.

The girls rode the bus to school in middle and high school. We drove them to elementary and some of high school. One day while Selena was in middle school, I received a call from the mother of a child who rode the same bus as Selena. It seemed she had gotten into a fight with one student on the bus but ripped the shirt of a student who was trying to help her out. I apologized profusely for Selena and offered to replace her son's shirt. The parent was quite understanding and just wanted me to know what happened. Selena was suspended from riding the bus for a week, which means we drove her to school that week.

In high school, Selena enjoyed band and school in general. She performed well academically, made excellent scores on her SATs, and upon graduation, had college offers from many schools, including North Carolina Central University, University of Maryland–Baltimore, University of Tennessee, Memphis, North Carolina A&T State University, and earned scholarships and financial aid totaling more than $250,000. She got a full ride to NCCU, where I was dean of the college of her major, the College of Arts and Sciences. She chose chemistry as a major. I knew nothing about the full ride, and the admissions team had no idea Selena was my daughter. They looked at her stellar high school record. After college, Selena again scored well on the GRE and received scores which made her eligible to receive scholarship offers of more than $300,000. She first went to the University of Tennessee to pursue a doctor of pharmacy degree. When that did not work out, she returned to NCCU and completed a master's degree in chemistry.

Selena was married to Lionel A. English in June of 2008. Lionel is an artist and painted a portrait of me for my seventy-fifth anniversary celebration. He is also a hotel manager.

Selena chose to attend the Ohio State University and matriculated there for one year, but discrimination in science classes and the Columbus, Ohio, snows, alone with being newly married all became too much, and she and husband Lionel returned to North Carolina in 2011. Their first child, Baby Lionel, was stillborn in June of 2015. However, in 2017, Lishelle Amani English was born and has been a joy to all of us.

Selena now works at Fuji Film, one of the companies that is producing a vaccine to fight the coronavirus. She is also in the second of a three-year doctoral program in leadership.

Cortez, Fatima, Corlissa, Larry, Bernice, Lishelle, Selena

Back Row: Fatima, Bernice, Larry,
Front Row: Corlissa, Selena, Lishelle, Lionel

My Professional Career in a Nutshell

The details of my professional career will be detailed in a book of my personal memoirs.

During 1978, Larry was asked to apply for the position of director of Black Church Affairs at the Duke University Divinity School. He took the position and moved to Durham, North Carolina, in September of 1978. The girls and I followed in January of 1979. It was one of the coldest and snowiest Januarys on record. Larry was living in a hotel until an apartment came open a few weeks later. We flew into Durham, but our luggage did not make it. I only had diapers in a diaper bag for eleven-month-old Selena. All stores in Durham were closed because of snow. Thus, my first introduction to Durham was not pleasant. I was unhappy for almost a year. That's when I got a part-time position at NCCU teaching one course in the home economics department.

I did part-time teaching for two years, then received a fellowship to pursue the doctoral degree in 1982. After three years of doctoral studies at University of North Carolina at Greensboro located fifty-five miles from Durham and while teaching three to four courses per semester at NCCU, I received the PhD degree in home economics education, leadership, and administration. I was then promoted from adjunct instructor to a tenure-track assistant professor position. In 1994, I was asked to take on a major administrative role: dean of the College of Arts and Sciences at NCCU, the largest academic unit in the university consisting of twenty-four academic departments. Only four of which were chaired by women.

This was an unprecedented move on the part of legendary Civil Rights Attorney and then Chancellor Julius L. Chambers, who himself had taken on a non-precedent position as the first non-PhD to serve as chancellor. I was an assistant professor with tenure but no experience in administration in an academic setting. I had served four years as a corporate vice president of the Women's Division, an international volunteer organization within the United Methodist Church. When I was administratively placed over department chairs who had been in their positions from five to twenty-four years, one can imagine the opposition I faced. In fact, when I held my first monthly meeting with the twenty-four department chairs, unbeknownst to me, several of the male chairs had huddled together in a scheme to trip me up at that first meeting. One of the five white chairs presented the deflection. I cannot remember exactly what I said, but it stopped him in his tracks. One of the male chairs who worked on the scheme told me after the meeting, "Once you set him in his place, the rest of us got in line."

Earlier details of my career at North Carolina Central University will be shared in my personal memoirs coming later. I climbed in my academic career from a visiting lecturer, with no benefits, to adjunct lecturer and professor, to assistant professor with tenure, to associate professor to full professor in terms of professorial ranks. Administratively, I moved from the dean of the College of Arts and Science to assistant vice chancellor for Academic Affairs, to assistant vice chancellor for Academic Services, founded and organized the University College and became its first dean, then on to associate vice chancellor for Academic Affairs, and finally upon retirement in January 2014, served as interim provost and vice chancellor for Academic Affairs, second in line to the chancellor.

Chapter 10

· · ○ · ·

The Eighth Child—
Octavris C. Duffy Jr.

Growing Up in Arkansas

I am Octavris Duffy Jr., the eighth of thirteen siblings. I was born October 1, 1946, in Augusta, Arkansas. During the early part of my life, I grew up kind of a sickly child. I was a loner. Because my thoughts were different from most children. I do not really remember doing many childhood things. I viewed most things that children did as things that did not make sense. I was gifted. I could perform most tasks on the farm better than most of my siblings, picking cotton, picking strawberries, chopping cotton, sawing wood, and the like. I was small in stature and stood at five feet and two inches tall and weighed ninety-seven pounds when I was sixteen years of age. I always tried to do the best of anything I was involved in. My early years in school were challenging. I did something that no other sibling of the family did. I repeated the first grade. I remember I was very small and was bullied by some of the students in the class. I think it was because of being bullied, I became withdrawn, and I just chose not to participate in class to avoid attention. I do not remember having a learning disability.

By repeating the first grade, my brother Edward and I ended up in the same classes from the first grade through the twelfth grade. My mother joined us in the twelfth grade, and the three of us graduated together in 1965. Many people thought Edward and I were twins. From the second grade through graduating from the twelfth grade, I was one of the smartest, if not the smartest person, in the class. I was plagued with a few health problems in the early years of my life that went unnoticed until the pain became unbearable to live with. I experienced so much pain that I would pray to die to stop the pain. I finally told mother about my illness, and she told Daddy, and it was arranged for me to go to the hospital and have my first of eight operations. In 1962, I had my first operation, and I was in the ninth grade. I had developed a hernia on my left side from lifting heavy objects, such as carrying sixty to eighty pounds of cotton on my back, carrying heavy logs to the wood pile after the two horses, Maude and Bell that normally did the work, died. I remember the hospital experience. Our family was very poor, and I knew neither Mother nor Father would be able to take me or go to the hospital because we had no automobile. To prepare myself for this new experience, I went to the library and checked out a book explaining what happens when one undergoes an operation. It explained the preparation phase, the process of administering the anesthesia, and how the patient feels after recovering. I had educated myself of what should happen and how I should feel. I had no fear whatsoever. I had a roommate, an elderly Black man that was scheduled to have brain surgery the next morning. He was very frightened of the operation. I was wondering if I would have been frightened if I had been him. I purchased a $6 transistor radio during the summer from funds I earned working in the fields and took the radio everywhere I went. The gentleman that was sharing the room with me asked me, "Do you ever turn that radio off?" And I smiled and replied, "No, I love music." He further stated, "You don't seem to be afraid of undergoing surgery tomorrow," and I replied, "No, I am not afraid. I made it through the operation fine and was glad to return home." Unfortunately, I returned to work too soon, and the hernia returned, which was a blessing in disguise, to be explained later. Additional details will be in the book to be published later.

Elementary and High School Days

My high school years were filled with the most joyful memories of my life. I was the president of five organizations from the seventh grade through the twelfth grade. I was seen by my peers as a leader, and they had great expectations for me, and I enjoyed meeting their expectations. I often read excerpts from my high school memory book and felt blessed that members of my class and friends thought so highly of me for my character and intellect. Teachers from Carver High School that greatly impacted my life: Mr. Plato E. Barnett, parliamentary procedures; Mr. George Edwards, science; Mr. Hershel Alcorn, mathematics; Mrs. Thelma Smith, English; and Mrs. Ruth Clemons, typing and shorthand. I knew I was prepared to accomplish any goal I set for myself with the educational background I received from Carver High School in Augusta, Arkansas. Carver High School was a segregated school, and it was a particularly good place to receive an education. It was in high school when I first experienced love beyond that of my family and spiritual life. To me, this was a transition from earth to heaven. The experience of unadulterated love to me was heaven without dying. In retrospect, I guess I was pushing it to the limit. I was in the eleventh grade and was dating a girl in the eighth grade. Many people wanted to ask me about my personal relationship. After seeing Helen and I together, they saw Romeo and Juliet, the perfect love couple. I was told some forty years after graduating by many of my friends, how teachers and the school administrators would try to catch me doing something that I should not be doing. I didn't even give it a second thought when I was in school about doing things that would get me in trouble. I was accepted by my peers and her parents. The relationship resulted in me having a lovely wife Helen; two beautiful children, Meshell and

O.C. III; four wonderful grandchildren, Courtney, Adrian, Ashley, and Tajoyra; and four great-grandchildren. I walked fifteen miles round trip three times a week to see Helen and sometimes the temperature would be nearly zero. I remember one night when I left Helen's house at midnight, the wind was blowing about thirty miles an hour and the temperature was about ten degrees Fahrenheit. I walked about two miles and realized that I was not going to make it home without freezing. I stopped at Mr. West's house (Mr. West was one of our bus drivers), and I spent the night there. But in my father's house, you must be home by the time you go to work. I got up the next day about 6:00 a.m. and made it home in time to go to work. To hear the rest of the story, you will have to read my book that will be out later.

After graduating from high school, I was fortunate to get a job working with the Soil Conservation Service in Augusta, Arkansas. This was the start of me being one of the few Black Americans from Augusta, Arkansas, to hold many positions in the federal government and corporate America. Once two of the engineers who were White, and I had gone to meet a customer and we stopped at a store for lunch. The store was in Tupelo, Arkansas, on US Highway 33. The two White engineers went in the store and ate their lunch and brought my lunch to me to eat on the steps of the store about four feet from where the traffic was moving. When we returned to the office, I went and told the manager what had happened. He stated that any place that I could not go, we were not to eat there. The two engineers did not like that, and what made things worse, the three of us rode in the cab of a pickup truck with me being in the middle.

Leaving Home, Going Off to College

In September of 1965, I left Augusta, Arkansas, traveling to Pine Bluff, Arkansas, to enter Arkansas AM&N College. I wanted to become a mathematics teacher. Therefore, I enrolled in the Mathematics Department. The transition from high school to college was quite an adjustment. I graduated high school number three out of forty-seven students. I did not have to study often when I was in high school to pass tests. I knew I was one of the two smartest persons in my class. When I enrolled at AM&N College as a first-year student in September 1965, there were more than 1,300 first-year students in my class, and it did not take me long to realize that I was not the smartest person in my class. Some students from large cities did not buy books because they knew most of the materials because they had learned it in high school. This was a motivator to me. I was determined that a student without a book was not going to outperform me. This was the first time I really had to study to learn the materials at the rate the instructors were covering it. There were four beautiful young ladies that I studied with daily, Thelma, Zelman, Velma, and Betty Curl. After midterm, the class had gotten to materials that those students with no books had not learned in high school. They fell behind, and I moved ahead. I accomplished my goal. After being the president for six organizations for five years, I promised myself I would not run for another office. That lasted one year. I ran and won the parliamentarian for the sophomore class.

In my sophomore year, two students from the Mathematics Department were selected to participate in the first Cooperative Education Program at AM&N College. The two individuals selected were chosen by the content of the letter they wrote explaining why they should be the chosen ones. Once the selection was determined, the students would sign a contract with the Little Rock District United State Army Corps, AM&N College, and the University of Arkansas at Fayetteville. I submitted my letter for consideration and knew I would be considered. I remember as if it was yesterday how I ended my letter and it stated, that if I am one of the chosen ones, the Lord will have answered my prayer. I knew I would be offered one of the positions and I was; the other student selected was Dan Johnson. Dan and I talked and promised each other that if one stayed so would the other. On September 12, 1966, I became the first Black Cooperative Education student at AM&N College. My first assignment was at the Pine Bluff Resident Office. It was my understanding that the federal government had mandated that federal offices must be integrated. I received all excellent evaluations for the first assignment. Dan was much smarter than me, but his supervisor from the Corps of Engineers gave Dan an awfully bad evaluation. Dan and

I were to hold a full-time job together. When I was in college, he would be working until we received our degrees in engineering. I returned for my second assignment with the Corps of Engineers. I was not pleased with how Dan's evaluation had gone. I approached Dan's supervisor and asked why Dan's evaluation was very poor. I knew Dan could perform the work, probably better than I had done. The supervisor replied, "He did talk with us. He just did not fit in." I became terribly angry and stated what does that have to do with his work performance. After that experience, Dan chose not to continue with the Cooperative Education Program, and I did not blame him.

On June 25, 1967, Helen and I were married. Things did not go too well, to say the least. My transmission went out of my car the morning of the marriage. I borrowed the mechanic's car that was repairing my car. His car stopped on the way to church, and I walked to the wedding. The temperature was ninety-seven degrees Fahrenheit, and my clothes were drenched in sweat. I remember people saying that boy does not look like he wants to get married. I was to report to work the next day. The car was repaired, and Helen and I arrived in Pine Bluff a little after midnight. I was at work at 8:00 a.m. that Monday.

On November 21, 1967, I was involved in a car accident just five months after the wedding. I had gone home, Augusta, Arkansas, to get my wife to spend the Thanksgiving holiday with me. See, Helen was in the twelfth grade, and I was a sophomore in college when we were married. No, she was not pregnant. Our first child was born a little more than two years later. Four of us were in the car driven by her cousin, my classmate from high school, who had agreed to bring me and Helen to Pine Bluff. The starter of my car needed replacing, and Burke offered us a ride to Pine Bluff, and I would get my car when we returned to Augusta. However, we did not make it to Pine Bluff. Approximately twelve miles before arriving at Pine Bluff, we were involved in an accident. The result of that accident was the amputation of my left leg midway my thigh. I entered the hospital November 21, 1967, and was released December 21, 1967.

Luckily, I was able to return to college after the amputation. In the midsixties, it was not often that you saw someone with an amputated limb. I remember how many of my sister's friends would break down in tears when they saw I had lost my leg. I understood why people would stare at me, and it did take some adjusting. Many people would look at me and ask, "How did you lose your leg?" I would tell them, "I will only answer one question." They would ask, "How did you lose your leg?" I would reply, "It was bitten off." Naturally, they would ask, "What bit it off?" I would reply, "I answered one question."

I was taking eighteen hours that semester, and after being away from class one month, I maintained a 3:20 GPA that semester. I transferred to the University of Arkansas at Fayetteville in September of 1969. I remember the long drive from Little Rock to Exit 13. Exit 13 was the exit where you left Interstate 40 and continued through the mountains to Fayetteville, Arkansas. I dreaded every mile of the way. I drove along, and once I passed Conway, I did not think I saw another Black person on the interstate. I finally arrived at Fayetteville about 5:30 p.m. Sunday evening. On Monday morning, I registered and did not see a Black student, faculty, or staff person. There were three hundred plus civil engineering students in the Civil Engineering Department, and I was the only Black person in the building. No Black janitor, secretary, or faculty person. This was a new world, and the adjustments were exceedingly difficult. This was the first time I was challenged to the maximum amount of my ability. I studied twelve to fourteen hours per day. Many times seven days per week. After the first semester, I realized how difficult this journey would become. First semester, my grades were three Fs, two Ds, and one C. A 0.73 GPA for the semester. The pressure is on because now I am on probation, and any semester I do not meet the minimum requirements, I will be dropped from the civil engineering program. I went to my advisor to select courses for the next semester. He told me, "I knew you were not going to pass all those courses. I just wanted to see whether you were a genius or not." I have always been one to keep my cool. I politely told him, "I did not need his advice. I could fail by myself." And from that semester to graduation, I selected the courses I would take each semester. I was called in by the faculty, and it was recommended that I be dropped from the engineering program. I thanked them for their recommendation and said, "You cannot see what's inside of me, and if I were you, I probably would say the same thing. I will not quit. If I fail, I will know why I am not in the engineering program, but if I quit, I will always believe I could have made it." Although the road was long and the struggle was rough, I fought that battle.

Now at seventy-four years of age, I can say that was by far the most challenging task that I have been confronted with in my life. I took the scenic route for my education. I started to college in September of 1965 and received my engineering degree in December of 1973. Was it worth it? Yes. I became the first Black student to receive a bachelor's degree in civil engineering from the University of Arkansas at Fayetteville.

I continued and completed the three-part program (completed one hundred hours toward a degree in Mathematics at AM&N College in Pine Bluff), five cooperative education experiences with the Little District Corps of Engineering, and completed the necessary requirement to receive a degree in civil engineering from the University of Arkansas at Fayetteville. After graduating, I was employed with the US Army Corps of Engineers Little Rock District as a hydrological engineer. I was the first Black civil engineer with a bachelor's degree to be employed with the Little Rock District United States Army Corps of Engineers.

My personal life has been more than wonderful. I never was one that took relationships lightly. I have dated very few ladies in my life. Most of my relationships were long term. After getting married at an early age and being married for forty-plus years of my life, I have lived a particularly good life. Once I experienced love, I promised myself that I would not live a day without being in love and being loved. I have held that promised to be true as of today. Helen was my first love, and that love continues today. Thanks, Helen, for the many years of heaven you brought into my life and our beautiful children:

Children:

- Meshell Duffy—accounts manager for TSI, IT support specialist @ ARcare, PT manager for Maurices
- O.C. Duffy III—owner, D3 Construction and Designs
- Spencer Duffy—orthopedic and podiatric specialist
- Katrena Jackson—nurse assistant

Grandchildren:

- Courtney Duffy—owner of Duffy Details
- Adrian Duffy—daycare teacher
- Ashley Duffy—minister, author, and owner of Ashleycreates2
- Tajoyra Clark—caregiver

Great-Grandchildren:

- Jayden Duffy, Deonate Lockhart, and Ah'Jrea Duffy (Adrian's children)
- Greylon Duffy (Ashley's son)
- Tristian Clark (Tajoyra's son)

Courtship and Marriage

And to the other major players in my life: Cynthia, Jeannette, Debbie, and the two wonderful Wandas were the other angels that allowed me to experience heaven. Debbie was special. I met her while she was working at a bank. After we developed a relationship, I asked her to quit her job with the bank and start working for me. I guaranteed her a job as the office manager for one year. I realized I did not know anything about operating a print shop, and neither did she. I must admit, she gave her all, but unfortunately, she did not meet my expectations, and she was terminated after six months. That decision did not adversely affect our relationship. Debbie and I continued our life together, and she gave birth to my second son, Spencer L. A. Duffy. He is named after my oldest brother. And now for the highlight of my life. I met a young lady that was introduced to me by my brother James. I have been a lover of music all my life. I am a DJ, owned clubs, and presently own an event center. I have always found myself surrounded with music and people. It was in this environment that I met Lora Campbell, the lovely lady I have been married to for thirty-five years. And with this marriage, I added another wonderful, lovely daughter, Katrina Jackson and two lovely granddaughters, Little Lora and Lorissa Jackson.

Lora and O.C. Duffy Jr.

Lora, O.C. Duffy Jr., and O.C. Duffey III

Church, Spiritual Life and Religion

My spiritual life provided me with the strength, the ability to love, and acceptance, understanding, and forgiveness of others. My parental training combined with my spiritual training opened my mind and my heart to climb mountains that were sportingly impossible to climb, to forgive the unforgivable, and to give more to others than to myself. I remember sitting in Jackson Chapel Church in Augusta, Arkansas. I was fourteen years old, and I wanted to start an organization called Save the Children. This would have been a nonprofit organization that would supply needed services to children that needed someone to care. I always have had the desire to do something to help someone other than myself. I also remember writing on a picture of mine, that the only sin I committed was to tell a joke. I was certain that telling a joke was a sin. I was taught that if it's not the truth, it is a lie. But I developed my own definition for a lie, and that is. if someone says something to hurt someone to benefit him or herself and it is not truthful, it is a lie. I started teaching Sunday School when I was sixteen years old. I really enjoyed teaching Sunday School. I was particularly good at explaining the scriptures where everyone could understand the meaning and also why it was written and how those words written in Jesus's days applied to the world of today.

The most memorable of my teaching and spiritual experiences was when the church decided to have an unscheduled and unrehearsed play. It was called Judgement Day 1980. I played God, and all the adult members of the church were facing me on Judgment Day. My father was one who, in most cases, carried on a one-way conversation—do this or don't do that. There was rarely any discussion. The response was mostly "Yes, Sir" or "No, Sir." This was my chance to tell Daddy about himself, and he could not retaliate because I was God. I called Daddy to come before judgment for me to judge him. My father had a way of saying things that would really hurt your feelings. I felt that he didn't really enjoy hurting people's feelings, but it was easier for him to say whatever came to his mind than to hold it inside. As God, I gave the person coming before me one of three choices. First choice, I can let you enter heaven. Second choice, I could allow you to return to your life and correct your sins. Or thirdly, I could send you to hell. The narrative went something like this.

"Brother, Duffy, I have many reports of how you have said things to really hurt your loved one's feelings, your wife, your children, and your friends. How do you plead?"

And Dad replied, "Guilty."

"What are you planning to do to correct those matters?"

Dad replied, "Please give me another chance, and I promise I will treat my loved ones and my friends with words of love and compassion."

After, being assured that he would return and keep his promises, I stated, "You may return to your life with a second chance to redeem yourself, but this is your last chance." My dad was so grateful that I did not send him to hell. I knew all the church members well, and I knew of each one's weakness, and they had to confess to the sin they had committed and promise to return and repent before coming before the judgment again. I remembered everyone's sins, except for my mother. I cannot remember why she was not admitted into heaven. If you want to know why mother was not admitted into heaven, you will have to wait for my next book.

The two great tests of my spiritual belief came when I was about thirty years old. The second occurred when I was about fifty years of age. One night at my club, someone took a stick and broke the windshield out of a car parked in front of the entry door. There were approximately forty people standing outside the building that witnessed the person breaking the windshield. The police arrived and asked, "Did anyone see the person that broke the glass?" No one said a word. The man that broke the windshield said if anyone had identified him, something bad was going to happen. The officer said, "I cannot believe all of you were here, and no one saw what happened." My spiritual conscience got the best of me. I remember the scripture that tells that the sin of omission is as bad as being one that commits the sin. I held my hand up and said, "I saw the person who broke the windshield." The police asked me to identify the person and asked if I were willing to appear in court and testify to the occurrence. I stated that I would. I can remember the expression on the face of that young man and how he looked at me.

The second time my faith was tested was when I received a call from Augusta that mother was missing. I was in Little Rock, Arkansas, about eighty miles from Augusta, Arkansas. I drove to Augusta thinking to myself what could have happened to my mother. I did not really think about it for very long. I remember like it was yesterday, and I said to myself, *If it's the Lord's will, let his will be done.* In other words, I was willing to accept whatever the condition I would find with my mother. After going to several places I thought she may have been with no luck in finding her, the thoughts became stronger. *If it is God's will, let his will be done.* That verse gave me consolation when I was in doubt. I found my mother safe but sitting on the steps of a church on the banks of White River.

I tested my faith very often by placing myself in harm's way. Looking back at race relations when I was in high school, things were not too good for Black people. I would walk approximately fifteen miles to see my girlfriend. Many times as I was walking, people would stop and say racial remarks. I realized what could happen to me, but I was certain that I was protected, and I never really feared. I probably have the record for picking up hitchhikers. I have picked up more than one hundred hitchhikers in my life, and no harm has come to me. Hitchhikers are remarkably interesting people to talk with. I would always ask them, "Why are you hitchhiking and where are you going?"

I remember I was driving from Little Rock, Arkansas, on my way to Cleveland, Ohio. I had gotten about twenty miles from Little Rock and picked up a hitchhiker. He rode with me about fifteen miles and asked me to pull over. I pulled over, and he got out and said, "You will never make it to Cleveland, Ohio." I had been up most of the night and was driving with about three hours of sleep, and I was running off the road at times and across the center line. I thanked him and drove on to Cleveland. The question I would always ask myself was, if Jesus were driving by in a four- or six-passenger car, would he pass by someone walking? My answer was always, no, he would give them a ride. I honestly thought, if one is to be Christ-like, he would do as Christ did.

My parents would worry about my safety when I would walk fifteen miles along at night, and I would tell them, "Maybe you trained me too well." I would say and I still hold that belief today, if I get killed or injured for doing what I know is the right thing to do, then my life has not been in vain. The transition in my spiritual life took a drastic turn when I was attending the University of Arkansas at Pine Bluff, and some of my new thoughts were reinforced when I attended the University of Arkansas at Fayetteville. I took a course in humanities while attending AM&N College. In that course, I learned about the nine great religions. In learning of each of their origin, Christianity was next to the youngest of the great religions. And from data and knowledge gathered from that class, I reevaluated my religious belief. I did not stop there because I was looking for the truth. It was not difficult for me to gather information, observe the behavior of Christian's people or so-called Christian people and analyze data and draw my conclusion about Christianity. The principles of how to treat people and how one should be treated were basic principles that I was taught from my spiritual training, and it plays a great part of my life today. Many of the Christian principles and beliefs I live by today. And then there are some of those which do not benefit me or my race, so I do not need them. I view my religious training, my home training, my educational training, and my experiences in life as guideposts to lead me in the right direction. I do not use all of them, but I take from them those things that make me a better person and I think that is the key to happiness and understanding. I remembered when I expressed my religious beliefs to my siblings and friends. Many of them said, "I am sorry for you because you are going to hell." My reply was, "If I happened to go to hell after I die, at least I will have experienced heaven on earth by being free to my belief. I hope there is a heaven, so you will not be disappointed if you wake up in hell."

Work and Professional Life

My professional life has been wonderful. I started working with the Soil Conservation Service in Augusta, Arkansas, immediately after graduating from high school. I was the first Black person from Augusta to work in the Soil Conservation Service there. I had my challenges. I remember we were performing precision land leveling. One of the areas we were to survey was blocked by burning grass, and I asked my supervisor what was I to do. He replied, "Walk through it," and I did. Being the first is not always easy. Another incident happened when I was working at the Pine Resident Office in 1968. My supervisor gave me an exceedingly difficult project to do. He really felt that I would not be able to complete the project. I surprised him and did an excellent job. When I handed him the project, he threw it in the trash can without looking at the project. I am extremely glad that I grew up in a very spiritual and forgiving family. My supervisor's desk and my desk were next to each other. There we sat face-to-face about five feet apart. I had heard of people that worked in the same office and did not speak to one another, but I could not imagine myself ever being in a position where I would change behavior to that point. I was wrong. For two weeks, we worked every day and never said a word to each other. The day finally came, and Charlie asked O.C., "What is wrong with you?" That was all I needed to tell him all the things I had wanted to say those last two weeks. When I finished what I had to say, he had tears running down his face like a baby. The setting where we worked was an accessible area where about six engineers were working. My voice carries well, and everyone in the office heard the entire speech.

You know, it is funny how your past can come back to bless you or haunt you. It was twenty-two years later while working at the University of Arkansas at Pine Bluff, I looked up one day, and who did I see, Charlie. I was walking on the sidewalk, and here is Charlie and he spoke, and I spoke very cordially. I must say I was surprised to see Charlie. He asked me if I had a minute, and I replied sure. He explained to me he needed a letter of reference from someone that was working at the institution in which he was trying to enroll. He explained further that he tried to receive a degree at two other colleges and failed. He said that the only way he could enroll at another college in Arkansas was to have a letter of reference from me. Naturally, I have a flashback and remember the project that he threw in the wastebasket. I gladly wrote a letter of reference for Charlie. He completed his four-year degree at AM&N College in Pine Bluff and continued his education and received a master's degree. I am happy for Charlie as being the first is not easy.

The next place I went to was the Dardanelle resident and I was the first Black student to work in that office. Everything went well, and everyone treated me with respect. The next work assignment with the Corps of Engineers Little Rock District was in Rodgers, Arkansas, in 1969. I was told there were no Black people living in Rodgers, and "You are going to have some problems." I don't really understand how I control my feelings. I remember replying, "No, I will not have a problem, and they may have a problem." I worked there for three months, and everything went well. The people in the Rodgers Office went overboard to show me that I was accepted. I finally told them, "I really do not need the extra treatment. Just treat me like anyone else." I did not live in Rodgers those three months. I lived in Fayetteville, Arkansas. My next work location was the Little Rock, District Office in Little Rock, Arkansas. This was my first position after receiving my civil engineering degree. I entered an eighteen-month rotational training program. In that program, you worked about six weeks in each of the departments. After completing the eighteen months training program, I chose to work in the hydrology section. I was a hydrological engineer and handled creating floods and seeing them through different cities and locations and assessing the damage caused by the floods. In 1975, a capsule was placed at Murray Lock and Dam. I wrote a letter to place in the time capsule to be read in 2075. They did not want my letter to go in the capsule, and I had to go all the way to the district engineer to have my letter placed in the time capsule. I will insert a part of the letter that is supposed to be read in 2075. You must realize when I was working for the Little Rock District of Corps of Engineers, I was the only Black engineer working for them. We were to tell how we thought the world would be in one hundred years.

I only worked at the Little Rock District Corps of Engineers in Little Rock for three years. I was told by one of my professors when I was in engineering school not to work for the government for more than three years. I wondered why he told me that, but after three years, I understood what he was telling me.

One day at lunch time, I walked to the Southwestern Bell Building, which was only two blocks away. I really had no intention of changing my career. I spoke with an engineer, and he invited me to come the next day for an interview and I did. Southwestern Bell offered me $10,000 more than I was earning with the Corps of Engineers. Therefore, I gave my letter of resignation. I worked for Southern Bell for twenty-two months. Then, Polytech Engineering out of Cleveland, Ohio, heard of me and wanted to open an office in Little Rock and asked me to come for an interview. I interviewed and Polytech Engineers offered me $10,000 more than Southwestern Bell was paying. I gave my letter of resignation to Southern Bell and started working for Polytech Engineer as the director of engineering. This change was a big gamble that I was willing to take. I was to hire the necessary staff and procure a minimum of $100,000 in engineering services by the end of the first year. I rented an office in the First Commercial Bank Building in downtown Little Rock. My office was an inside office where there were no windows, just four walls. I worked extremely hard and did everything that I thought should be performed to secure engineer contracts. The end of the year is approaching, and the number of contracts secured is zero. I received a call from the principal that I was reporting to who informed me that I needed to come to Cleveland, the corporate office, and the purpose of the meeting was to close the Little Rock office. I knew I had done all I think anyone could have done.

Remember, Polytech Engineering Firm is a Black-owned enterprise, and to get engineering in the south would not be easy. Let me give a little information of how engineering contracts are evaluated. There is a committee made up of probably six people with no one on the committee being black. The major criteria are the capacity of the firm, how many projects have you completed of this kind, and how many have you completed in this area. The odds are against you from day one. Those who know me know that I am a gambler. I faced the three principles with a two-page typed report of the things I had done, and I spoke to the three principles.

"What more would you have done?" I requested an additional year, and if I did not meet the goal, I would recommend that the office be closed. I was given another year to reach the goal, and I tripled the goal. I am presently employed with the University of

Arkansas at Pine Bluff. I have been employed there for the last forty years. Working with a HBCU is an extremely rewarding experience. I am assistant professor for the Department of Industrial Technology Management and Applied Engineering. My department head was once a student of mine. When we inherited the department, the enrollment had decreased from 121 students to forty-three, and the department was on the verge of being terminated. Under the leadership of Dr. Charles Colen, we were able to rebuild the enrollment from forty-three students to 225 students in less than nine years. Not only has the enrollment of the department increased, but the percentage of students being employed in their major increased from near 0 to 90 percent. The average student graduating from the department can expect a starting salary of approximately $70,000 plus. Students often asked me, "Why are you teaching when your students' starting salaries are more than yours and you have been working here for more than forty years?" My reply was, "Do you think I am working here for the money when you have seen companies offer me more than $150,000 to work for them?"

I guess the greatest reward I have received while working at UAPB is that students named me the Distinguished Teacher of the Year for the first five years of my being employed. Secondly, every year since I have been teaching, one to five parents ask me to promise that I will remain at UAPB until their child graduates. It is an honor to have the respect of parents, many of whom I have not seen. Yet they ask me to remain at UAPB until their child graduates. I often wonder how many other teachers are asked by parents to remain until their child or children graduate. I am approaching seventy-five years of age, and I know my years are limited, and I am preparing a transition plan to assure that the work I have done will not be in vain.

I am the owner of Tri-State International Building Systems, Inc. The company was set up in February of 1993. Tri-State International Building Systems, Inc. is a construction base company that is licensed to conduct residential and commercial work in Arkansas and Mississippi. The company has been truly fortunate to have projects totaling more than $1,000,000 for the year of 2021. I am the cofounder of Assists with Helping Hands, a non-profit organization established on April

15, 2015. The organization is registered with IRS as a 501(c)3 status. Assists With Helping Hands was established to assist elderly citizens with minor home repairs. The total funds for the operation of the non-profit are donations from friends and business associates. One hundred percent of all donations are spent on materials, labor, and supplies. If you would like to contribute or donate your service or time, we welcome you. Your contributions can be sent to Assists with Helping Hands, 5001 west Thirty-Fourth Street, Little Rock, Arkansas, 72204. Make all payments with check or money orders. For more information, you may call O.C. Duffy Jr. at 501-590-8414 or e-mail me at ocdoct@ aol.com. Just remember one's worth is not determined by what he or she gains, but how much one has given.

I will end my chapter with a poem that I wrote in 1972 while attending the University of Arkansas at Fayetteville in a parking lot.

THE SCREAMER

One night as I was walking through the park
I heard a scream a terrifying noise
As it became closer, I begin to creep
And there it stood right next to me
I was so frightened I could not speak
As the screamer came closer to me
It made a noise that sounded so loud
I noticed that it had no mouth

My feet started moving because I wanted to run
But by now the struggle had begun
It tore my nose from my face
And blood was running all over the place
It placed its foot in my chest
And that was when my body let go of my neck

I prayed oh God take away the pain
And that's when the screamer started acting insane
It ripped my ears from my head

I said oh God I wish I was dead
It broke my arms twenty times
By now I am practically out of my mind

It said to me the play will begin
Now I will pay you for all your sin
It ripped my throat, it clawed my chest
And said you still look better than the rest

Again I screamed to the sky
Oh God please let me die
It continued to drag me through the park
Again making the terrifying noise
It finally released me and let me go
And then the pain was no more
With a weakened eye I looked at my face
And slowly dragged me into a grave
For I did not want anyone to see
What the screamer had done to me

This letter was supposed to be placed in a time capsule June 9, 1975, at Murray Lock and Dam in Little Rock Arkansas. I did not see the letter placed in the time capsule. Therefore, I can't really say it is in the capsule. I kept a copy just in case.

From the Eyes of a Black Man

This letter was placed in a capsule by the Corps of Engineers, Little Rock District at Murray Lock and Dam in Little Rock, Arkansas, on June 9, 1975. This capsule will be opened on June 9, 2075. There were individuals who did not want this letter to be a part of history. I had to take the matter to the district engineer to get permission to get this letter entered as part of the materials to be stored for one hundred years.

This letter read as follows:

From the Eyes of a Black Man

I AM A Black Man, and I shall summarize my life experiences as a black man. I was born October 1, 1946, in Augusta, Arkansas. I can remember events that happened as early as 1948. I am from a family of 13 children with me being the eighth child. I was fortunate enough to live with the oldest member of the family as well as the youngest member of the family. My seven sisters and four brothers live throughout the United States.

My family has always been poor, but I predict by the time this letter is read that the Duffy's will be a wealthy family. I remember many days when the family only had Kool-Aid mixed with cornbread for an evening meal. We walked several miles to get to school with shoes that had no soles. Later, we were bussed to the nearest black school. At this time bussing is a big issue, but Black children have been bussed all their lives.

By some stretch of luck most of us had intellectual levels beyond that of the average student in our class. Five out of twelve children that lived graduated as valedictorians, and four salutatorians of their classes. The rest were in the top ten of their classes. I graduated number three out of fifty students.

The race relation situation has come a long way. I remember when a black man could be killed for the mere fact of whistling at a white woman. I remember the days when I had to sit on the back seat of the bus. I remember the doctor's office with the "colored" waiting room, the white restaurants that you wouldn't dare to stop in and eat. This is the age where Black Men are no longer allowing anyone to call them "Boy." Just a few years ago you were a boy if you were ninety-five years old and Black.

I went to a second-grade segregated school. My family was so poor that we didn't have the money to buy pencil and paper at times. The only heat in the house was in the living room and the heat provided by the cook stove when meals were cooked. Many days the temperature would fall below freezing inside the house. We picked cotton with the cotton frozen in the boll. But we all are model citizens today. Most of my sisters are teachers, educational administrators, social workers, and bankers; one brother is a scientist, another brother, a psychologist, and counselor for the University of Maryland at College Park. I am a Civil Engineer, a Tax Specialist and a D.J. I have tried to do many things simply because my parents were not allowed to do them.

My father is retired, and my mother works in the kitchen of a white lady.

I played a great part in increasing the enrollment of Black's Students at the University of Arkansas at Fayetteville. I am proud of what I have become.

I have straightened a road that was full of hills and curves. At times I wanted to give up on life but being an image that was looked up to by many, I had to keep pushing forward. The secret to my success was two-fold: (1) I have enough faith in myself to realize that if the hill were to fall, I must start digging, and keep digging until the job is completed. (2) I plan my life in ten- and five-year's intervals. By during this, if I happen to get off key at least I know where I hope to finish.

As I close, remember whatever you do or learn from birth to twenty-one, will determine how your health and life will be from twenty-one to death. Listen to the elders for they are wise but do what you must to fulfill your obligations to yourself. Find yourself while you are young and enjoy yourself while you are growing old.

I predicted I would die at the age of 36. I have held this belief for 12 years, how close was I?

I believe that life exists on other planets. Have any of you fellows found out whether or not this is true?

I am the only Black Engineer with the Little Rock District Corps of Engineers. I was the third black student to graduate from the Civil Engineering Department and the first to graduate with a bachelor's degree in civil engineering.

I am twenty-eight, father of two, and a daughter five, nearly six years old, Karen Meshell, and a son Octavius III, one year old. I was once married to Helen W. Duffy who is the mother of my children. If there are any descendants of the children of Helen or my children, please do me the favor of seeing that a copy of this letter be sent to each of them.

With Love from "1975"
June 9, 1975
Octavris C. Duffy Jr.

Chapter 11

The Ninth Child—Edward Duffy

I was born November 29, 1947, in a sharecropper's house out-side of Augusta, Arkansas, a small delta farming town in the eastern part of the state that, then, and now, has about two thousand inhab-itants. The town sits on the White River, a tributary of the mighty Mississippi, and river barges still carry cotton and grain grown in those moist, lowland fields to markets in Memphis, about eighty miles away, and then on to New Orleans.

The population is roughly half White and half black, but my world was entirely black. Our family, friends, my father's work col-leagues, my schoolmates, and friends, all were African American.

Whites would not be a big part of my life until the day I was drafted into the army and sent to Vietnam.

There were fifteen in my family, including my mother and father, twelve brothers and sisters, myself, and a cousin, Gloria Dean, whose mother died in childbirth and who was taken in and raised by my parents. Though she was about twenty years older than me, I always viewed her as my oldest sister. After her, there was Spencer, Eliza, Cora, Edna, Henry, Leona, Bernice, O.C. Jr., then me, Edward. Younger than me were Nancy, Mary, and James. I had one sister between Nancy and Mary that lived only six months and died.

Even in my name, I felt singled out from the rest of my siblings. I'm the only one whose name doesn't correspond to a family member or friend. My brother O.C. was named for my father. No one could ever figure out exactly where the name *Edward* came from.

Growing Up on the Farm

I was born on that farm just outside of town where my father worked as a sharecropper raising cotton.

Life was hard for my parents, but it became even harder due to something I did at age four. I was in the living room with my younger sister Nancy. The very next year, I would be going to school, but as I was not old enough yet, I was still at home, as was Nancy and my next younger sister Mary who was only a year old. My youngest brother James has not yet been born. The other eight kids were all at school, and my daddy was working.

Mother always had a cloth hung over the mantle above the fire-place. It was from that mantle that I pulled down some matches.

As I said, my sister and I were kind of bored, so we took down those matches and started lighting them one at a time. I took the box of matches from Nancy on my turn and lit a match. I guess I must have swung it out too wide because it came near enough to the curtain over the mantle that it caught on fire. Though I was only age four, my reflexes took hold of me, and I patted the flame down to the point I thought it was out. Satisfied at my firefighting skills and relieved Momma didn't see me, I went outside to continue to play with Nancy. At one point, I looked over and saw that our house was engulfed in flames. The only thing I could think about was the whooping I was about to get from Momma.

The first thing Momma did was get my baby sister out. Nancy knew that she hadn't set the fire so, even though she kept it a secret, she wasn't afraid to go up to Momma while the house burned down. But I stayed hidden because I was convinced I was about to get the beating of my life. But then, I heard Momma's frantic cries, calling my name. She couldn't find me and thought that I was in the house burning up. It hurt me greatly to know that Momma was so worried about me, but I also could tell she had no idea that I had set that fire. So I came out and told Momma, "Here I am!"

I didn't say anything more than that. I wouldn't say anything for the next sixteen years until I was a grown man of twenty-one because I knew I'd get a good whooping, even as a teenager, if I had fessed up.

We didn't have a telephone or electricity, so there was no way of calling the fire department, though we were only a mile out of town. Some folks saw the smoke and got hold of the fire department, but by the time they got there, the walls of the house were falling in.

I couldn't have known at the time, but that fire changed our lives. Before that fire, I had gotten a tricycle for Christmas, but after that, I don't remember getting anything more than some candy or an apple. I felt bad later, knowing that something I had done had made my parents life harder.

Another way that fire changed our lives is that within a couple of days, Daddy had found a home about twelve miles out from Augusta. Before, my siblings could walk to school. After that, we all had to ride the bus. But that was a good thing for me. Between all the unfair comparisons at home and the teachers constantly needling me about not getting as good of grades as my siblings, my only refuge was that school bus. The only happy time I could remember was those hours sitting in those hard seats. Sometimes I would wish that the bus ride would never end. I fantasized that I could be on that bus forever. When I was on that bus, I didn't have to measure up to anything. I could just sit there and ride. I cherished that time.

Though we managed to become even poorer after that fire, I learned we were already among the poorest people in the community. The night of the fire, my siblings and myself were split up amongst folks in the community who agreed to take us in. A neighbor named Ms. Page agreed to take me in. This was the first time I realized that anyone had such a thing as an indoor toilet. I also learned that some children go to sleep in their own bed. In our home, there were three bedrooms: one for the boys, one for the girls, and one for my parents. All of us boys slept in the same bed, using each other and horse blankets for warmth.

From the age of five, I worked on the farm, chopping cotton as well as rounding up the cattle each morning that had wandered off the night before. Unlike our neighbors, we had no barbed wire fence in which to keep our cattle.

Cows are the dumbest animals. All the other animals—the chickens, the pigs—knew to go back to where they were fed during feeding time. Cows, however, would wander off and get lost. They needed to be brought back every morning so they could be milked, so we would have milk to drink.

As I said, starting at five years old, my assignment was to track down the missing cattle. Sometimes they would have wandered a mile away in thick woods far from any road or stream. I soon had to learn the basics of tracking, of knowing how to find a hill from which vantage point I could spy out my surroundings, how to listen carefully for the sound of a lost heifer, how to tell the scent of a cow from the scent of any other woodland creature or livestock. All these skills would serve me well in later years, not in the thick woods of Arkansas, but in the thick jungles of Vietnam.

Once I found the cow, I would make a large ark to get on the other side of the animal so I could drive it toward the house, and then they would get their hay. After a while, the effort got easier because the animals came to recognize where they were going and to realize there was food coming if they just kept going toward the house. If the cows were smart enough to know that, why didn't they know to stay near the house in the first place? I never understood why the cattle would wander off at night.

I worked as hard as I knew how, but somehow, it was never good enough for my father whose approval I constantly sought. In the house we lived in after the fire, we usually stayed in the front room during winter because that was the only room with a fire constantly lit in the wood-burning stove. My brother Junior and I were playing in the front room one day when my father was talking to a couple of his friends. After a little while, one of my father's friends pointed to me and said, "O.C., I have half a mind to take that boy home for myself. He looks like he could be a strong worker."

"That boy?" my father said, looking straight at me and I at him. "You don't want that boy. You want that one." He pointed at my brother. "That's the one you want. This one?" His father now indicated to me again. This one doesn't work worth a nickel."

Though I tried my hardest, I never seemed to measure up to my brother, neither in the classroom nor the cotton field. I would work my hardest all day and pick ninety pounds of cotton. When we got to the scales to weigh, my brother would have picked 180 pounds. On my best day, I probably picked no more than 150 pounds, but my joy was soon banished because my brother had picked two hundred!

That evening, we had a hearty meal of beans and cornbread, but I couldn't even enjoy that. "I wish you'd work like you'd eat," my father said sternly. "If you worked as hard picking as you did eating, you'd have two hundred pounds easy."

School Days

My father's low opinion of me was shared by some of my teachers at school. I had the misfortune of having four of my eldest siblings named class valedictorian. I was, therefore, always subject to the question, "Your name is Duffy. Why aren't you smarter?"

One of the problems I faced is that even though I was such a "poor worker" in the eyes of my father, I had to do plenty of it. I never got to go to school until my chores were done. In my fourth-grade year, school had started in September, but I arrived in October after the harvest. My teacher's name was Ms. Raspberry, a matronly lady of around fifty years of age.

She was adding large numbers on the chalkboard on my first day back in class, and she called me up to the front of the class. I don't particularly remember what the exact numbers were, but it was something like 589 + 477. I knew that 9 + 7 was 16, but I didn't exactly know how to show that on the chalkboard.

"Carry the one," Ms. Raspberry insisted.

I looked at her, completely lost.

"Carry the one!" she said, as if saying it more loudly could make me understand.

"Where do you want me to carry it?" I asked honestly.

The classroom burst out with laughter, and in no time, I was feeling a strap on my behind.

After I sat down, my brother Junior asked me why I was trying to be so funny. "I wasn't trying anything," I told him. "I didn't know what she meant by carrying the one. I still don't know." Though I would eventually learn, I was often made to feel not good enough. All too many days, the teacher would stand in front of the class and call out the grades while handing back papers.

"O.C. Duffy Jr., 92," she would say, handing my brother his paper with a big red A on it.

"Edward Duffy, 64." Mine would be handed back with a big red D.

"Look at your brother," Ms. Raspberry would say. "Why can't you do as good as him?"

I think today that those teachers had my best interests at heart, that they thought they could inspire me through jealousy, but in the end, that just discouraged me. I thought I couldn't win, so why try? And I don't want to make it sound like all the teachers were negative about my abilities. I remember fondly one of those kind teachers. Her name was Willie Mae Bryant, and her temperament was very much like my own mother's, kind and compassionate. If I made a lower grade than my brother in her classroom, which was often, she would put her arm around me, and say "I know you worked hard. You'll do better the next time."

Looking back on it, Ms. Bryant had a son of her own who was two or three years younger than me. He had issues with learning and had a sister who made better grades than he did. I felt better having a teacher show empathetic understanding.

Of course, even with those teachers who were harsh, it was likely because they knew the harshness of the world I was going out into. We went to Carver High, the Black school. The White kids went to Laura Conner High, the White school. Our books were their hand-me-downs. Our buses were the old buses the White schools had replaced with newer ones. Those teachers lived almost their entire lives in a segregated world where they had to work harder just to make it. They wanted me to use every ounce of brain power and motivation to be the best I could be. But in the end, they sapped me of motivation.

Between my inability to please my father and constant mockery from my teachers, my happiest place was on that school bus, on the twelve-mile rides to and from school. I could be in my own world. As I said before, my world was a world mostly inhabited by African Americans or "colored folk" as the popular term was used back then. Much of my interaction with White folks was when I would be hired out to work for them after the harvest was finished on my father's land.

Going to Town on the Greyhound

When I was six or seven years old, it was common practice to wave down a Greyhound bus to get where we were going. Daddy would then pay the bus driver for our passage. When we got on one day, I took a nice front seat for myself that was next to an open window because I wanted to look out. But almost immediately, everyone was telling me I could not sit there. My sister came up and told me I had to get up and come with them to the back of the bus. At the time, I was too young to completely understand why I couldn't sit up there when all I wanted to do was look out the window.

Working in the Fields

Once, when I was around ten years old, I was chopping cotton for a man named Reese Jones along with my sister and mother. Often, after I had finished the harvest on my father's farm, I was hired out to other folks' farms to do chopping or harvesting for them. Most young folks today are used to picking up a job to pay for a car or cell phone or something they want to do. The thought of keeping the money never crossed my mind. I was working to support our family. Usually, the money went straight to my folks, but even when it was paid out to me, I knew that every dime had to go to my mother and father to pay for our food and clothing.

Reese's wife brought us some water to drink in a big bucket, but first, she stopped to give her dog a drink from the bucket. After that, she offered my sister a drink out of a dipper pulling water from the same bucket the dog just drank from.

Now, my mother was a very even-tempered lady, meek and easygoing. I rarely saw her angry and almost never angry with folks outside the house and certainly never with White folks. But I could hear the anger in her voice when she told the lady, "We don't drink after dogs!" A dog was the lowest animal on the farm. A dog wasn't allowed in the house, much less allowed to eat anywhere near anything you were to eat, and here this lady was treating us like one of her dogs.

But I was fearful because we were always taught, we had to speak respectfully to White folks. We never called them by their first name, only "Mr." or "Miss" and that applied even to White children who were the same age. And if you didn't, it didn't just affect you. Your whole family would suffer, especially your parents. But here my mother was, standing up for her daughter to a White lady.

It was in that moment I was afraid of what sort of reaction Ms. Jones would have to my mother, but to my surprise, she seemed shocked and apologetic. It was almost like she had never realized that Black folks would be offended by being given a drink out of the same bowl a dog just drank out of. Not only did she seem apologetic, but she also told my mother she was sorry and went and got another bucket of water to offer us.

Despite not having money, my parents sacrificed greatly to make sure all of us kids had a chance at college. Looking back, I believe that most of that encouragement came from my mother. Although my mother did not finish high school (my father only went to third grade), her father went to Branch Normal School, the Black college that became Arkansas Agricultural, Mechanical and Normal College (AM&N) and then University of Arkansas at Pine Bluff. This experience made my mother understand the doors that college could open for us children.

The Washing Machine

My rivalry with my father came to a head one day when I was home on break from college. I was walking into the house as mother was walking out of the house, her eyes full of tears saying that she was leaving.

I calmed her down and asked her to tell me why she wanted to leave. She told me that she had bought a washing machine, but Daddy demanded she take it back. I walked into the room where he was. I stood up and said, "Why can't my mother have a washing machine? Do you want her to spend her life washing everything by hand? If it's too expensive, we can raise the money and pay you back."

"It's not the cost of the washing machine," Father said. "It's the cost of the electricity to run it."

I was stunned. As hard as my mother had worked, she finally had saved up to buy a machine that would take some of the drudgery out of her life, and Daddy wanted to deprive her of it because the machine needed to be plugged in and would use, at most, a few dollars of electricity a month.

"My mother can have a washing machine, and if you don't like it, you can leave," I said firmly. I still remember the look in his eyes. I was challenging the master of the house, and this was the decisive moment. Would he strike me? Would he give in for the first time in my life? We were in the kitchen, and the stove was in between him and me. He took one step toward me, and I tensed up, preparing for a physical confrontation. Father had to know that I was now physically stronger than him. I could almost feel the thoughts running through his head as he came closer. He stopped and suddenly turned and walked out of the house.

My mother indeed could have a washing machine. I had successfully challenged the master of the house, but there would be a price to be paid. My relationship with my father was never good, but it would never be the same after that day. It became almost as if I were an enemy in his home.

Serving Time in the United States Army

After being drafted into the army, I was sent to Fort Polk, Louisiana, for basic training, followed by infantry training. At the end of the training, we all received orders with our MOS (military occupational specialty, the job we had to do) and the location of our next assignment. When I first got my orders, I didn't quite understand what it meant.

I went to the sergeant to ask him "What is 11, Bravo?"

He answered, "You will be a bushbeater."

I said, "What is a bushbeater?"

"A bushbeater is a foot soldier, so basically, you will be in the infantry. You will be in the fighting part of the army."

The sergeant had said that since I was a college graduate that I would get a better MO. I had been asked if I was interested in going to warrant officer school to train in flying helicopters. At first, it sounded like an appealing option, but one of the Black sergeants said, "We are losing warrant officers faster than we can train them."

After I heard that, I told the commander that I didn't want to go to warrant officer school. The commander got upset. He asked, "Are you refusing to be an officer in the US Army?" I didn't say anything, but the answer was "yes." I was more concerned about staying alive than being an officer in the army. A little while after that incident, a telegram arrived at the offices of my higher ups saying I was accepted into the Peace Corps. I had applied to the Peace Corps my senior year in college and knew that if I was accepted, it would mean that I didn't have to go to Vietnam.

The Peace Corps telegrammed the acceptance to the commander. I was called into his office and the first sergeant was standing there. Incidentally, both were White men. "What do you think? Should we send this young man to the Peace Corps?" the commander asked the sergeant.

The sergeant looked at me. "He didn't want to serve as an officer in the US Army. No! Send his ass to Vietnam." At that point, I was genuinely concerned. The statement at the bottom of my orders indicated I was being sent to Vietnam as part of the American division. In preparation for going to Vietnam, I gave away all my possessions, all my clothes, everything I had. I really believed that I might not make it back because there had been so many people I had known who had been killed in the war.

The day I left to begin my journey to Vietnam, my mother, father, and brother Junior were in the living room. I remember distinctly standing behind my father. In the few years that had passed since I had confronted my father about the washing machine and his treatment of my mother, he had barely spoken a word to me.

"I'm leaving for Vietnam, Daddy," I said, staring at the back of his head while he sat in his chair in the living room. I thought that this would break the ice, that he would want to give me a hug for what could be the last I would ever see him. But he just sat there, silent.

My brother and I walked out the back of the house, and my mother had tears in her eyes. She gave me a package. "Take this with you," she said, gently placing the box in my hands. "Don't open this until you get to Vietnam." I hugged her goodbye. Junior and I walked out into the backyard. "I will see you when you get back," he said definitively.

"I hope you are right," I said, completely uncertain if that would turn out to be true.

I had almost forgotten about my mom's order that I not open my package until I got to Vietnam. Well, here I was in Vietnam, so I opened it. Inside was a small Bible, one of those that only had the

New Testament, along with the Old Testament books of Psalms and Proverbs. There was a marker placed on Psalm 23, one of Mom's favorites. I would often pull out that Bible to read that Psalm after some hard battles.

> Yea, though I walk through the valley of the
>   shadow of death,
> I will fear no evil: for thou art with me;
> Thy rod and thy staff they comfort me.

When I was a youngster, I was often trying to get wayward cattle to come back home, and at that job, I was largely successful. But when I came back home, I often didn't feel like I was truly home. I didn't live up to the hopes of my father. I did not meet the expectations of the community. In many ways, especially in school, I did not meet my own expectations.

After returning from Vietnam, I felt like a stranger in a strange land, a feeling compounded by the racial resentment I experienced at the University of Arkansas and in the rest of my native country. Over time, however, I began to become comfortable with who I am, settled in my own skin.

I have resolved my experiences in Vietnam. I have done this primarily by going to the Veterans Administration for counseling and by meeting with a group of veterans for about ten years. We meet twice a month. I find it therapeutic to talk to men who have gone through the same experience that I have. The things I say, the things I had to do to stay alive in the jungles of Vietnam that haunted me long after I returned, are not shocking to them. I have found that, as bad as my experience was, many of my fellow veterans had even worse experiences and that has helped me to keep my problems in perspective. When I first returned, no one wanted to hear about the realities of war. I had to live with those demons. Talking about them with my fellow veterans has largely exorcised them, and today I feel free.

Married Life and Reconciliation with My Father

Lorraine and I were married in Washington, DC, on July 25, 1981, and we have two children, Edward and Chardae. We have four grandchildren: Letia, Lorrin, Richard, and Carmelo.

My father and mother came to Miami, where I raised my family when my son was six months old. I had settled into an excellent job at Miami-Dade College. I could tell my father was able to see me from a different perspective. He had feared that because I had difficulty obeying his every command when I was growing up, therefore I would have a tough time making it in this world, but he could see I was successful in life. As we spoke, I realized that he was speaking to me in the respectful tone of a man and not the belittling tone he took with a young boy.

My mother later confided with me that the happiest moment of her life, happier than when I stood up to my father about the washing machine, happier than when I came home alive from the war, was the day she saw her son and her husband laughing and joking together as father and son and friends.

Richard, Carmelo, Chardae, Randy, and Edward

Lorraine and Edward

Chapter 12

· · ◦ · ·

Tenth Child—Nancy Mae Duffy Blount

Growing Up in Augusta

I am Nancy Mae Duffy Blount, the tenth of thirteenth children born to O.C. Duffy. Sr. and Leona Stith Duffy on January 13, 1949, in Augusta, Arkansas. I was very young when the house we lived in located in Augusta burned down, and we moved to a community called Cavell about three miles from McCrory. My parents were sharecroppers, and we spent days working in the fields, chopping, and picking cotton and cutting Johnson grass out of soybean fields from sunup to sundown, Mondays through Fridays, and sometimes a half day on Saturdays. Sundays were always reserved for church. Some of us younger ones stayed home with a couple of the older siblings who looked after us. When we were not working in the fields, we found creative ways to entertain ourselves. My two brothers, Edward and O.C. Jr., and I played together because we were closest together in age. I can remember when we took an old car tire and tied a rope around it and then found a strong tree limb, running horizontally, to tie the rope to that limb so the tire could swing from it. It made a very good swing. We would take turns pushing each other so we could swing very high. Then we decided we wanted to seesaw. So we took one of Daddy's wooden horses and placed a board on it, and one of us would get on each end and seesaw. We soon grew tired of the swing and seesaw and decided to play cowboy and Indian, which required us to have a bow and arrow for the Indian. We took a strong stalk of sugarcane, a filed-down nail that was inserted into the stalk of cane for the arrow, and we took an old inner tube from an old worn tire and cut strips and attached the rubber to a strong, but limber tree limb to make the bow. After making the bow and arrow, we had to try them out. So the two brothers, Edward, and O.C. Jr., had to decide who was going to play the Indian and who would play the cowboy, and I would be the lookout for Mom and Dad. Edward decided to play the Indian and O.C. decided to play the cowboy who would be running from the Indian and the Indian would try to capture him with the bow and arrow. O.C. Jr. started to run, and as he turned the corner of the house, Edward shot the arrow at O.C., and all we could hear was a scream around the corner. The Indian had shot the cowboy. It was just a little scrape. A true example of "God taking care of fools and babies."

As we grew older, we became curious about fire. One day, Edward and I set some grass on fire beside the house, then we could be firefighters and put it out before it got to the house. Edward started the fire while I watched for Mama. The fire started burning much faster than we had thought, but we finally put it out right at the house. Sometime later, Daddy noticed the burned area, and when he questioned us about it, we blamed it on the White neighbor who lived down the road a piece behind us.

We were dangerously creative in our youth. I remember one Saturday when Mama went to town to shop. She had just bought and put down a new linoleum black and white kitchen rug. It was so pretty and shiny that we couldn't resist running and sliding on it. We were having so much fun that we didn't notice that we were sliding so hard that the color was coming off the rug. Boy, were we in trouble, we thought. But the older siblings who were supposed to be watching us were the ones in big trouble, specifically Bernice, Leona, and Henry. When Mama saw the rug and asked what happened, the older siblings claimed they were trying to clean it and the cleaner must have taken the color off. That was the end of that. When we were not entertaining ourselves, we had certain chores assigned to us daily. The girls had to wash clothes, hang them on the line to dry, and take them in and iron them. We had to do house cleaning and cooking also. The boys had to cut wood; feed the horses, cows, hogs, and chickens; and keep the yard clean. All their work was outside the house and the girls' work was primarily inside. I can remember when I was about nine years old, and Mama was teaching me how to cook biscuits. I made my first batch, which didn't turn out so well, so I threw them out to the dogs.

The dogs came up to them, looked at them, smelled them, looked at me, and walked away. Even the dogs knew those biscuits were not fit to eat. I also remember the girls being assigned certain days to wash the dishes and clean up the kitchen. When it was my sister Leona's day to do the dishes, she would try to make me do them for her. She was about five years my senior and about twenty pounds thinner, but we would fight over who was going to do the dishes, and of course, I always won the fight because I was bigger and stronger. I was the tomboy of the family. It seemed like Leona, and I found something to fight about almost every day, but the fights were friendly, and soon after, the fights we were back friends, playing together as if we had never fought.

My School Days

As we became school age, I can remember walking almost a mile from the house to the highway to catch the bus to go to school in Augusta, which was about ten miles away. I can remember standing at that bus stop in all kinds of weather. While Mama and Daddy didn't have the opportunity to get a high school education, they insisted that we did. They instilled in us the desire to learn and become productive citizens. They didn't want us to have to work in the fields of the "White man" all our lives. I attended elementary school at Carver Elementary School in Augusta. My favorite elementary teacher was Ms. M., a robust but very kind-hearted lady. She would pay for my lunch and buy me snacks. I became so fond of her that one day I decided I would purposely hide in the room after school to miss the bus so I could go home with her for the night. But when she noticed that I was still at school and everyone else was gone, she had another teacher take me home. Mom and Dad were pretty upset with Edward and O.C. Jr. for coming home without me, but they were so glad to see me that they forgot about the boys. I didn't pull that trick again.

When I got to the fourth grade, I became interested in music. I wanted to learn to play the piano. The music teacher was Ms. R. L., who also taught private lessons. Mama worked something out with Ms. R. L. for me to be able to take lessons. We couldn't afford to buy a piano for me to practice at home, so I took a large shoe box and drew a keyboard on it, and that little invention allowed me to practice at home. Ms. R. L. was very proud of my progress until I wanted to add to the script and put extra notes to the bars to jazz up the music a bit, but that wasn't allowed. I struggled through that year and then stopped taking the lessons but continued to play on my own. When I got to junior high school, I became a member of the school choir. I sang second soprano and alto. During my junior high school years, I also became involved in sports—track and softball. Our father was very old-fashioned and protective of his girls. Thus, I could only take part in sports that were held during the day. I was a track sprinter who won several awards for the school. In softball, I played center field. Our softball team won several games against neighboring Black school districts.

When I arrived at Carver High School, I continued to be involved in extracurricular activities. I was a member of the debate team. I always enjoyed discussing controversial issues and trying to convince the opposition to come to my way of thinking. In addition to school activities, I was involved in the 4H Club. Daddy was involved in Farm Bureau Events and always had a good relationship with the extension agent, who provided him with transportation to meetings and the County Fairs each year.

I often entered various competitions at the Fair. One of my most memorable demonstrations was "How to prepare a chicken for barbecuing," which I was the first-place winner. One year, I decided to try the music competition. Daddy wasn't too much in favor of us singing secular music, but that's what all the contestants were singing. So I performed my rendition of "The Sea of Love" and won third place. When they announced the winners, I could see how proud Daddy was of his little girl winning a prize. There were about a dozen of us competing for those prizes. When I got to the tenth grade, I started working hard to prepare myself for going to college. I knew that education would be my ticket out of those cotton fields and cleaning houses for rich White folks for forty cents an hour. I would study and work hard in school. I wanted to learn all I could to ensure my success in college. At that time, I didn't know what I wanted to be in life, but I knew that I didn't want to pick and chop cotton the rest of my life. Then, one day while chopping cotton with that hot sun bearing down on me, I made a promise to God that if he got me out of those fields, I would dedicate my life to helping children growing up very much like me.

In May of 1966, I graduated valedictorian of my class of fifty from Carver High School. My life's journey was just beginning. I applied for a scholarship to AM&N College, Presently University of Arkansas at Pine Bluff. After passing the entrance exams with flying colors, with a high score in reading, I decided to become a teacher of English and foreign languages (French and Spanish). To earn extra money for items the scholarship didn't cover, I cooked and sold hamburgers and hot dogs for the lady over the dormitory, Ms. S. I was so happy to get out of the cotton fields that I went to school year around and graduated in three and a half years. In January 1970, I received my BA degree in foreign language with a minor in English. Since I had finished my course of study the first semester of my last year, I landed a job as secretary of the Education Department on campus.

At the end of that semester, I still had a thirst for more knowledge, so I applied for a graduate assistant position at the University of Arkansas in Fayetteville, Arkansas. I took the Graduate Record Exam and passed it. I got the position and went on to pursue a masters in French. When I arrived at the university, to my surprise, there were thousands of students on campus with a faculty of approximately five hundred with only two African American professors. Out of the thousands of students on campus, there may have been fifty African Americans. I was the only African American student in the master's program in French. I was the only African American graduate assistant, teaching first and second level French to college students during the day and taking my graduate courses in the evenings and at night. After a year and a half of study, I received my MA degree in French. After finishing my masters' degree in Fayetteville, I returned to Pine Bluff and applied for a job at Timex Corporation in Little Rock. I purposely only listed my bachelors' degree so that I would not appear to be "overqualified "for the job. When the manager interviewed me and saw that I had a teaching degree, he was very hesitant to hire me, but I reached back and got my debate skills and convinced him to hire me. He said to me, "I know you are not going to stay here with your credentials, but I am going to give you a chance." And I replied to him, "If I get a teaching job, I won't leave here until you have a replacement for me." I continued to apply for a teaching position, and in September of 1972, I received several calls from the superintendent of schools, Mr. K. in Marianna, Arkansas, asking me to please come for an interview. I went to Marianna for an interview and was offered the job that day, but I asked him to allow me to go back to my job at Timex and resign, move to Marianna, and come to work the following week.

The superintendent agreed. I went back to Timex Corporation and asked the manager if we could talk, and before I could tell him that I had a teaching job offer, but that I would stay with Timex until he had a replacement for me. He smiled and said, "I have someone that I can put in that position because I knew I wouldn't be able to

keep you long. Good luck, Ms. Duffy!" I finished working the rest
of that week and then left and prepared for the move to Marianna.
In September of 1972, I began teaching at Lee High School in the
Marianna School District, located in one of the poorest counties in
the state and continued working there for thirty-three years before
retiring. My promise to God had been fulfilled. I taught English,
French, and Spanish over the course of my career. During my teaching career, I also served as an adjunct faculty member at East Arkansas
Community College in Forrest City, Arkansas, and Phillips County

Community College in Helena, Arkansas

While teaching, I had the wonderful opportunity to do additional
studies at Memphis State University, Memphis, Tennessee; University
of Illinois/Champaign-Urbana; University of Arkansas at Little Rock;
University of Arkansas at Conway; University of Lausanne, Lausanne,
Switzerland; and Instituto Centroamericano De Asuntos Internacionales,
San José, Costa Rica. During the summers, when I wasn't teaching or
taking students on field trips, I managed to compose a few poems that
were published in my brother Spencer's book of poems *Windows of
My Mind*. I later wrote and directed a religious play "Celebrating the
Homegoing of Satan," which was performed at some local churches in
Memphis and at an open-air theater in Memphis. After retiring from
teaching in 2005, I decided to try my musical talent by composing religious music. So I wrote the lyrics to nine songs. My daughter, Laquita
wrote the lyrics to one, and we did our rendition of two old hymns. In
2008, two of my sisters, Marie and Leona; my daughter, Laquita; and
the church organist and I recorded a CD "Witnessing for Christ" in Los
Angeles, California. Since the recording, Nancy Blount and the Duffy
Ensemble have performed concerts in Arkansas and Tennessee with the
proceeds going to the Duffy Scholarship Fund.

Family Life

A couple of years after working in Marianna, I met a guy
who owned a service station. I had been taught to do business with

minority-owned businesses as much as possible. I was having trouble with a Datsun station wagon, and I took my car to him for repairs. After he torn down the vehicle, he found he couldn't get it back together. Only to learn later, he intentionally torn it down to keep me coming to the station every day. He even managed to talk me into working after school and during the summers at the service station (Blount's Super Shell). In 1973, Sam sold the service station and we moved to West Memphis, Arkansas. Sam started to work with a Toyota Dealership in Memphis and did some professional modeling while I commuted to Marianna every day for my teaching job. I often carpooled with another teacher. We decided to get married in 1975. We decided we didn't want a big formal wedding. So we went to the Crittenden County Court House. I wore something old and something new, something borrowed, and something blue. A judge performed the ceremony. I will never forget Sam, asking him, "What do I owe you?" The judge responded, "Well, what is she worth to you?" Sam gave the judge $20. We moved forward and raised my daughter Laquita to adulthood. In 1978, we had a premature baby girl who was stillborn. We never had any more children.

In 1978, we purchased a funeral home in West Memphis on Eighth Street. We decided to name it National Funeral Home. Two years later, we opened a branch of National Funeral Home in Marianna, Arkansas. His mother managed that office for us. A few years later, we opened an additional funeral home, People's Funeral Home in Forrest City, Arkansas, about twenty miles from the Marianna Funeral Home. We have been in the funeral business for over forty years and the business is now considered one of the most successful funeral homes in the Tristate area.

Family Reunions and Sisters' Summit

The Duffy Family held family reunions on the odd years, and we had sisters' summits on the even years. Those were fun times with all the family together, having picnics, going on tours, and attending banquets and concerts. At those events, we really got to know each other. We learned to celebrate the things we had in common and to respect and appreciate our differences.

One summer during a sisters' summit at one of the sister's summer home in Las Vegas, Nevada, we went to a Motown Show at a theater in one of the Casinos. A group from Australia was performing Motown Sounds. They were excellent performers. About halfway through the performance, they wanted to involve the audience. So one of the performers came down in the audience to choose someone to go on stage and perform with them. My last thought was that it would be me. But when I looked up, the singer was coming down the row where the sisters were sitting, and to my surprise, he stopped right in front of me and extended his hand and said, "Will you be my girl?" After I got over the shock, about ten seconds, I said, "Sure!" and accompanied him to the stage. First, we talked a little about me, and then we danced a little and then we performed "My Girl." When he would say, "My girl," I would say, "My guy." The audience thought our performance was so good that I had to be part of the show. That was one of the most memorable Sisters' Summits and a most enjoyable event that I will always cherish. After the performance, I had a difficult time remembering. What happens in Vegas, stays in Vegas. As a gift for my performance, the group gave me a copy of their CD, autographed by the guy who chose me to go be his girl that night.

I have had and continue to have a good life, and I hope that I have been a beacon of light to others growing up like I did. My best advice to my students in school and youngsters in the church and community was, "It's not where you are from, but where you are going that is most important. Education is the key that unlocks the doors to success and happiness."

I am a living witness that these statements are true. And by the grace of God and a loving and supportive family, happiness, and success have been possible for me.

Laquita, Tre, and Nancy

Sam and Nancy

The Striblings: Finis IV, Finis III, Laquita, Kylan, and Tre

Politics

My first political office was Lee County coroner. I was the first female and the first Black to be elected Lee County coroner. I served four two-year terms (1991–1998). This was an historic event because I was also the first female and first Black to be elected county coroner in the state of Arkansas. A few years later, I decided to run for state representative for District 52. Backed by an excellent campaign team, we were victorious. So I became the first Black female to represent District 52 in the Arkansas House of Representatives.

I will never forget a certain day that two other Black representatives and I were walking the halls of the Arkansas Capitol admiring the photo composites of the various general assemblies. When we came across our composite, I said to one of the guys, "You know, I never thought that I would be walking the halls of our state's capitol and looking at our pictures hanging on the walls and the list was not a most wanted list." We chuckled and continued admiring the composites.

During my tenure in the Arkansas House of Representatives, I proudly served on the House Education Committee, Cities and Counties and Local Government, and Joint Legislative Audit. I served as the chairperson of the Early Childhood Education Subcommittee, and vice chairman of the House Education Committee, and chairman of the Legislative Black Caucus. During that time, I was proud to have sponsored and cosponsored several bills that made significant improvements in education, provided financial support for volunteer fire departments, boys' and girls' clubs, senior citizen centers, and various health facilities in the state. I was also instrumental in getting several African Americans appointed to State Boards and Commissions and grants to small African American nonprofits. The most outstanding pieces of legislation that I sponsored, and of which I am most proud are Lifetime Teaching License, ARKIDS (Health Insurance school aged children), and the Minority Contractors Mentor Program (ACT 950), which formed a partnership between large contractors and small and individual minority contractors. When working in those cotton fields, I could never have imagined that I would serve in these public service positions. I never thought that I would be able to attend the inauguration of two presidents of the United States, President Bill Clinton and President Barack Obama.

Service

Currently, Nancy Duffy Blount serves as the CEO of the Duffy Scholarship Fund, which is a scholarship foundation established in 1977 by the Duffy Family as a dream come true for our mother, Leona Stith Duffy. This scholarship is awarded to needy students wanting to continue their education beyond high school. She serves as chairperson of the Arkansas Education Association Federal Credit Union, UniServ director for the Arkansas Education Association, an insurance agent, funeral director, notary public, co-owner of Marianna Funeral Home, and a member of True Love Outreach Ministries in Memphis, Tennessee, where she serves as the director of music and pianist, and where her husband, Bishop Sam E. Blount is the pastor. Nancy is also a member of Eta Sigma Omega Chapter of Alpha Kappa Alpha Sorority, Inc. in Marianna, Marianna Rotary Club, Lee County Branch NAACP, lifetime member of Arkansas Education Association, National Education Association, American Association of Retired Persons, and the Lee County Retired Teachers' Association.

Awards and Recognitions

Icon of the Delta December 5, 2020—Theta Tau Lambda Chapter of Alpha Phi Alpha Fraternity
Outstanding Legislator Award 2007—2009 Arkansas Municipal League
Bill Thomas Outstanding Legislative Leadership Award—2008 Crossroads Coalition
Outstanding Leadership on Behalf of Public Education 2005—Arkansas Education Association
Arkansas Education Association Human and Civil Rights Award 1994
Trailblazer Award 1991, 2005, 2019 Ladies of Essence Outstanding Educator of the Midsouth 1983

Chapter 13

The Twelfth Child—Mary Louise Duffy-Lewis

Biographical Information

My name is Mary Duffy-Lewis. I am the twelfth of thirteen children born on May 18, 1951, to O.C. Duffy Sr. and Leona Stith Duffy in Augusta, Arkansas. I was told that the house I was born in burned down in 1953 when I was only two years old. I was told I was in the bed asleep, and Mama came in to get me with flames all around the bed. She got me out, along with our cousin Gloria (Janie), and her son Nick. We were the babies in the family then.

Growing Up in Augusta and Cavell, Arkansas

Growing up on the farm in Cavell, Arkansas, about eleven miles from Augusta and midway between Augusta and McCrory, Arkansas, was quite a unique experience. On this farm, my daddy was a share-cropper. We lived in a house owned by the landowner, Mr. Willis. We grew cotton mainly, and it was our job to pick it. We also had cows, pigs, chickens, and horses that were used to work the fields. My daddy did not allow us to ride the horses.

On the farm, we picked cotton, although my baby brother, James, and I were too small to do a lot of work and were not in school yet. We had croker sacks and put cotton in them until we got tired and would fall asleep on the end of my mama's sack, and she would drag us down the cotton row until her sack was full.

Another chore James and I had was picking wild berries, mostly blackberries to take to Mama who would use them to make a cobbler for dinner. We had a cobbler, cake, pies, or cookies every day for dessert. Cobblers were and still are my favorite desserts. Since we had a fruit orchard, peach cobbler was my favorite dessert. We had a fruit orchard of peaches, pears, apples, and plums.

Speaking of the fruit orchard, we could hardly wait until the fruit was ripe to pick for Mom to make a cobbler for us to eat. One day, Nancy and I eyed some almost ripe peaches. We wanted to get some to take back to our rooms and eat later. My daddy had told us not to eat those green peaches because they would give us a stom-achache. Well, being kids we decided we were going to get some anyway. The trick was to get by Daddy sitting on the front porch after working in the fields all day. So Nancy and I decided to hide the peaches in our underwear. While passing by, some of the peaches fell out of our pants, and we were caught. He didn't have to discipline us because the peach fuzz did that for him. It gave us quite an itch. We didn't do that again!

Another fond memory of living on the farm was when my mother's father, Grandpa Henry Stith, would come visit. He would make animals from pea casings James and I kept from shelling purple hull peas. He came to visit us in Augusta a time or two before his health declined and went to St. Louis to live with my mother's sisters. He lived to be ninety-nine years old about six months shy of his one hundredth birthday. He died in 1965. He was born in 1865. I really loved him. He was the only grandparent I knew. Daddy's mother and father died long before most of us were born.

I really loved living on the farm in Cavell. My siblings O.C. Jr., Edward, Nancy, James, and I often played and got in mischief together. We used to walk about two miles from the farm to Patterson to buy candy at a local grocery store there.

Another memory I have is that one time my sister Edna was milking our cow. I had a pet pig named Peggy. My pig ran in the stall where she was, and she yelled at me to get my pig and get out of her way. The cow didn't appreciate us either and swiftly kicked me and my pig out.

Although, I didn't say anything then, it really hurt my feelings. Later, Edna was courting a guy named Walter. He drove a fancy black pickup truck and always looked nice, all dressed up with his shoes shining and all. My siblings, O.C. Jr., Edward, Nancy, James, and I decided we did not care for Walter because when they were courting, we couldn't sit in the living room where they were. We decided to push his nice black pickup out into the pasture where the animals grazed. When he left, he had to walk to the pasture in the dark and try to find his car. It was a while before he returned. We never told Edna what we had done until we were grown.

We didn't have very much in the form of entertainment, so we had to make our own. We did not have a television, just a radio. One day, my siblings Henry, Leona, O.C. Jr., Edward, Bernice, Nancy, and I decided we would take a number 2 tub up on the pitch of our red barn where the animals stayed and where my father dried his peanuts on the tin roof. Henry decided someone should get in the tub, and they would release it to slide down to the flat part of the roof. I volunteered. When they let the tub go, I went flying down that tin roof, and the tub stopped just a few inches from the edge because of the peanuts. There was a thirty-foot drop, and if the peanuts had not been up there, I may not have been here to tell this story. Our parents did not know about this until we were grown either because if they had, my daddy believed in not sparing the rod and all of us would have received a whipping.

We moved from the farm back to Augusta again on February 9, 1960, which was my brother James's sixth birthday. Since we moved in February, I was eight and would not be nine until my birthday in May.

I had to adjust to not being able to roam from our property to our neighbors since we were in town and not on the farm. However, we had a big front and backyard and a lot next to the house where my father had a big vegetable garden. Mr. Harris, the neighbor to the north of our property, had a vacant lot and let us set up a softball field. He was a nice man and told Daddy that he didn't mind us playing on his vacant lot. We would play on that field every Friday and Saturday, but not on Sunday. Sunday was a holy day, and we did not play softball or basketball, only board games.

We were raised in the Christian Methodist Episcopal Church (CME) faith. Our family was the makeup of the church: Daddy was the Sunday School Superintendent for over sixty years, Mama was one of the two stewardesses, and my sisters served as secretary of the Sunday School as we came of age. A few of our cousins and other friends of the family were also part of the congregation. We would attend Sunday School, evening programs, and Christian Youth Fellowship (CYF).

I really liked our church and looked forward to Sunday services. Our family made up the choir. One of my favorite pastors was Reverend Curry. He was genuinely nice to us and would come pick up the older children and my parents from the farm to come to the church in Augusta before we moved there.

Mama made the Communion unleavened bread. She would place the flour mix (no salt) in between wax paper and iron it out flat until it was crisp and slightly browned. This was the best communion bread I had ever tasted, and if there was some left, she would bring it home, and we could eat it and drink the rest of the grape juice that was left from communion.

At age six, I attended Carver Elementary School. The first day of school, I got lost trying to find my classroom. Nancy, my older sister, had to help me find the right building as the school included five separate buildings. The principal's office was in the center of the campus; it was the only two-story building on campus.

In elementary school, I had great teachers. I will never forget my second-grade teacher, Ms. McDaniel. One day, she was teaching us spelling, and the word for the day was "wind." She went around the class of twenty-five or so and asked each student what "wind" spelled, and no one knew. She was a disciplinarian too. She lined us all up outside the classroom, had us hold out our palms, took a ruler, and gave us several licks in our hands. She then sent us back into the classroom. I will never forget the word "wind" as long as I live.

My favorite elementary teacher was my third-grade teacher, Ms. Marshall. She was kind and smart. I sometimes wonder what happened to those teachers.

Fast forward to age fifteen. There was a grocery store owned by this African American couple, the "Spears." My sister Leona was the first girl from the family to work there. When Leona graduated, Ms. "Mutt" hired my sister Bernice then Nancy then me. They were very nice people, and we only lived a block from their store, Spear Grocery. I would work at the store during the lunch hour during the week making sandwiches for the students that came there for lunch. I could hear the bell signaling a return to school from the store and would always return to my class on time.

Another favorite memory of homelife while working at Spear Grocery was that on Saturday, the store closed at 10:00 p.m. My parents, James, and I were the only ones at home. The others had graduated and left home for college or the military. I would bring home two pints of Yarnell's ice cream and vanilla wafers for us to enjoy as we watched the 10:00 p.m. news before retiring for bed.

When we lived two blocks from school, we always walked to school. I never understood why my father would come down the hallway telling James and me to get up at 6:00 a.m. because the school bus had gone by. The bus was going to pick up kids in the rural area, where we used to live and get them back to school by 8:00 a.m. when school started. As an adult, I now know why he did that. There were four of us at home and only one bathtub. Each morning before going to school, we had to eat breakfast. This time was needed for us to get ready and get to school on time.

I will speak briefly about my courtships in high school. I remember asking my mother when I turned fifteen if I could have company (that's what they called dating). She told me no and that I shouldn't even know the difference between a boy and a girl. A year later at sixteen, one of my neighbor's that my parents knew, had a son, Eddie, who worked downtown at the drugstore. Eddie asked me if he could court me. I told him I had to ask my parents. My mother said yes, but only at our house and when one of my parents was at home.

My father worked doing carpentry work around town and my mother worked as a domestic worker all day. Therefore, there was no time either of them would be home, so that relationship went nowhere.

At age seventeen, my senior year of high school, I was still working at the grocery store and a friend of the man called Mr. Willard would bring a young man, the same age as me, with him to sit around the store and talk with the owner and some of the customers. James, my brother, used to come walk me home, but I met another James, and he began walking me home. This was the only time I would see James. Shortly before I graduated, he and I lost interest in each other, and I left for college in the fall of 1969.

Because most of my siblings had attended and graduated from AM&N College in Pine Bluff, Arkansas, I knew that was where I would go. I tried to decide on a major. My twelfth-grade teacher, Ms. Tabron, said that I would be good in home economics. During that time, home economics was mainly the art and science of cooking and sewing, and neither of which I felt I was very good at. My mother did most of the cooking, especially the meats, I would do the vegetables, set the table, and wash dishes. Washing dishes was my main job, and I still don't mind doing them to this day.

Another chore I had was doing the family's laundry. We did not have an automatic washer, so I used a tin wash board and later a glass washboard. The laundry was done in two number 2 tubs. One for washing and one for rinsing. The clothes were then hung on a line to dry. We later got a wringer washer. I was so happy I didn't have to rub my knuckles raw on that old wash board anymore! I also ironed the dresses and shirts that were mostly white for my dad and my four brothers that were at home at the time. Dress shirts were only in white until years later when they finally made pastel dress shirts. Boy, was I delighted to see pastel shirts!

Leaving Home and Going Off to College

In September of 1969, I entered AM&N to begin the four years that I would spend earning a college degree. I began my major my first year. I had classes every day and labs on Monday, Wednesday, and Fridays. Some of my classmates did not have classes every day and would tease me, especially when we had breaks for the holidays, since they had to wait for me since my labs were usually not over until 5:00 p.m.

For cooking classes, I had to wear a white smock, white hose, and white shoes. My classmates would tease me saying, "There goes nurse Mary." It was not mean, so I would just laugh it off and continue to my class.

I had a loan for my first year, and we were not allowed to work. However, the next three years, I completed work study and earned grants to pay my tuition, room, and board. When I graduated, I only had to repay tuition and fees for the one year I had a loan. My work study assignment was to be a messenger for the head of the Home Economics Department, Dr. Greenhouse. I enjoyed this job. During my senior year, my friend Shirley and I worked with Ms. McCray on her research as she pursued her doctorate degree. Shirley and I are still close friends to this day.

We would get a ride to Pine Bluff, which is ninety miles from Augusta, with some of my siblings' friends. We did not have a car in our family then. However, when my brother James came on campus my senior year, he had a car. He did not want the girls—my friends and me—bugging him to take us downtown for shopping, so he let me keep it on weekends. My friends and I would go downtown and shop for little things like health and hygiene items we needed.

During my first year, I lived with two roommates, Contha from Earle, Arkansas, and Darlene from Crawfordsville, Arkansas. They were both very nice and the three of us got along well together. My sophomore year we could choose a roommate and I had met Lynda, and she and I decided to become roommates. Lynda was from Washington, Arkansas, near Hope where my father had a lot of cousins. He used to tell my brothers, "Don't go messing around with those girls from Hope. They may be your cousin." As Lynda and I were talking, she knew some Duffys. Her mother's first cousin was married to my father's first cousin, Andrew Duffy, so we started telling everyone we were cousins, but we were more like sisters.

When I went to AM&N, I was joined by three other classmates, Sharon, Joyce, and Peggy. We remained friends and hung out with new friends we met. Sharon had an older sister, Gwen, who became our transportation to and from school on breaks. She had another sister, Dot, who lived off campus since she was married. She and her husband John had a daughter, Chrystal. Chrystal was Sharon's niece, but we all loved her as though she was our niece too.

My favorite memory of college life besides my many friends was graduation day. I graduated May 22, 1973, four days after turning twenty-two. I graduated cum laude. Our school merged with the University of Arkansas at Fayetteville, home of the Razorbacks, my junior year, so when I graduated, we were now the University of Arkansas at Pine Bluff, no longer AM&N as it was called when I began there. We were the transition Class of 1973.

On my graduation day, my parents came to campus for the ceremony. Once it was over and we were heading to the car to leave, they presented me with a silver stuffed pig. My mother made, and it was stuffed with $50 in Kennedy halves. I received a lot of other gifts that day, but this was the most precious of them all.

I am still shy of visiting all fifty states in the US before venturing outside the USA. Some of the attractions and places I have been include the following: The National Civil Rights Museum in Memphis, Tennessee, and in Detroit, Michigan; Hot Springs National Park, Hot Springs, Arkansas; The Washington Monument; Lincoln Memorial and other museums in Washington, DC; The St.

Louis Arch (I actually rode up to the top and looked out over the city); The San Diego Zoo, California; Disneyland, Disneyworld, Orlando, Florida; The Pier, St. Petersburg, Florida; The Hoover Dam, Nevada; Grand Canyon National Park, Colorado; Red Rock Canyon, Las Vegas, Nevada; downtown Chicago's Water Tower; and the International Civil Rights Center and Museum in Greensboro, North Carolina.

Love and Marriage

Before I tell you about love and marriage, I must tell you how I got to Indianapolis. My first job after graduation was teaching school in West Memphis, Arkansas. It is six miles across the Mississippi River from Arkansas to Memphis, Tennessee. I taught family living and consumer economics. The foods teacher there was Paula, and we became good friends and remain so to this day. She was from a large family like me. Over breaks, we would visit with each other's family.

After teaching for one year, I looked to change careers. I didn't feel I was being all I could be. I was recruited for a job as a benefit authorizer with the Social Security Administration (SSA) in Kansas City, Missouri. My classmate, Sharon, had begun work there after graduation and was renting a two-bedroom house. I moved from Augusta to Kansas City, Kansas, to begin work in early June with the SSA.

Lynda was working in Chicago and had applied for the job with SSA as well. Neither of us knew that the other had applied until we received the notice to report there in June 1974. So Sharon, Lynda, and I were together once again. Since our job was in Kansas City, we would travel from Kansas City, Kansas, to Kansas City, Missouri, daily. It was a short commute.

For this position, we had sixteen weeks of intensive training in the old TWA building in downtown Kansas City, Missouri. Once the training was over, we moved to the floor where we were assigned to unit supervisors for our hands-on training.

We would go bowling most Saturdays and some Sunday evenings. On two separate occasions, our house was broken into. The thieves took most of our clothing, bed linens, towels, and even food from our pantry. After the second break-in, the three of us discussed that we should move. Sharon didn't want to, so Lynda and I decided to find an apartment in Kansas City, Missouri.

After a month of being on the floor and working cases without phones or contact with people, we grew tired of this and tired of Kansas City, Missouri. The summers are extremely hot, and we knew the winters would be bitter cold. Almost every weekend, we would come to Indianapolis to visit my sister Bernice and her family. My niece, Fatima, was a year and a half, and we enjoyed playing with her. Bernice said that since Lynda and I came here almost every weekend that we should just move to Indianapolis, Indiana. So we did. My brother-in-law Larry was pastor of St. Paul Methodist Church, which later became St. Paul Brightwood United Methodist Church. Larry founded Brightwood Community Center, which is still operating today.

I was somewhat familiar with Indianapolis during the summers while I was in college. I worked three summers at the Brightwood Community Center. On October 22, 1974, we made the move to Indianapolis. I had a 1974 Toyota Corolla, and it was packed with all our clothes and personal possessions. A moving company later brought our furniture that we left in storage. I bought my Toyota from my brother-in-law, Sam, who is married to my sister Nancy. It was a plain white Toyota until I picked it up and Sam had a full checkerboard vinyl roof put on it. Since I am such a huge Indianapolis 500 race fan, this was perfect. I gave my car the nickname Yoda. So me and Yoda came to Indianapolis (Naptown) to live.

Some of the first people I met in my new city were the Floyds—Sheila, Beverly, Valerie, and Rochelle. Both of their parents are deceased, and the Floyd girls continued a close relationship by hosting the family dinners on various holidays. Ken Lewis and I are close friends, and we also take part in these gatherings. We have curtailed them since the coronavirus pandemic. They are like family to us as well.

I had been living in Indianapolis since 1974 when Larry, Bernice, Fatima, and Selena, moved to Durham, North Carolina, in

February 1979. Selena was just a year old. I really missed them, but I had decided I would remain in Indianapolis.

I had a few courtships, but none were serious until I met Ken. Ken's sister, Beverly, was head of the Department of Home Economics at North Carolina Central University (NCCU) where Bernice worked. She was Bernice's supervisor. Ken was living in Durham after completing his master's at NCCU. He was working as a claim representative for the Hartford Insurance Company. His job transferred him to Indianapolis. Beverly said that he would be moving to Indianapolis and needed someone to show him around.

He moved into Riley Towers in downtown Indianapolis in April 1982 and worked in what was the Indiana National Bank Tower; it is now Regions National Bank. He called and we agreed to meet in a public place. Lynda and I met him for lunch at St. Moritz Steak House downtown. Ken, Lynda, and I became fast friends, and we all hung out together for about a year before Ken and I decided to date. We dated for five years, and in 1988, he went home to Augusta with me and asked my daddy if he could marry me. My daddy must have said he could because he proposed to me in April of 1988. Once we were officially engaged, we began making wedding plans. Lynda and another friend, Cynthia, gave me a wedding shower. My beautician at the time, Doris, made sure my hair looked good. I received several nice gifts. I chose a friend, Virrither, to be our wedding coordinator. My friend Liz and her husband, Steve, had a daughter, Kia, who served as our flower carrier. The best man, Randy, Ken's best friend, had a friend that had a son, Ryan, who served as the ring bearer. We were married June 17, 1989, at Scott United Methodist Church by Rev. Thornton. Our reception was at the Historical Madame C. J. Walker Legacy Center here in Indianapolis. We honeymooned in Kauai, Hawaii. We hope to return to Hawaii one day, maybe Maui. It is every bit as beautiful as it is pictured!

Since Ken transferred to Indianapolis and I was already here, we decided we would make this our permanent home. Some thirty-one years later, we are still here and happily married. We do not have any children. Although I was nine weeks pregnant in 1991, I miscarried on Father's Day in 1991. This was a challenging time for us as we both wanted children, but since we were in our late thirties, we knew we may not and have gotten used to it being just the two of us. We love all our nieces, nephews, great-nieces, and nephews and now great-great-nieces and nephews and spoil them rotten, then send them home.

Ken and Mary

The year of 1991 turned out to be a difficult one for me. A few years before our wedding, I flew home and took my parents to Los Angeles in September 1978 to visit my sisters and brothers-in-law there. They took us to the San Diego Zoo and other attractions, including Hollywood. I am so glad we had that time together because on December 14, 1991, my daddy passed away. I will never forget how I would go home almost every Christmas before I got married and would put up the Christmas tree. If any of the other siblings got there before me, Daddy would say, "Don't put up the tree, Mary will put up the tree." My other siblings would tease me about that. My mother said she didn't know how, but each of us children were a little spoiled in one way or another. Another thing Daddy told me during one of our talks on the front porch was, "Whenever things get too bad, you can always call on Old Dad." Daddy was a disciplinarian who believed in "spare the rod and spoil the child."

Sept. 1978—Took parents to Cal.
Left to right: Mary, Daddy, Mama, Cora

Even though I never heard him say the words "I love you," he showed he loved us by his actions. When we visited, he always had a big hug for us. He was very protective of us, especially his girls. He loved all his children. At Christmas, he would make sure I had a duck for dinner. My sister Cora and I joke about how he had her dig in a local grocery store's freezer just to get a duck for me. He said he knew it was a duck in there because he had seen one a few weeks ago. In the meantime, he would be standing on his cane talking to people he knew or didn't know. Daddy loved to talk to anyone about all types of things. He would sit on the front porch and wave to those who passed by. He knew almost everyone in Augusta, Black and White.

He and my mother always taught us the Ten Commandments and the golden rule, including never to judge anyone by the color to their skin. I have always tried to live by that and the biblical teachings they taught us and as a result, I have many, many friends of all races.

My mother passed on October 11, 2011, at the age of one hundred. The day of her wake, October 20, 2011, was one of the worst days of my life. Ken and I were on our way to Forest City, Arkansas, where my sister Nancy and her husband Sam lived. They owned a funeral home and were doing the funeral services for our mother. On the way there, I was driving, and a big truck passed and threw a large rock that cracked the windshield, mostly on the passenger side, but as we traveled, it traveled over to the driver's side of the car. I called Nancy and inquired about getting it repaired, and she contacted Sam, and he had someone waiting for us at the house to repair it. I had said to Ken, who was driving at the time, "Don't speed because this is a small town, and the cops are out." He didn't listen and shortly afterward, we were pulled over for speeding. The officer was going to cite us for the cracked windshield as well, but I pleaded with him not to because we were on our way to my mother's wake and was already late. He gave us a ticket, and we were on our way. By the time we got to Nancy's, the family car was in the driveway and waiting for me to get in and leave for the wake. Ken did not get to go since he stayed to get the windshield fixed. I remember a saying my mother used to say, "Father, I stretch my hands to thee, no other help I know." I found myself saying that over again and composed myself before going to the wake. I miss my parents so much, but I know though absent from the body, they are present with the Lord.

Ken has a much smaller family than me. He has one sister, Beverly, and her husband, Ted. She has a daughter, Tammy. Tammy and her husband, Jimmie, have two sons, Simeon and Savion. They are very close, and I love them just like my siblings and their families. Both of our parents are deceased. Ken is from St. Petersburg, Florida. His aunt and uncle stood in for his parents at our wedding and his mother and stepfather came to the reception. They had visited us in Indianapolis and were so happy for our marriage. I loved his mother just as much as my own. We both draw our strength from our parents and know they are looking down on us.

Professional Life

When I first moved to Indianapolis, I did substitute teaching, first at Broad Ripple High School where my sister Bernice taught foods and nutrition. I subbed for one of the home economics instructors that was out for six weeks due to an illness. From there, I went to Harry E. Wood High School and subbed for another six weeks and spent a short time at Arsenal Technical High School and Shortridge High School in their Home Economics Department.

Lynda and I moved to our own apartment on the city's Southside around April 1975. We both interviewed for caseworker positions with the Marion County Welfare Department on a Friday and were hired and told to report to work on Monday, March 17, 1975.

I stayed in this caseworker position for sixteen years. I had six different supervisors over the first six years, and then for the last ten years, I had one supervisor, Diane. My first supervisor was Tina. She was genuinely nice, and once I was having problems with the Human Resources Department about my college degree, she spoke up for me. At that time, you had to have a college degree in some field to be a caseworker. My job was to determine eligibility for clients receiving cash assistance, food stamps, and Medicaid. We wrote case summaries by hand and a clerical unit typed the summaries for them to be a permanent part of the case file.

I met Beverly while I was a caseworker. She was in a unit that was in a room next to mine. She had to pass behind my desk to get to her desk. For several days, she would walk by and not speak. One day, I said to myself, if this girl doesn't speak to me, I'm going to trip her. Well, she must have heard my thoughts because the next day, she spoke. We became friends and today are best friends.

Once Beverly, Lynda and I became friends, we met her mother, whom I refer to as Mom Sanders because she was and still is like a mother to me. Other friends I met while working for the welfare department were Henrietta, Frankye, Carolyn, Mary, Fred, Bill, Wille, Chris, Coco, and Helen whom I call Podner. Henrietta, Beverly, Frankye, Carolyn, and I call ourselves old school, and we get together for each other's birthdays. We eat, laugh, talk, and try to catch up on each other's lives. I treasure this fellowship and enjoy our time together.

I was advised by Diane to apply for a supervisor position. I always earned complimentary reviews of my work and took time and effort to process my cases and met the necessary deadlines. I always received favorable evaluations and recommendations for a promotion. I became a supervisor in 1991. In this position, I supervised seven to ten caseworkers that determined eligibility for cash assistance, Medicaid and food stamps, just as I had done sixteen years earlier.

I remained in the supervisor position until 1995. I received another promotion to division manager and our agency became the Family and Social Services Administration, Division of Family Resources (FSSA/DFR). As division manager, I supervised seven to eight supervisors of caseworkers. Our offices were in downtown Indianapolis. In 1999, the administration decided to open branch offices, and I was assigned to manage the office located at 3500 Lafayette Road, about ten minutes from my home. This was great—no more fighting traffic to get downtown. I did enjoy walking around downtown during my lunch hour. Even though the office on Lafayette Road was near a few eating places, I would still drive to lunch rather than walk across a busy street. The director of DFR was Julia, and we are still friends to this day.

In 2003, I was given an opportunity to apply for a grant and work on my master's degree in social work. I enrolled as a part-time student and continued to work full time at DFR. I had evening classes and one class on Saturdays. I graduated with a master's degree from Indiana University Purdue University Indianapolis (IUPUI). My degree says IU. After graduation, I was to work in Child Welfare; however, there was not a position for me there. I graduated in December 2005.

Since I had thirty years of service, and I was age fifty-five, I met the Rule 85 Clause that said if you have thirty years of service and are age fifty-five, you could retire with full lifetime benefits. So I retired from FSSA/DFR December 1, 2006. Since it would be ten years before I could get Social Security benefits, I started searching for a new career.

I began working for AFLAC in 2007. I studied and passed the insurance exam to be an insurance agent. I met another good friend and mentor, Barb. We worked together for two years. I was getting discouraged with this job because some days I would drive one hundred miles and may or may not make any money as I worked on commissions only. Barb and I were talking one day, and she said that she had a friend at United Healthcare that was looking for agents. I met with her friend, Tom, and was hired. In 2008, I began work with United Healthcare as an agent and remained there until I retired in May 2017. At this point, I am sixty-six years old and eligible for my full Social Security and have my retirement for life.

After forty-four years of employment from teaching one year, working thirty-one and a half years for FSSA/DFR, eleven and a half years insurance work, I am happily retired and spending my days doing what I want to do. I keep busy around the house, visiting relatives, taking trips with my spouse, and doing volunteer work. I am resting and enjoying the fruits of my labor.

Church Life / Role and Responsibilities / Community Involvement

I have attended Scott United Methodist Church since 1974, when I moved to Indianapolis and began participating in various church activities. Lynda and I officially joined as members in February 1979, and Reverend Thornton was our pastor since Larry and Bernice had moved to North Carolina. I have been a member of this church for forty-one years. I treasure my church family and have far too many friends to name them all.

Some activities I have been involved in include giving the Children's Message during service for about ten minutes, joining the United Methodist Women and becoming the secretary, then vice president and today, president of the local unit since 2012.

Our local United Methodist Women (UMW) group usually has our weekend the third Saturday with a prayer breakfast and on that Sunday and has a guest speaker, who is usually a United Methodist Women from the Conference, District or even National (UMW). We had to cancel the event in 2020 due to the pandemic. In 2019, our National President of UMW, Shannon Priddy, was our Sunday speaker. Shannon is from Indianapolis, and we were so happy to have her. She represents us well in the New York headquarters for UMW.

I held a conference office with UMW as education and interpretation coordinator for four years. I held the office of chair of the nominating committee for the North Central Jurisdiction for four years. I thoroughly enjoyed both duties and did quite a bit of traveling. I said I wanted to see all fifty states in the US before I traveled abroad, and I am well on my way!

When I was chairperson of the Committee on Nominations for the North Central Jurisdiction, I served for four years on the Board of the Lucille Raines Resident in Indianapolis, which is a local mission institution that helps men and women work toward sobriety from some form of addictions. It is owned, operated, and maintained by the Indiana United Methodist Women. Their long-term director, Carolyn, is a good friend to Bernice and me. This was my first time serving on a board of directors, and I learned a lot. It was a humbling and rewarding experience. I got to interact with the residents. Our local unit did a talk, tour, and lunch with them and got to hear one of the residents' story.

With United Methodist Women, I went to Minneapolis, Minnesota, twice, North and South Dakota, Michigan, Wisconsin, Illinois, Tennessee, Ohio, and Louisville. I have attended assemblies in the following cities: Cincinnati, Ohio; Louisville, Kentucky; Orlando, Florida; Philadelphia, Pennsylvania; Des Moines, Iowa; and, St. Louis, Missouri. The assemblies are every four years. I went to my first one in Indianapolis when my sister Bernice lived here. I really enjoyed it and have only missed two since.

I am a communion steward. I work along with four other members, Jo Ann, Ruby, Gail, and Kevin. We are a good group that work together well, and we get together from time to time to socialize.

Since I have immediate family living from coast to coast, I have been to Miami; Cleveland; Durham and Raleigh; Washington, DC; Beltsville; Little Rock; Forrest City; Los Angeles; and Gardena, California.

While living in Indianapolis, I had opportunities to visit Oklahoma; New Orleans; Jersey City; New York City (saw "The Wiz" on Broadway); St. Petersburg; Sioux Falls, South Dakota; Hilton Head, North Carolina; Tuskegee, Alabama; Montgomery, Alabama; Las Vegas, Nevada; Colorado; Biloxi; Houston, Texas; and Savannah, Georgia. I have about fourteen more states to visit to reach my goal of seeing all fifty states in the USA.

My main hobby is reading, developed from when my mother used to read stories to us as children. She also had a subscription to *Reader's Digest*. I loved the stories, and I still subscribe to this magazine today. Other hobbies are traveling and photography. I am unofficially the family photographer for our reunions. Just about everyone has a camera now, so I am not so much the photographer anymore. I am a library express volunteer. I check out and carry books to homebound patrons. I have been doing this since 1999.

I am a member of Church Women United. A local group of ecumenical church women who are responsible for putting on an event the first Friday in March, called World Day of Prayer This service rotates among several churches in the city and each year we highlight a specific country with indigenous songs and messages of how to help the country with such issues as education, health, childhood hunger, public safety, redistricting, hate crimes, and other issues. These are issues we as United Methodist Women work with as well. Our slogan is "Hope, Faith and Love in Action." We are working with women, children, and youth, locally, nationally, and internationally.

I also belong to our local alumni chapter for University of Arkansas at Pine Bluff (UAPB) Alumni Association. I serve as cochair of the scholarship committee. We had an active chapter in the 1980s, but due to illness and death of our long-term president, no one started up the chapter again until 2019. The University of Arkansas at Pine Bluff is a Historically Black College (HBCU), and our family has supported it with a Duffy Scholarship Fund since 1977. For our 1977 family reunion, a *Reader's Digest* reporter interviewed each of the twelve children and wrote an article because of his time with us called An American Dream. The article was published in the July 1977 *Reader's Digest*. A woman who read the story made a sizeable donation to the fund. We began giving $1,000 scholarships to students who attended UAPB. In 2016, we changed it to $2,000, one for a student attending UAPB and another for a student attending any school in the United States, to reach other students in need. Each of the siblings donates to this fund annually to keep it going in memory of our parents. This is one way we can give back to an institution that has given so much to us.

Our mother authored a book titled *The Eternal Dream,* which highlighted her life with our father and the birth of each of her thirteen children. The book was self-published in 1982.

Outstanding Contributions to Society

In 1977, then Indianapolis Mayor Bill Hudnut asked Bernice and me to come to his office in the City County Building downtown Indianapolis. There, he presented us with a Key to the City after he read the article about our family in *Reader's Digest.* He was thrilled that two of the Duffy daughters were living in Indianapolis. I still have that key and wear it with pride.

Our family was so loved and had left such a mark on the city in Augusta. My sister Nancy, who had been a state representative for that district and some coworkers, got a street renamed Duffy Drive in Augusta. It runs by our former church, Jackson Chapel, and another church, Ward Chapel, that my parents joined after we all left home, and Jackson Chapel closed. Each of us has this sign and proudly displays it in our homes.

Another contribution I made to society was after a speaking engagement at my friend Carolyn's United Christian Women's Ministry District Conference on May 4, 2019. I did not charge a fee, but they gave me a donation that I in return gave to a charity, Horizon. At the end of my speech, my friend Carolyn and three other friends that had given a donation to a charity of their choice each year, presented me with a $1,000 check for the Duffy Scholarship Fund. I was very honored, and our family really appreciated this donation.

Deaths

I have lost so many family members, including parents, a sister, and brother, aunts, uncles, cousins, nephews, who are far too many to name. However, I must mention a few. My best friend Lynda passed on February 9, 1995. I will always remember this day since it is her sister, Brenda's birthday and my brother James's birthday. I really miss her.

My brother Henry passed away on September 27, 2005. I will never forget him not only because he is my brother, but because I was taking my last class for my master's in social work, and I got the call from my sister Nancy. My professor was very understanding and made sure I got all class assignments sent to me by one of my classmates, so I did not miss anything. I really miss my brother too.

I had a sister, Everlee, that died before I was born. She was born in February 1950 and was only six months old when she passed in 1950. She was between my sister Nancy and me. I often wondered how it would have been had she lived.

Most of my father's siblings had passed before him except my Aunt Nancy that would visit from Chicago and my Uncle Ishmael. Uncle Ishmael passed on Christmas Day in 1974. I still have the small leather bound Bible he gave me for my high school graduation. I am still close to his children's children. His last child, my cousin Florita, passed May 25, 2020.

My mother was from a family of five, four girls and one brother, James, who died in 1951, when she was pregnant with me. Her oldest sister, Aunt Mae, had passed too before I graduated high school. I was very close to her sisters, my Aunt Armentha, we called her Aunt Ment and her sister, Aunt Eloise, we called her Aunt WeWe. Aunt WeWe had one daughter, Jean, who preceded her in death. Aunt Ment had one daughter, Louise. She and I are more like sisters than first cousins. We call each other every Sunday and talk and catch up with what is happening in the world and with our families. My cousin, Gloria Dean, we called Janie, passed while I was in college. Her daughters, Dorothy, Tereatha, Helen, and Brenda, attend the family reunions, and I still see them and keep in contact with them. I don't see their brother Nick that much.

Other cousins I remain in contact with are my father's great-nieces and nephews; Julia, Pearl, Billy. Julia and Pearl and their mother, Hazel, attend family reunions. I haven't seen Billy since they left Augusta and moved to St. Louis.

I was so happy that we got to have our 2017 family reunion in Detroit, Michigan where my cousin, Florita, and her children live. My cousin Florita, passed May 25, 2020, from COVID-19, a virus that has killed so many Americans. I really miss her too because she was like a sister to us too. Her brother, James, preceded her in death, and we used to call him number 13 and her number 14.

As I said about my parents, for all of those who have gone on before, although you are absent from the body, you are present with the Lord.

Chapter 14

The Thirteenth Child— James William Duffy

Early Childhood

My life began in Cavell, Arkansas, a small community in Woodruff County, just west of McCrory and Patterson, Arkansas. I was born in a tin top house with brick siding on the outside of the house. It had walls with wallpaper. I really mean paper, not plastic or plastic coated—just paper. When the wind blew hard, the paper would move back and forth. Mice was a part of everyday life especially at night you could hear them in the ceiling and behind the wallpaper.

I enjoyed farm life, the animals, and the wide-open spaces. Daddy was a sharecropper, and Momma was a housewife and worked in the fields. You would never see much money as a sharecropper because at the end of the year, you owed just about as much as you made. Daddy and Mom, however, would make sure to get us some goodies from time to time. Daddy would go to town driving a mule and wagon. This was his only mode of transportation other than his feet. Sometimes he would walk to Augusta, seven miles away, and sometimes to McCrory, two miles away. He would always bring the kids something back. He would bring Cracker Jacks, peppermint sticks or maybe a raw coconut from time to time. At Christmas, Mom and Dad would muster up enough money to buy me a cap pistol, girls would get dolls.

I would play outside all day, eating wild greens and wild onions for lunch and rabbit grass. At five years old, I remember going hunting for deer with a stopper gun. Also, at five years old, I was introduced to my first cotton sack and the cotton field. I had a burlap sack, and Daddy meant for me to pick enough cotton to fill it up. Everyone had to work. When I was too young to pick, Momma would pull me on her cotton sack. Like I said, everyone had to work.

One day my brothers, Edward and O.C., were in the backyard. I was sitting on a five-gallon bucket turned upside down. Next thing, I know Edward and O.C. were running. Someone had shot a hole in the bucket I was sitting on. I didn't know it until they showed me the hole. We moved to Augusta on my birthday. It was to be a birthday present for me; however, I did not want to leave Cavell and the *red* house. I said nothing of this to my family.

From where we had been living, it was like moving to the big city although the population was only about 1,800 people.

Although we moved to town, we did not have running water except for the toilet in the inside of the house and kitchen sink. However, it was a step up from the outhouse. I remember my first day of school at Carver Elementary. Mary, my sister, took me. I wanted the teacher to call me by my nickname, Bimbo. That didn't happen. Later, I wanted to drop the nickname, and it was not easy.

Other children began to meddle at me about how large my nose was. This gave me an inferiority complex. Sometimes I got in fights I never started. I was not a fighter. Mom and Dad taught me not to start a fight. So usually I let the other kid throw the first punch. The first one was usually devastating, and I was no good the rest of the fight. So I lost most of the fights I was involved in. I never started a fight.

Clothing was a problem. I had to pull off my clothes after school, hang them up, and put them on the next day and I had to wear them at least two days. Mom had to wash clothes by hand. There was a program called 89-10 where low-income families could get free clothes. I could only get two pair of blue jeans two flannel shirts and some brogan shoes. I hated the clothes. To this day, I will not wear blue jeans or flannel shirts. I know jeans are popular now, but I prefer khakis.

At the age of seven, I was amazed with fire. One fall, I was playing out in the vacant lot where Daddy would plant his garden. The grass was dry, and I took a match and made a small fire. The wind started to blow, and the fire began to spread out of control. I ran and told my siblings who tried to put it out. The entire lot burned before they could get it under control. Fortunately, Daddy was not at home. I was so afraid Daddy would kill me when he got home. Thanks to my sister and brothers quick thinking, I was not punished. They told Daddy the fire was set on purpose to keep someone from throwing cigarette butts out of their car and starting a fire. I can't believe he bought it. I never played with fire again.

At the age of nine, I had my first trip out of Augusta with my sister Mary to visit my sister Cora and her husband. It was great to get out of Augusta. They lived in Camden, Arkansas, about a two-hour drive, and I loved the ride.

I remember in the fifth grade we would have a talent show on Fridays. There was a popular group of boys that would sing. They called themselves the Impalas. I had a group called the Bugs. There was a constant battle between the two groups. The teacher, Ms. James, would decide who won the contest. The Impalas would always sing popular love songs. We were the Bugs and would sing songs like "Secret Agent Man" and the Beatles song like "When I Saw Her Standing There." Ms. James loved the songs we sang, and we always won.

High School

During the seventh and eighth grade in junior high school, I remember my friend Burl and I picked up papers after school for our weekly lunch ticket. Mom and Dad did not have much money. Mom worked as a maid for White folks, and Dad did odd jobs and carpenter work when he could get it. He built an extra room onto the house, screened in the front and back porch, and insulated the house through and through. He took pasteboard to insulate my room and allowed me to paint it. I painted it a light blue, and it looked good. We had a wood heater in the living room and a wood cook stove. So at night, I would have to get warm and go to my room and jump in the bed under a ton of cover. I had previously shared this room with two brothers, and we all slept in the same bed. I slept in the middle. Although I missed my brothers when they left home. I enjoyed having the room and bed to myself. Every day after school I had chores, mainly stacking what we called stove wood. This was wood for the kitchen stove about eighteen inches long and three inches thick. I had to stack what seemed like hundreds of pieces each day. I then had to take enough wood in my arms to stack on the porch for Momma to cook with the next day.

My daddy was very handy and smart, even though he only had a third-grade education. You could not tell it if he didn't tell you. I liked working with him but could never seem to please him. I would be told to measure a board and cut it. I would measure it and cut it, and it never seemed to fit. When he measured the board, it would always fit perfectly. I tried so hard to please him. I do remember on a few occasions when I did something right and he acknowledged it, and it made me feel good. It was hard to communicate with him. I remember one time we were having dinner, and I bumped the table leg with my knee. He said, "Knock the table down," I said Daddy,

"I didn't mean too." He replied, "Boy, you are talking back?" I said, "No, sir."

Another occasion, we were at the dinner table eating and had beans as the main course. This was the case most of the weekdays. There was a big bowl of beans in the center of the table. I loved beans, and I kept getting the bowl and putting beans on my plate until I got down to the last little bit. After I scooped up the rest of the beans, he looked at me and calmly said, "Are you through?" I said, "Yes, sir." He said in a gruff voice, "Now take a big bite out of the table!" Sometimes you didn't get a chance to speak before he took action. I remember when I was about thirteen or fourteen years of age, I came from the neighborhood store, and I ran and quickly pushed open the back door. Daddy was behind it, and the door hit him. Before I could say sorry or anything, he slapped me. This really hurt my feelings more than the slap. He had whipped me with a razor strap many times but never hit me with his bare hand. I don't remember him ever telling us he loved us, but we knew he did. We loved him despite his mean streak. Mom, on the other hand, was calm and gentle and very seldom hit us. I just remember Momma whipping me one time with a switch. I don't even remember the reason for the whipping.

About the eighth grade, I went to my first wedding. My sister Bernice was getting married at Jackson Chapel CME Church. This was the church I attended every Sunday for Sunday School and morning worship and Wednesday night for prayer meeting. The day of the wedding finally came. After the wedding, the girls came outside stood in front of the church, I stood behind them. Bernice came out and threw the bouquet in the air. I jumped up over everyone and caught it. What an embarrassment when I was told I was not supposed to catch it!

I had no luck with girls in junior high school. I never had a girlfriend, and my face broke out with acne. My face had not caught up with my nose, still big. Other kids meddle at me because of the acne also. One guy had it worse than me, but because he was one of the popular guys, no one meddled at him, but he had the nerve to meddle at me. They would often call me Nokie or Pinocchio. I began to pay attention to my brother O.C. as he had no problem with the other sex—they loved him. I started to try to look like him. I would try to have my hair cut like his. It didn't work. I wasn't O.C.

In the tenth grade, I got my first real girlfriend, KG. She was a cute, shy little girl. She really liked me, and I liked her. She was in the eighth grade. When she was in the ninth grade, she invited me to take her to the freshman ball. I could not dance. So I practiced at home with a broom until I could do something that resembled dancing. Her father brought her to the dance escorted her directly to me. He stayed and watched us the whole time, and after it was over, I had to deliver her directly back to him. No good night kiss or nothing. Later, I took her to the movies and wow! There I had my first kiss. It was wonderful, I saw fireworks! There was another guy who called himself liking her. He said if I came to the movie, he was going to beat me up. She was so beautiful I was willing to take the chance. Thank God he didn't show. We went together about a year and a half. I don't know what happened to the relationship. No falling out; it just kind of fizzled out.

When I was in the eleventh grade, all Augusta schools were integrated. I went from Carver High to Augusta High formerly Laura Conner High. They didn't change anything but the name of the school. Our trophies were not brought over to the new school. We did not have our colors or part of our colors, and they kept their school mascot. Ours was Bearcats; theirs was Red Devils. Our colors were purple and gold; theirs were red and white. Lunch time the Black people would be on one side and the whites on the other. I don't remember many violent or abusive situations. For the most part integration was peaceful.

I had started working after school at a store called Night and Day Food Mart that was White owned and operated. Jim was my boss, and he taught me to speak up. I was always told I talked low under my breath. I would be stocking shelves, and he would say something to me, and I would talk low. He would say, "James, you are mumbling again?" So I started to speak up.

I had been walking to school with my friend Ralph, whose mother owned and ran a neighborhood store about two blocks from where I lived. Since I started working at the store, I saved some money and was able to buy the retired Black principal's 1960 black Ford Falcon. This was on the weekend; we couldn't wait until Monday to drive to school. Monday morning came, and Ralph got in the car. I started the car and pulled out the yard, got about one block when the car went putt, putt, putt. Ralph said, "Give it some gas, Duffy." I accelerated. The car went, um putt, putt, putt. Ralph said, "Put it to the floor, Duffy." I did, and it went putt, putt, and died. We still had to walk to school and was late. Later that evening, I got it home and had it repaired. Next day, we were riding high to school.

I had a friend named Eddie who was a bit radical. He was to speak at a Black history program after he had fought to have it. The Black teacher who was over it had written a speech for him. He made her believe he was going to read the speech she gave him. When it came time to speak, he put that speech down and spoke from his heart. It was great.

I made my first D in algebra 2 in the eleventh grade. This was also the first year of integration. I did not have the support and help I had at Carver High.

Then came my senior year. I went to the prom with an eleventh grader. She had a guy that was an eleventh grader who had a senior girl to bring him. She left me on the dance floor and got with him. Quite embarrassing. Senior high school days were not very pleasant.

I had one girl RM I was sweet on, but she only wanted to be friends. We would go riding in my Falcon on the weekend and sometimes after school. She had a child already. I remember the senior play she was not allowed to be in it because she had a child. So she worked with the lighting. She was really hurt when she couldn't be in the play. I took her riding that evening, and we talked, and she felt so much better. There was never romance until one night I got up enough nerve to ask Daddy if I could go the game in McCrory. Surprisingly, he said yes. We won the game but loss the fight they tried to turn our bus over. On the way back, we talked laughed and had an enjoyable time when we were almost back to the school, she surprised me with a passionate kiss. I thought I had died and gone to heaven. It didn't, however, change the relationship she still just considered me a friend and continued to see other guys. One in particular DW. He would laugh in my face because he was with her romantically the night before. I would be mad for a while and not speak to her, but I always would go back to where we were before I heard about her and him. Everyone said I was a fool and maybe I was. Blinded by what I thought was love. So here I was in the twelfth grade and never really had a girl to call my own since tenth grade. She became pregnant again soon after we graduated. Not mine. I backed off for a while.

Then one Sunday, she asked me to go to church with her, an evening church service. I did not know she was going to bring the baby. When we came in all eyes were on us. Then we sat down, and she put the baby in my lap, and you should have seen the looks. I didn't think it was a big deal, but undoubtedly everyone else felt it was.

Daddy didn't believe in you doing much of anything on Sunday but going to church, no basketball in the back yard, no ironing, no washing clothes, no horsing around. Ralph and I were playing at his house. The dog ran after him, missed Ralph, and jumped me. My face and nose were skinned. When I got home, Daddy made me go to a night program at church. I was all scarred up, but he did not care.

Then came graduation. I remember coming down the aisle, and my young niece said, "Look at his nose." This was very hurtful. But I kept marching to my seat. I was always self-conscious about my long nose. I tried taping it down at night. Other students constantly meddled at me about my nose and bad acne. I had low self-esteem because of it all through high school. I tried everything on my acne. From acne cream to my urine. I would talk to Mom about it she would try to console me. I was scared to talk to Daddy about anything.

After graduating from high school, we went our separate ways. I went to the University of Arkansas at Pine Bluff, and she went to Arkansas state university in Jonesboro. The first college homecoming, I brought R. M. to Pine Bluff, and she stayed at the girls' dormitory. I do not remember spending much time with her—no kiss, nothing.

College Life

In September 1972, I entered the University of Arkansas at Pine Bluff (UAPB). It was the first year of the merger. The college had been AM&N. My sister Mary and I graduated from UAPB, six of my siblings graduated from AM&N. I was the first one to attend the college all four years since it was named UAPB. My scores on the (ACT) test indicated I was not college material. I ended up taking remedial math, English, and reading. But I really did not need any of them. I aced all three courses without trying.

Without a background in chemistry or physics, I struggled with college chemistry and physics. The White school counselors did not prepare me for a major in science. I did not have any chemistry, or physical science. I did have sense enough to take biology 2 in high school and did well in it.

I bought a car, a 1965 Chrysler from my Uncle Ishmael. Then I sold the Falcon I had to my friend Joe. I would leave my car at the lady's dorm for my sister Mary to use since I didn't have anywhere to go. I also told Mary if she needed something to let me know and I would write a check as I had saved money from working at Night and Day Food Market while in high school. Mary was graduating the next year, and I figured by then I probably was going to need her help. I did, and she was always there when I needed her. Many times, unexpectedly I would receive a check from Mary (right on time).

I remember right off the bat there was a boycott. The president of the student council and his hinge men didn't want anyone going to class. I was a green first-year student I was going to class. They were throwing students that were trying to go to class in the fishpond by the student union. Somehow, I managed to avoid that. Later, I would take part in a picket of then Governor Bumpers. The governor would come each year and speak at a rural life conference. They would spruce all the buildings up. He was taken only to see the outside of the newest and best-looking buildings. And he never went inside any of the buildings. Therefore, the college was not getting the money needed to remodel or repair. A student who was a veteran and older guy organized the boycott. We had signs saying things like

"Rats and roaches are not a part of the university system; I can't study with rain dropping on my head."

At the time, my sister Cora was working for Governor Bumpers. We marched to the student union, the governor was speaking so we stood behind the ropes and raised our signs high. He ignored us and kept on speaking. The leader said, "Let's march one by one in front of him and hold the signs directly in his face." We crossed the roped-off area and one by one paraded in front of him raising our signs and then marched out. The next day, governor said he did not know the condition of the buildings, and soon after buildings were repaired or remodeled and some new buildings sprang up, I was afraid of what Mom and Dad would say and what Cora would say as it was covered with pictures of us in the *Arkansas Gazette*. Fortunately, I suffered no backlash from Mom, Dad, nor Cora.

My first year I was introduced to fraternities. One group I was particularly leery of was the Omega Psi Phi or the Q dogs. I was in the library. The head dog was with a bunch of pledgees, and they told the pledgees to get me. I told them if you mess with me, it is going to be a fight. They didn't bother me.

I had no real girlfriend in college. Still had some students meddling with me about my nose. I used to go over and visit my home boys at their dorm, and before I left, I would get angry because they would meddle at me about my nose and have other guys from other places join in. Sometimes they called me Pinocchio. Finally, I figured out if I didn't let them upset me, they would get no pleasure out of meddling at me. The next time I went over to my homeboy's dorm, and they started, I would smile and say, "That's all right. I don't have no problem breathing." After that they, stop meddling since they could no longer get a rise out of me.

I was in the work study program the whole time I was in college. I worked as a RA (residence assistant). One night, I was working at the desk answering the phone, and this crazy guy jumped up on the desk and shot a gun with tear gas in my face. The first two years were rough. By my junior year, things got better, and I moved off campus with two friends. I did not know one had a bad temper. I was watching TV one night, and he came in with his girlfriend. Without saying anything, he changed the channel. I told him I was watching something. I don't remember the show. I turned the TV back. He got mad and turned it back again. I told him he was just trying to show out in front of his girlfriend. That really angered him, and he jumped up, and before I knew it, he popped me in the eye. I had a blackeye for a week. I didn't go to class for a couple of days. My homeboy said, "I wondered what happened to you." He said, "By the way, what happened to you?" I told him what had happened. I moved out and moved in a duplex with him and purposely left a large phone bill. My ex-housemate came over to collect. He stood outside the door yelling. I told him to leave. He wouldn't leave. About that time, my homeboy came to the door with a pistol. He had a junior deputy card for one of his classes that allowed him to carry a gun. I told him he had better leave or my friend would shoot him. I then pushed him out the door so that he would not get shot. He then went and called the police. The police came but found that the ex-housemate had no case. He never bothered us again. Since then, I got word through the other roommate that he was deeply sorry for what happened. I told him, "Man, that was when we were young." I thought no more about it and told him, "Don't worry about it. We cool."

The fraternities were always inviting my homeboy and me to their smoker. This was a party to try to get new pledgees. We went to all their parties but never joined. We pledged wine Omega and women Psi Phi. Because of how we could slow dance they called us the party makers and the back breakers. I finally was starting to somewhat enjoy the college experience.

My last year of college, I worked at a liquor store. I worked with another college student I think she was a senior. I was not working the cash register one night when an undercover police officer and a uniformed officer came in. Plain clothes officer walked up to the counter told her she had sold liquor to a minor, handcuffed her, took her out of the store, came back in, and said, "We saw you sell liquor to someone who looked like a minor." I said, "Looked like a minor? Okay."

Later, an older lady about forty years old was hired to work with me. She was genuinely nice, and we had an enjoyable time working together. Since we were underpaid, we made up for it at the end of the night. Whatever we wanted to drink, we got it at the end of the night. There was an old security guard that worked there. He would be in the back room looking from a two-way mirror. It was right behind our head. He once told us if someone come in and try to rob us to duck, and he would shoot through the mirror. Both of us thought he was crazy and said if someone would try to rob us, we would give them whatever they wanted.

I did have some enjoyment with two ladies who would wait to go out to the club with me after I got off at midnight on Friday and Saturday and dance the night away. I really thought I was something I would come in with two ladies on my arms. They both would dance with me and would not dance with the other guys. They liked the way I danced. It was not a romantic relationship. We were just friends.

I graduated from the University of Arkansas at Pine Bluff in May 1976 with a bachelor of science degree in biology.

Life after College

I continued to work at the liquor store part time, but it would not pay my part of the rent and utilities. I remember my housemate and I got down to a can of sauerkraut and hominy. I didn't like either one but had no choice but to eat it.

I soon landed a job with the cooperative extension service. A government program that helped farmers and gardeners. I worked as a horticulture aide, assisting gardeners with planning and raising gardens. It didn't pay much, and after the bills were paid, there was nothing left. I begin traveling to Little Rock to apply for jobs. I took all the merit exams (exams required to be eligible to work a state job) for the jobs I was qualified for including lab tech, lay meat inspector, and sanitarian. Fortunately, I scored the highest on the sanitarian exam. It was the highest=paying job of the three—$9,000 a year. My brother-in-law was the head of the employment security commission. He contacted the head of the Health Department at that time, and the next thing I know, I had an interview with the director of sanitarian services.

In January of 1977, I was hired as the first state hired Black sanitarian. I was to begin my first day of training on January 17 and was excited and started out that snowy morning driving to work. I got about four blocks from the state office and couldn't make it up the hill and had to call in and let my supervisor know I couldn't make it. I was so disappointed; however, the next day, I begin my training, which consisted of reading regulations all day. This went on for four weeks until the county supervisor rescued me. He convinced my supervisor to let me come over to the county unit and go out with the sanitarians in the field. I was really excited about that. The next day, I begin my training in the field riding with and observing the field sanitarians. Each day was exciting, from restaurant inspections to investigating sewer break, garbage complaints, and dog bites. I trained another four weeks and was ready to go to work in my assigned county.

I was to begin work in St. Francis County but ended up in Lee County. The sanitarian that was to work Lee County was reassigned to St. Francis County since he had attempted suicide and shot himself in the eye. They wanted to keep him close to home. I remembered riding with him one day. He would swerve from one side to the other and thought it was funny. I told him if he wanted to kill himself to let me out. I very much wanted to live. He straightens up after that, and we made it to our destination. I never rode with him again.

I lived in the back of an older lady's house in Marianna, Arkansas, on Mississippi Street. She had added a small living room, bedroom, kitchen, and a shower. I would come home each day to my lonely apartment. One day, I went across the vacant lot to talk to a young lady I went to college with. We were just friends. I was standing in her yard when I saw two beautiful young ladies wearing short shorts about two blocks away. They were walking down the street going the opposite direction from the house. One was tall light-skinned with short hair. The other one was short with long black hair with a brown streak. I asked my friend which one she thought I would have the best chance with. She told me the short one she doesn't have a boyfriend. I said, "Good. That's the one I was looking at." I told my friend I was going to go and tell her that she said to pick her up and give her a ride home. I said maybe then she would get in the car with me. To my surprise, it worked. She got in the car with me, and I asked her name. Her name was Yvonnie (ie *is silent, pronounced* evun). Her nickname was Sue. It was only about four blocks to her house, so it was a short trip. I stopped in front of her house and asked for her phone number. She gave me hers, and I gave her mine. I was going to an Arkansas Public Health Association meeting in Hot Springs, Arkansas, the next day. I told her I would call her when I got back. She said okay. I was so excited I almost backed over her. I went to the three-day convention as well as a lot of educational sessions. The night life was exciting. Free drinks, wild women, and dancing. Although it was a lot of fun, I couldn't wait to get back to call Yvonnie. We didn't have cell phones at that time, and it was very expensive to call long distance on a land line.

I returned and called her and waited to see if she was going to call me back. From problems with my experience with getting to know young ladies, I found I would move too fast. So I told myself I was not going to call her anymore unless she called me. My theory was if she doesn't call, she's not interested. A week or two passed and she did not call. One day I was just riding around with my young friend Steve who stayed right behind my apartment with his grandmother we called Miss Laura. I purposely drove by Sue's house and saw her walking down the street. I started talking to her and asked if she wanted to go riding. She said yes, and I had Steve to get in the backseat. I quickly took him home. Sue and I rode and rode, and we really enjoyed each other. After that, she called, and I called daily.

Her uncle and aunt were going to a class reunion Saturday night, and they asked Sue to bring me. She did, and after sunrise, I wanted to kiss her but did not want to move too fast, so we just said our goodbyes, and I went home. Later, she said she wondered why I didn't try to kiss her. I told her I didn't want to move too fast and scare her away. Next time I saw her she came over to my house, and we kissed and kissed. Later, she would spend the night from time to time. I told her your parents are going to get you go home. She insisted it was all right and refused to go home.

I remember one of my early inspections was of the Lee County Jail kitchen. I went to the jail to inspect it and was met at the door by the jailer who was the chief deputy's wife. I told her who I was and that I was there to conduct an inspection of the kitchen. She told me to go ahead. There was a Black lady cooking in the kitchen. I spoke to her and then began to look around. The next thing I knew was when I turned my head, I was facing a large pistol on the side of the chief deputy who was about 6'6". I was about 5'11" at that time. I continued my inspection, and he continued to walk beside me. He didn't say a word and nor did I until I saw a dog feeding dish with food in it on the floor. I asked the chief deputy if he fed the dog in the kitchen. He replied in a rough voice, "Yes, I feed him in here. That dog is cleaner than some people." I was offended because I felt he was referring to Black people or the lady working in the kitchen. I was offended, but I kept my cool and responded, "Regardless of what you think of the dog, it's a violation for him to be in here." He then went to his office, and I continued the inspection. When I finished, I went to his office to explain the inspection. He sat quietly as I went down the line pointing out each violation including feeding the dog in the kitchen. When I finished to my surprise, he said, "Yes, sir. We will take care of everything."

I knew if I showed any fear, I probably would never be able to conduct a complete and thorough inspection in the county. Especially of any White owned establishment.

In another incident, I went to check on a resort area that had been closed for years. The man trying to reopen it was of Indian descent. I went by to make him aware he needed to submit plans to the health department in Little Rock before continuing to work on the restaurant and installing a new swimming pool. He took the information for submitting plans.

I returned a month later, and he was still working on the restaurant and installation of the pool. I gave him orders to cease and desist. He told me directly, "We don't need Little Rock to tell us what to do." He said, "We can work this out." I told him he must have his plans approved by the state health department in Little Rock before I could do anything. He cursed me out, and I left. I returned the next day with my supervisor. He began to rant and rave again. My supervisor became angry also, and they entered a shouting match. He then told us to get off his property. We left, and my supervisor who was an ex-boxer told me, "I started to knock him out, James. I don't know how you could stand to talk to him period." I would go by from time to time to see if he was continuing construction. My supervisor said he was being financed by his wife or girlfriend, and she had stopped financing the project, and the banks would not give him any money. He said he thought this project would die on the vine. He said just keep checking on him. One day, the man called my office and left a message that if I set foot on his property, he would kill me. He called me again, and I was in the office. He spoke with me and asked me to come out, so we could work this out. I asked him why I would come out when you called the office and left a message that if I set foot on your property, you would kill me. He denied it. I told him my secretary did not have a reason to lie.

A week later, I got a call that he was continuing with the work on the restaurant and pool. I started to go by and talk to him again but was about to go on vacation for a week. I decided to wait until I came back from vacation. The Sunday before the Monday I was to return, I got a call that he had killed his wife, children, and committed suicide. I thank God I didn't go back before I went on vacation. From then on, I took all threats seriously.

In September of 1978, I was accepted to the University of Arkansas School of Law and was so excited. I did not move or transfer to Little Rock. I got permission from my supervisor to leave work at 4:00 p.m. a half an hour early. I had to be in class at 6:00 p.m. I had class four days a week Monday through Friday. This was hard as I had to take that hour and half trip back to Marianna. After one year, I was named new sanitarian of the year.

After the first semester, I transferred back to Little Rock so that I could be close to the law library. I told Sue I didn't believe a long-distance relationship would work, and we would just be friends. After about a week, I missed her so much. I began calling her every day sometimes more. I would go get her to spend the weekend with me.

As for law school, the move was too little too late by now my grades had really suffered since I did not have access to the law library the first semester. After the second semester, the inevitable happened. I dropped out with fourteen hours completed.

I remained in Little Rock, and my phone bill was getting higher and higher. I finally realized it would be cheaper to marry this woman than to keep up this long-distance relationship. May 1, 1980, we were married at my sister Cora's house in front of her fireplace, intended to just have a quiet wedding with a few family members and friend. Cora and my brother O.C. weren't having it. Her large living room was packed, and she had a reception prepared after the wedding. She also hired a professional pianist. It was great.

James and Yvonnie (Sue)

I moved my bride to Little Rock and adopted Tina, her four-year-old daughter. I wanted her name to be Duffy. If we had any more children, I didn't want her to feel any different from any of the other children. I loved her as if I were her biological father. After renting here and there for two years, my brother Edward provided me with a down payment to buy a house. We acquired the service of a realtor and found a house in Southwest Little Rock. The house had been recently remodeled and was very nice. The house is now paid for, and we still live in it.

Eight years later after marriage, we had given up on having another child and had a beautiful baby girl. We named her after my sister Cora Jamehla Duffy. She looked just like her mother. Jamehla is Arabic for "most beautiful."

Eleven years later, I was offered a supervisor's position in the Forrest City Regional Health Office. I was interviewed, hired, and moved back to Marianna, located seventeen miles from the office. We stayed with her parents for three months and then bought a used mobile home. We were so excited to have a home to call our own. I was proud of being the first Black sanitarian in Arkansas and now first Black sanitarian supervisor in Arkansas.

The job didn't come without challenges. I was hired to supervise an all-White crew, six men and one woman who told me if she had changed her part-time status, she could have been the supervisor. All the six were sanitarians with me and had been sanitarians longer than me, and most of them applied for the position. One sanitarian just knew he had the position.

They resented me being their supervisor and would tell me they should have gotten the position. I stood my ground and eventually gained their respect, and we worked well together. My plan was to work in Eastern Arkansas for only two years and then transfer back in a couple of years as one of the two supervisors were planning to retire in two years. One supervisor retired, and the decision was made to not fill the second supervisor position, and now there was only one supervisor, and the remaining supervisor was already in that position. I ended up in Marianna another eleven years. I had eight counties that I was responsible for. My wife was getting tired of Marianna, and after two years of the eleven years, she and the children moved back to Little Rock. I would again stay with her parents a couple of nights and the other nights and weekend I would be at home. Sue soon grew tired of me staying in Marianna, and I began to travel back and forth from Marianna to Little Rock every day. I would leave Little Rock at 6:30 a.m. to travel eighty-six miles to get to my office in Forrest City by 8:00 a.m. Then leave for home at 4:30 p.m. unless I was in another county at the end of the day. Sometimes it would be 8:00 p.m. before I got home. There was not much time to spend with the family. Cora was seven, and Tina had graduated and left home. Sue was asked to keep Tina's two children, one three-years-old and the other one four-years-old.

I realized that was a lot of responsibility for her. I begin applying for various positions in Little Rock I thought I could get. Finally, after two years of applying for various positions, I was able to return to Little Rock again as a sanitarian. Although not happy about going back to my old position, I was glad I did not lose my supervisor's salary. After two years, I was given the opportunity to become the administrator of a county health unit. I gladly accepted it. My salary stayed the same, but I was still making more than the other administrators. This was during the time of the September 11 tragedy. I remember sitting in my office doing paperwork, and suddenly on the news, I see planes flying into the Twin Towers at the World Trade Center in New York.

We were on lockdown all day, especially since we were near the airport. It was unusually quiet. The health department begin to offer a 70 percent discount on tuition for employees to attend the University of Medical Science College of Public Health. The second year after the college opened, I applied and was accepted. The boy who they told was not college material was now in graduate school and would later, at the age of fifty-five, graduate with a master's degree in public health. After two years, the clinic closed due to low turnout. Again, I returned to the field as an environmental health specialist, formerly called sanitarian.

A year later, I was asked to go to work at the state office as an environmental program specialist responsible for the plan review program. I would review plans for all food establishments for the state of Arkansas. I spent my last two years in this position that I enjoyed. After thirty-seven years, I retired from the Arkansas Department of Health after an interesting career. I had worked in local health units, the Regional Health Office, and ended up in the state office. I had seen all facets of the Health Department and was glad I did not retire in the same position I started in. Six months after retirement, I decided to work part time as a security officer for the Little Rock School District. I worked at the famous Little Rock Central High School with two other officers at various locations after school to watch the children that were waiting for their parents to pick them up.

When I first started, it was easy as I worked in front of the library. This is where the most manner able children waited for their parents to pick them up. A few months later, I was moved to the gym, where the athletes hung out until their parents picked them up or after they finished practice. This was the rowdy crowd, and I hated it. I remember the first fight I broke up. It was two girls, and they were arguing over a guy and had gone around the corner. I told them to come back around to the front and that there would be no fighting on my watch. I was wrong. As soon as I turned my head, they went at it. I immediately jumped between them. They grabbed each other's hair. I grabbed the wrist of each girl to keep them from pulling each other's hair out.

We were walking up a ramp. I was between the two girls still holding their wrists when we fell on concrete ramp. The girls didn't let go of each other's hair, and I didn't let go of their wrist. Finally, the school resource officer, who was a Little Rock police officer, came from the gym to assist. We were still having a tough time pulling them apart. A parent who was a former football player joined us, and we finally pulled them apart. The resource officer had threatened to tase them.

After they were apart, I was holding one girl, and the officer was holding the other one. The one the other officer was holding broke loose and punched the other one in the face. He handcuffed them and took them away. If I learned one thing that day, it was as not to jump in to break up a fight before I radio for help. My only injury was a hurt thigh from falling on my keys. I realized quickly this was not for me. The children were rude and disruptive.

After the first semester, I remember another incident where students were sitting on the gym steps and a basketball game was about to start. I asked them to move to the side so that those coming to the game would be able to come up the steps to get in the gym. There was one guy who just sat in the middle of the steps. I continued to tell him to move. He just ignored me. This surprised me because this guy had been quiet and had not given me any trouble. I finally went inside and told the coach. He came out and cursed them out and told all the students to get totally off the steps. He asked the young man (who was one of his players) what was wrong with him. My supervisor had been telling me I know you are a Christian, but you got to get tough with these kids. Curse them out.

That just wasn't my style. I knew I was going to have to leave this job. After the first semester, I was given the key to the office, a golf cart to ride around in and check on the other officers and the authority to decide if we could leave early if all the children had been picked up. I was given these privileges over those who had been there for years. I would also check the building that was about two blocks long and five stories high at the end of the day to make sure no one was left in the building. I was running up and down five flights of stairs each day.

I lost ten pounds. Not that I had any to lose. After the second semester, I was asked to come back to the health department and to work part-time in my old position as program coordinator for plan review. I gladly accepted it and worked off and on until July 2019 when my wife has two strokes a week apart. The first one was mild and barely noticeable. The second was more severe although she was able to walk from the living room to the back to get on the gurney. When she got to the hospital, they got her up to go to the rest room the first day. After that, they said she was a fall risk due to her weight and inserted a catheter and a fecal tube. She stayed in the hospital three months, rehab for two months, would go home for a week or so during the next year and back to the hospital and rehab. I stayed at the hospital and rehab each day and night during her stay. She never walked again after they inserted the catheter and fecal tube. The first rehab doctor started giving her blood thinner injections two times a day in her stomach. He said she would have to be on them the rest of her life.

She began some serious bleeding. The doctor who was a blood specialist said if she didn't stop bleeding, he would have to take her off the injection, but it would be a significant risk of her having another stroke. I prayed and prayed she would be all right. Day 1 went by, no stroke. Day 2, no stroke, but bleeding continued. Day 3, the bleeding stopped and no stroke. The painful shots begin again. The same doctor told me at some point I should consider comfort (hospice). I did not receive that and dismissed it. Soon afterward, she went to another rehab facility. I asked the doctor there for a second opinion on the injections to the stomach twice a day. He told me he had never heard of taking that medicine long term. He said it is usually used after surgery and only for a month or two. He put her on two pills a day. She is doing fine two years later and no strokes. I think all the doctors had given up on her. She had gone through a lot. In addition to the strokes, she has experienced serious bed sores that required surgery, her kidneys were failing, aspiration is where she had to be fed through a feeding tube. I never gave up, and now, she's eating by mouth, kidneys functioning normally, and bed sores healed. I never lost faith and kept my faith in God, not man. She finally came home from rehab March 17, 2020.

When the rehab facility personnel were about to kick me out due to COVID-19, I decided if I couldn't stay, she would not stay. She would not do well at all by herself. I knew her mental state would totally decline. She has not had another hospital visit since. She was on hospice care for six months because I was told it was no longer for a dying person. They would manage the care, and I would be able to get more therapy since the insurance company had denied any additional therapy for home health. I enrolled her in hospice with this in mind. I later found out I could get no therapy for her, and they constantly concentrated on dying. I told them not to discuss anything about death around her. I was told she was aspirating, and food was going into her lungs and eventually would deplete the lung capacity. Two x-rays, months apart, were done and no aspiration was detected. The lungs were clear. Oxygen levels were constantly checked and were always good.

Seven months later, I took her off hospice care, and she is doing fine except for some serious anxiety from time to time, and we are working with a mental health specialist on this. She is confined to the bed and a wheelchair, and she cannot stand to get in a car. I had problems getting her to doctor appointments. My loving sisters and brothers purchased a wheelchair accessible van. My brother O.C. built a deck and wheelchair ramp. She enjoys going out on the deck. All my sisters and brothers have supported me financially, emotionally, and I love them dearly.

I thank my daughter Cora, who moved back from Indianapolis, Indiana, to help care for her mom. She married and moved out last summer, and now she and her husband have a sweet baby girl named Promise. She named her Promise because her doctor had told her she would not have any children. She had had a miscarriage two years earlier. I thank my oldest daughter, Tina, who comes and helps with her mom every chance she gets, and if I need anything, she will see that I get it. I thank my granddaughters Charise and J'Kaylan, who have been very supportive. A very special thanks to Tashiera, who moved from Indianapolis, Indiana, after her grandmother had her strokes and have put her career and her life on hold to help me take care of Sue. Most of all, I thank God for keeping Sue and keeping me. There is no doubt that it is because of God's grace and mercy that I still have my loving wife with me today.

Chapter 15

· · ·○· · ·

Family Reunions—the Duffy Scholarship Fund: The Duffy Family Investment Club (DFIC)

The Family Reunions

The reunions started in 1973 and the first one was in Little Rock, Arkansas, at home of Sister Cora and her husband Henry. Persons attending included all the siblings, aunts, nieces, nephews, and cousins. At first, reunions were held every year, but in 1987, it was decided that every year was too often and imposed too great of an expense on some members of the family, so we started having reunions every three years in odd numbered years. This two-year rotation is still followed today. We held reunions at the homes of the siblings which allowed us to move around across the United States. We did this until Mom and Dad were not able to travel long distances. Then we moved the reunions to Augusta or Little Rock, Arkansas.

The reunions include time for fun fellowship, introduction of new members of the family, plenty of good foods, sometimes including Mama's famous butter roll, a banquet program featured one of the siblings speaking, beginning with brother Spencer in 1977. In addition, each sibling and a representative of each family present would present their talents in dance, song, poems, skits, or games. Mom and Dad would give words of wisdom and then we would close with rounds of singing of hymns and gospel songs. All family members could sing. One year when the reunion was held in California, we made a CD called "Songs Our Father Taught Us." Unfortunately, it was after Dad had died; therefore, his bass voice was not included.

Photos

Duffy Family Reunion 1983, Little Rock, Arkansas
Back Row: Lawrence Johnson, Leonard Carter, Henry McHenry, O.C. Jr.,
Leona M., Nancy, Henry EC, Maria Duffy, Barbara, and Spencer Duffy
Second Row: Cora, cousin Helen with baby, Ferroll Marie, Felicia
Duffy, Laquita Blount, Meshell Duffy, Fatima Johnson, Joseph Paul
Third Row: James, Andre, Leonard, Lorraine, Aunt
Eloise, Aunt Mint, Cora, Edna, Louise, Leona
Front Row: Selena, Randy, Chardae, E. Marie, O.C. Duffy
Sr., Leona S. Duffy, Bernice, Mary, Cousin Hazel Lee

Duffy Family Reunion (children and grandchildren)
1991, Little Rock, Arkansas

Duffy-Stith Family Reunion 2017, Detroit, Michigan

Brothers, male cousins, and male in-laws at a reunion

Mom Duffy and ten of her children at a reunion

Sisters: BR: Leona, Nancy, Bernice
FR: Edna, Cora, Marie, and Mary

The Duffy Scholarship Committee

The committee meets during the reunion and conducts business relevant to the scholarship fund. This committee awards two $2,000 scholarships annually—one to a student attending the University of Arkansas at Pine Bluff, and the other to a student attending any accredited university in the United States. Since 1977, we have awarded $50,000 in scholarships to college students.

The Duffy Scholarship is a dream come true for the late Leona Stith Duffy. The scholarship fund got its start from a story "An American Family" printed in the *Reader's Digest* in the July 1977 issue by reporter Joseph A. Blank. After the story ran, the Duffy family received many letters and contributions from friends who came to know us through the article and wanted to help us in this endeavor.

The largest contribution came from an elderly lady, Ms. Wilba D. Marley of Florida. When she read the story about the Duffy family in *Reader's Digest,* she was so touched by it that she wanted to contribute. In September of 1978, we received a letter from her lawyer stating that Ms. Marley had passed away but left $15,000 to the Duffy Scholarship Fund. These funds were immediately deposited. The Fund has an annual fundraiser each year on the birthdays of our parents, Mrs. Leona Stith Duffy on April 30 and Mr. Octavris C. Duffy on September 18.

The Duffy Family Investment Club (DFIC)

The Duffy Family Investment Club (DFIC) was established in 1995 and is the brainchild of our matriarch, the late Mrs. Leona S. Duffy. The purpose of the DFIC is to invest in the future of the family by establishing an avenue to financial independence with a focus on financial education and financial security. The DFIC Scholarship Fund provides scholarships for members of the Duffy-Stith family who desire to continue their education beyond high school and to establish an avenue for financial independence for its members. The DFIC started with sixteen members and $2,000, and now has thirty-five members and a net asset value of nearly $400,000. Dues are $240 per year. The DFIC has awarded more than $20,000 in scholarships to members of the Duffy-Stith families seeking higher education. The DFIC Scholarship Fund is available only to members of the DFIC or children of members of the DFIC.

President Edward Duffy leads the DFIC in helping family members achieve and fulfill their dreams of obtaining a college education and financial security through active participation in the Investment Club.

Chapter 16

• • • ○ • • •

Summary and Key Words

We told our stories in our own words through the lenses of our eyes and memories of our unique experiences within the Duffy-Stith Family. One sibling Everlee died in infancy, and brother Henry died in 2005. The Duffy-Stith children, born of the same mother and father who grew up in rural Arkansas, tell stories of how they related to each other and to their parents. These stories are real. They bear account of actual events and activities that happened in a time-span from 1934 to 2021. We rejoice that we made it through the challenges faced in the time of wars, segregation, Jim Crow, racism, economic and social injustices, and moral decline. Our stories were written during the COVID-19 pandemic, and we believe we used time wisely in writing this book with the hope that others who read our stories will be inspired to write their own stories.

Yes, we grew up in the same community, with the same mother and father, yet each of us established and maintained a different relationship with our parents and each other. Our parents were not outwardly affectionate toward us, but there was no doubt that they loved and cared dearly about us. They did all they could for our well-being and sacrificed much for us to have the necessities of life. They were nurturing and mentoring parents and great teachers. They wanted a better life for us than they had, and therefore, education was the number one goal for each of us. In other words, there was no dropping out of school and no remaining at home after high school graduation. The choice was to go to college or get a job.

We all followed that line of reasoning and finished high school and at least two years of college. We became fathers, mothers, and grandparents. We became professionals in engineering, education, environmental science, health sciences, human sciences, the ministry, and social sciences.

Through monthly Zoom meetings, we discussed progress on our individual chapters, the outline to follow, and the timelines for completion. We also updated each other on our health, needs, joys, concerns, and retirement triumphs. Through these exchanges and individually working on our chapters, we produced the book *The Duffy-Stitch Family: From Arkansas Cotton Fields to Global Investments.*

Key Words

1. *Butter Roll*—a savory desert made by encasing a soft dough with rows of butter sprinkled with nutmeg and cinnamon. A milk mixture or syrup mixture is poured over it for baking.
2. *Canning*—preserving food, mainly fruits and vegetables, by cooking the food in a pressure cooker, then placing and sealing food in sterilized glass jars.
3. *Clay dirt*—a non-sandy-type of soil baked on a wooden stone and eaten.
4. *Chopping cotton*—the process of using a hoe to remove grass and weeds from young cotton stalks, without chopping up the cotton.
5. *Cotton sack*—a linen/canvas like piece of cloth sewed on three sides. The fourth side has an opening to pass the cotton from the stalk to the sack. The sack is about six feet long with a long sown in strap that goes over one shoulder. When filled with cotton, it can weigh up to eighty to ninety pounds.
6. *Gathering cows*—going into the woods to bring calves back to get milk from their mother, after the cow has been milked for the family's share of milk.

7. *4H Club*—a program delivered by the Cooperative Extension Service, which provides experiences where young people learn by doing, using their head, heart, hands, and health to raise the level of living for themselves and their community, state, nation, and world.

8. *Greenest people in the world*—Daddy's way of telling us that a college education had not made us smart.

9. *Hoe*—a metal blade with a long wooden handle used to chop weeds and grass from fields and gardens and to till soil.

10. *Milking cows*—hand process where a person sits beside the cow and get milk from cows by using an up/down motion applied to the cow's teats and milk flows into a bucket.

11. *Outhouse*—a small wooden house located outside the regular house and usually at a distance. It has a stall with a hole cut in a wide board for sitting. The hole is over a pile of ashes where waste is deposited from the body.

12. *Picking cotton*—using both hands to remove cotton from bolls (with sharp edges) which hold the cotton and placing it in the cotton sack strapped over the shoulder. The picking is done in the fall of the year.

13. *Picking strawberries*—removing strawberries from the strawberry vines and placing the berries in pint- and quart-sized containers.

14. *Pumping water*—prime the pump by pouring some water in it, then use up and down motions of the handle until water flows from the mouth of the pump.

15. *Shotty head*—Daddy's phrase for uncombed hair, especially if there were small curls around the edges of the head.

16. *Slop jar*—a metal pot or ceramic jar used for human waste at night when you could not go to the outside to use the outhouse. It was emptied often.

17. *Tin tub*—A large metal tin tub (referred to as number 2 tub) about two and a half feet in diameter and two feet tall used to take baths and wash clothes.

Appendix A

· · ◦ · · ·

Family Recipes—Originals and Modified Ones

MAMA'S BUTTER ROLL
(Mary's and Bernice's Version)

Ingredients:

1 c. sugar (plus the sugar for the syrup or milk sauce)
butter (5 sticks) or 1 ¼ lb.
1 tb. cinnamon (reserve ½ tsp. for the syrup or milk sauce)
1 tb. nutmeg (reserve ½ tsp. for the syrup or milk sauce)
1 tsp. vanilla flavor
2 ready-made piecrust (or make your own favorite piecrust)
1 ½ c. (2% or whole milk) if using milk-based butter roll

Syrup	or	Milk Sauce
1 ½ c. water		1 ½ c. milk
1 ¼ c. sugar		¾ c sugar
½ stick butter		½ stick butter
½ tsp. cinnamon		½ tsp. cinnamon
½ tsp. nutmeg		½ tsp. nutmeg.
1 tsp. vanilla		1 tsp. vanilla

Directions:

You will need a round pie pan or rectangular ovenproof baking dish. Roll dough out to form a 12-by-7-inch rectangle. Spread ½ stick soft butter over rolled out piecrust with a brush or back of spoon. Sprinkle nutmeg and cinnamon on top of soft butter and smooth the spices into the butter. Cut the crust into 2–4 strips lengthwise. On each strip, line the middle with pieces of butter, then sugar. Next, sprinkle on cinnamon and nutmeg. Fold the strips over, then close the ingredients in and crimp the strips closed. Lay the strips in a circle or straight lines in the baking dish with the crimped side down. Brown the pastry at 375 degrees for about 20 minutes. While the pastry is browning, make the syrup to pour over the pastry.

To make the syrup:

In a 2 qt. saucepan, add 1 ½ cup water, 1 ¼ cup sugar, 1 tsp. vanilla, ½ stick of butter and sprinkle with cinnamon and nutmeg. Bring to a boil until thickened. Once pastry is browned, pour hot syrup over it and let rest for a few minutes, letting the syrup soak in. Serve hot. Makes 6–8 servings.

For a Milk Sauce Version:

Once the rolls have been arranged in the pan, brown in a 375-degree oven for 10 minutes. Melt the ½ stick of butter in a 2-quart saucepan, add the milk and let it get hot. Combine the sugar, nutmeg, and cinnamon in a small bowl. Mix well. Add to the milk mixture and heat this mixture just below boiling. Add the vanilla flavor. Pour mixture over the hot pastry and return it to the oven and cook for 30 minutes or until browned. Let it rest as the liquid soaks into the pastry. Serve hot. Enjoy. Not for the faint of heart. If you are watching your weight, take only a few bites. It is very sweet and rich.

CORNBREAD
(Bernice Duffy Johnson)

Ingredients:

2 c. yellow or white regular corn meal (not the mix)
1 c. of milk
1 c. sifted flour
2/3 c. vegetable oil
2 tb. sugar
1 large egg, beaten
1 tb. baking powder
½ tsp. salt (optional)

Directions:

Preheat oven to 450ºF. Pour oil into a 9-inch by 13-inch pan and place in a preheated oven for 5 minutes. Sift and mix all dry ingredients into a medium sized mixing bowl. Stir in milk until blended well. Add the beaten egg and stir until blended with other ingredients. Carefully remove the pan of hot oil from the oven and pour the oil in with the blended ingredients, leaving a little in the pan. Stir at once to prevent eggs from beginning to cook. After oil is blended in with other ingredients, pour the mixture into the hot pan, then put the pan of bread in the oven for 20 minutes. Let it rest for 5 minutes before cutting. Yield: about 12 medium slices and 16 small slices of bread.

HOT WATER CORNBREAD
(Lora Duffy)

Ingredients:

1 ½ c. of self-rising corn meal
boiling water
cooking oil (vegetable oil or shortening)

Directions:

Place a pot of water on the stove and start boiling the water. Make sure water is boiling hot. The recipe may need 2 cups of water or less. While the water is boiling, start pouring self-rising corn meal in a bowl. Do not add any other ingredients. After the water has boiled, start pouring a little water at a time on the meal and start stirring until the meal is like dough, not wet. After the meal is mixed, spoon it or roll it. Hands can be used to roll the dough. Let it cool down for 2 minutes. Place the cast iron skillet on the stove (or use a deep fryer) with oil halfway skillet. Heat skillet at 350 degrees until oil is glistening. Start dropping bread in the skillet. Let the first side brown then flip it over and cook the other side until brown and crispy. Drain on a paper towel and serve. Best eaten while warm.

Serving size: four people. Remember: If cooking for a large group, add to the recipe.

Seven-Up Cake
(Bernice Duffy Johnson)

Ingredients:

Cake
1 ½ c. butter or margarine
3 c. plain flour
3 c. sugar
¾ c. 7-Up
5 eggs
3 tb. lemon flavor
½ tsp. almond flavor

Directions:

Cream butter and sugar in a mixing bowl. Add eggs, one at a time, beating after each. Add flour to the creamed mixture alternately with 7-Up, beating after each addition. Stir in lemon and almond flavors and beat well. Pour mixture into a greased and lightly floured 10-inch tube or Bundt cake pan. Bake in a preheated 325-degree oven for 1 ½ hours or until a wooden toothpick inserted in the center comes out clean. Cool thoroughly on a wire rack.

Glaze
3 ½ c. powdered sugar.
1 tsp. vanilla
¼ tsp. almond flavor
3 tb. lemon juice
¼ c. cold 7-Up

Directions

Using an electric mixer, combine all ingredients and mix until smooth. Drizzle over cooled cake.

CHILI
(Bernice Duffy Johnson)

Ingredients:

2 lbs. lean ground beef
1 pkg. McCormick chili seasoning mix
1 medium size onion chopped
1 29-oz. can tomato sauce
2 stalks of celery chopped
1 12–16 oz. can diced tomatoes
½ green pepper, chopped
1 12–16 oz. can kidney beans
1 tsp. cumin
1 12–16 oz. can mild chili beans
2 tbsp. chili powder
4 oz. uncooked spaghetti (about 30 noodles)
2 tbsp. vegetable oil
1 ½ c. water

Directions:

Use ½ cup of water to rinse tomato sauce and bean cans and add that water to the chili mixture as directed. In a large saucepan, sauté onions, celery, and green peppers. Sprinkle it with the cumin and chili powder. Drain and remove from the pan. In the same saucepan, brown the ground beef until all pink is gone. Drain excess fat from the meat, then add the drained vegetable mixture to the meat. Add the McCormick Chili Seasoning mix, then stir in one cup of water. Cook for about 5 minutes until ingredients are blended. Add the tomato sauce, diced tomatoes, chili and kidney beans, and water from rinsing the bean cans. Bring to a boil. Lower the heat and simmer for 20–25 minutes. Break the spaghetti noodles into 2- to 3-inch pieces. After 10 minutes of simmering, add the broken noodles for the remaining cooking time. Remove from heat and let it rest for 5 minutes. Makes 12 healthy servings. Serve with crackers or cornbread and a salad.

FAVORITE BEEF LOAF
(Mary Duffy-Lewis)
Ingredients:

1 8-oz. can tomato sauce
dash dried thyme/dash dried marjoram, crushed
1 ½ lbs. ground beef
½ can 8 oz. Rotel peppers with green chilies (mild)
½ c. of medium cracker crumbs
½ c. finely chopped onions
2 beaten eggs
2 tbsp. chopped green pepper

Directions:

Add ½ can of the Rotel peppers to the tomato sauce. Save the other half for later. Then combine all ingredients and I teaspoon salt, mix well. Shape mixture into a loaf in a 12-inch by 7½-inch by 2-inch baking dish. Bake at 350 for about 1¼ hours. Makes 6 to 8 servings. Spread the remaining Rotel peppers over the baked loaf. Bake for 10 more minutes. Let the loaf rest about 10 minutes before serving. Makes 8 servings.

MARY'S HAWAIIAN CHICKEN RECIPE
(Mary Duffy-Lewis)

Ingredients:

> 6–8 strips of boneless chicken breast
> 16 oz. can of Dole pineapples in heavy syrup
> 1 large green bell pepper (can use red too for coloring)
> minced onion
> ½ c. granulated sugar
> ½ c. light brown sugar
> ¼ stick of butter or margarine
> 2 tb. cinnamon

Directions:

Season and brown chicken strips. Drain pineapples and pour syrup in a mixing bowl. Set pineapple chunks aside. Cut up bell peppers into chunks. Set aside with pineapple chunks. For the sauce, mix the pineapple syrup, sugar, butter and cinnamon and heat on low heat until the syrup thickens. Add the bell pepper, minced onion and continue heating and mixing until all are well blended. Add the chicken chunks and continue heating and mixing until all ingredients are well blended. Serve over a bed of rice of choice or noodles. Serves 6–8. The original recipe came from a can of Dole pineapples. A few ingredients have been changed to make it my own recipe.

Buttered Steamed Carrots

Ingredients:

2 c. baby carrots
1 c. water
2 tb. brown sugar
1 tb. honey
2 tb. butter
½ tsp. cinnamon

Directions:

Wash carrots and set aside. Bring the water, brown sugar, cinnamon, butter, and honey to a boil. Add the carrots and cook on medium heat for 30 minutes or until fork tender. Serves 4.

Steamed Cabbage

Ingredients:

½ head of cabbage
½ onion sliced
½ tsp. pepper
½ tsp. no salt seasoning dash nutmeg
cooking spray
2 tb. butter or margarine
½ c. water

Directions:

Wash ½ head of cabbage and cut into coarse pieces. Place cabbage and onions in a glass casserole dish sprayed with cooking oil. Sprinkle the cabbage and onions with pepper, nutmeg, and no salt seasoning. Add water, cover with lid or waxed paper, and place in a microwave and cook for 9 minutes. Stir after 6 minutes. Stir in butter or margarine. Cook for 3 minutes more. Serves 4–6.

ICED TEA

Ingredients:

> 4 family size Lipton teabag (or 10 reg. teabags)
> 1 qt. water
> juice of two large lemons
> 2 qt. water
> 2 c. sugar
> 1 lemon sliced

Directions:

Bring one quart of water to a boil in a medium size saucepan, then add the four teas bags. Simmer for 15 minutes then stir in the two cups of sugar gradually and carefully with a long handled wooden spoon. Add the lemon juice and continue to simmer for 5 more minutes. Pour the tea mixture into a gallon pitcher with 2 quarts of water. Stir it thoroughly. Finish filling the gallon pitcher up with ice cubes. Pour in tall glasses garnished with lemon slices. Makes about 10–16 servings.

Appendix B

• • ◦ • •

The Duffy-Stith Connection
A Growing Family Tree

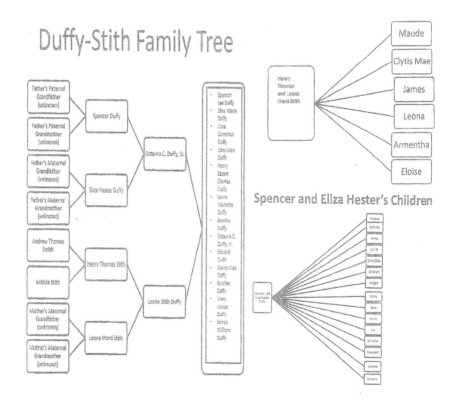

Duffy-Stith Family Tree

Father's Paternal Grandfather (unknown)
Father's Paternal Grandmother (unknown)
Father's Maternal Grandfather (unknown)
Father's Maternal Grandmother (unknown)
Andrew Thomas Smith
Mitilda Stith
Mother's Maternal Grandfather (unknown)
Mother's Maternal Grandmother (unknown)

Spencer Duffy
Eliza Hester Duffy
Henry Thomas Stith
Leona Ward Stith

Octawis C. Duffy, Sr.
Leona Stith Duffy

- Spencer Lee Duffy
- Eliza Marie Duffy
- Cora Cornelius Duffy
- Edna Mae Duffy
- Henry Ezzard Charles Duffy
- Leona Marretta Duffy
- Bernice Duffy
- Octawis C. Duffy, Jr.
- Edward Duffy
- Nancy Mae Duffy
- Everlee Duffy
- Mary Louise Duffy
- James William Duffy

Henry Thomas and Leona Ward Stith

Maude
Clytis Mae
James
Leona
Armentha
Eloise

Spencer and Eliza Hester's Children

Spencer and Eliza Hester Duffy

Pierceie
Tommie
James
Chris
Mary Ellen
Woldyn
Maggie
Bahia
Cora
Nancy
Lee
Ignatior
Hayward
Sherree
Octawis

240

Duffy-Stith Family Tree

Spencer and Eliza Duffy and Henry and Leona Stith

Octavris C. and Leona (Stith) Duffy
Grandchildren (Second Generation)

Name	Parent
1. Andre' Duffy	Spencer
2. Felecia Duffy	Spencer
3. Diane Callihan	Spencer
4. Brenda Blalock	Spencer
5. Ferro] Robins	Marie
6. Leonard Carter	Marie
7. Joseph Paul	Marie
8. Dwight Jones Bunzy	Marie
9. Stephanie McHenry	Cora
10. Robert (Duffy) Carter	Henry
11. Eric Duffy	Henry
12. Henry Duffy Jr	Henry
13. Leslie Duffy	Henry

14. Michael Harris	Leona
15. Sylvester Harris Ill (Pookey)	Leona
16. Fatima Ania Johnson	Bernice
17. Selena Efia Johnson	Bernice
18. Meshell Duffy	O.C. Jr.
19. Octavris (O.C.) Duffy Ill (BUG)	O.C. Jr.
20. Spencer Duffy (Little Spencer)	O.C. Jr.
21. Katrina Jackson	O.C. Jr.
22. Laquita Blount Stribbling	Nancy
23. Latina Michelle Davis	Edward
24. Edward Randolph Dennard Duffy (Randy)	Edward
25. Chardae' Larell Dennard Duffy	Edward
26. Adriaka Duffy (Tina)	James
27. Cora Jamelah Duffy (Little Cora)	James

Octavris C. and Leona (Stith) Duffy
Great-Grandchildren (Third Generation)

Name	Parent
1. Jeremiah (Jay) Duffy	Andre
2. Christian Duffy	Andre
3. Ariel Duffy	Andre
4. Israel O.C. Duffy	Andre
5. Desiree Duffy	Andre

6.	Andre Duffy Jr	Andre
7.	Michael Wheeler	Diane
8.	Sharon (Nichole) Wheeler Jenkins	Diane
9.	John Brooks Jr.	Brenda
10.	Kiona Perry	Brenda
11.	Charmane Blalock	Brenda
12.	Kingi Santiel	Ferroll
13.	Portia Carter Lewis	Leonard
14.	Shannon Carter	Leonard
15.	Jaela Paul	Joe
16.	Jordan Paul	Joe
17.	Byron Duffy	Henry Jr.
18.	Tina Duffy Carter	Robert
19.	Tyshun Duffy Carter	Robert
20.	Joshua Duffy Carter	Robert
21.	Daniel Duffy Carter	Robert
22.	Asia Duffy Carter	Robert
23.	Michael Duffy Carter	Robert
24.	Eric Duffy Jr.	Eric Duffy Sr.
25.	Eris Duffy	Eric Duffy Sr.
26.	Chazmin Harris	Michael
27.	Kyra Harris	Michael
28.	Lashay Harris	Michael
29.	Brandon Harris	Michael
30.	Maurice Harris	Michael
31.	Courtney Duffy	Meshell
32.	Adrian Duffy	Meshell
33.	Ashley Duffy	Meshell
34.	Tajora Duffy	Meshell
35.	Finis Stribling IV	Laquita

36.	Kylan Stribling	Laquita
37.	Tre' Jaden Stribling	Laquita
38.	Tashiera Mc Kissick	Tina
39.	Jakayla Williams	Tina
40.	Demetria Cherise Duffy (ReRe)	Tina
41.	Jayden Anthony Molina	Little Spencer
42.	Nicholas Octavris Duffy	Little Spencer
43.	Richard Terrell Edward Bowan	Chardae
44.	Carmelo Wayne Justice	Chardae
45.	Alissa Jones	Dwight
46.	Adrian Jones	Dwight
47.	Camille Jones	Dwight
48.	Corlissa Avery	Fatima
49.	Baby Lionel Lamont English	Selena
50.	Lishelle Amani English	Selena
51.	Promise Talia Henson	Cora (Mehla)

Octavris C. and Leona (Stith) Duffy
Great-Great-Grandchildren (Fourth Generation)

Name		Parent
1.	Jayden Duffy	Adrian
2.	Deonta (DJ) Lockhart Jr	Adrian
3.	AH' Jrea Duffy	Adrian
4.	Tristian Duffy	Tajora

5.	Greylon Duffy	Ashley
6.	Latia Michelle Davis	Latina
7.	Lorrin Marshai Rudawn Potter	Latina
8.	Logan Elijah Lewis	Porsha
9.	Layla Lewis	Porsha
10.	Nela Santiel	Kingi
11.	Jasmine Santiel	Kingi
12.	Jonah Santiel	Kingi
13.	Kori Saraye Arnett	Cherise
14.	Kailynn Dior Arnett	Cherise
15.	Alayah Robinson	Cherise

Octavris C. and Leona (Stith) Duffy
Nieces and Nephews (First-Degree Cousins)

Name		Parent
1.	Hazel Bledsoe	Dora
2.	Doris Bynum	Dora
3.	Helen William	Dora
4.	Elmira Coleman	Dora
5.	A. C. Robinson	Dora
6.	Hollis Robinson	Dora
7.	Lillie Mae (Duffy) Strickland	Ishmael Sr.
8.	Joseph Duffy (Died in Infancy)	Ishmael Sr.
9.	James Ellis Duffy	Ishmael Sr.
10.	Norita Mae (Duffy) Perryman	Ishmael Sr.

11. Ishmael Duffy Jr.	Ishmael Sr.
12. Charles Gardner	Clytis Mae
13. James (Jimmy) Stith	James
14. Erma Jean Malcolm	Eloise
15. Louise Triplett	Armentha
16. Celeste (Tyson) High	Elizabeth
17. Lucy (Tyson) Hunt	Elizabeth
18. LB Tyson	Elizabeth
19. Evelyn Tyson	Elizabeth
20. Eleanor Waller	Elizabeth
21. TW Tyson	Elizabeth
22. Nettie B. Tyson	Elizabeth
23. Queen Esther Tyson	Elizabeth
24. George Biggers	Elizabeth
25. Mamie Prunty	Elizabeth
26. Gloria Dean Duffy Bratton	Elmira

Octavris C. and Leona (Stith) Duffy
Great-Nieces and Nephews (Second-Degree Cousins)

Name	Parent
1. Kim Triplett	Louise
2. Robin (Triplett) Dawson	Louise
3. Taundelya (Tiny) Malcolm	Jean

4.	Vronnie (Ducky) Malcolm	Jean
5.	Steven (Stevie) Malcolm	Jean
6.	Brian Malcolm	Jean
7.	Pearl (Bledsoe) Phillips	Hazel
8.	Julia (Bledsoe) Goodman	Hazel
9.	Billy Bledsoe	Hazel
10.	Paul Bledsoe	Hazel
11.	Theodore Robinson (Teddy)	Helen
12.	Carl Strickland	Lillie Mae
13.	Homer Strickland	Lillie Mae
14.	Tad Strickland	Lillie Mae
15.	Direne Strickland	Lillie Mae
16.	Loretta Strickland	Lillie Mae
17.	James E. Duffy Jr	James E. Sr.
18.	Teresa Duffy	James E. Sr.
19.	Michael Duffy	James E. Sr.
20.	Ernest Eugene Duffy	Florita Mae
21.	Polinius Booker	Florita Mae
22.	Dorothy Tyson	Luther James
23.	James Tyson Jr.	Luther James
24.	Norma Jean Tyson	Luther James
25.	Bobby Tyson	Luther James
26.	George Tyson	Luther James
27.	Louis Prunty	Mamie
28.	Mathis Lee Prunty	Mamie
29.	L. C. Prunty	Mamie
30.	Nettie B. Prunty	Mamie
31.	Jimmy Prunty	Mamie
32.	Paulette Doreen Booker	Florita Mae
33.	Demetrius Booker	Florita Mae

34.	Clifton Anthony Catching Ill	Florita Mae
35.	Michelle Duffy	Ishmael Jr.
36.	Dorothy Jean Ferguson	Gloria
37.	Robert Thomas (Nick) Bratton	Gloria
38.	Teretha Roddy	Gloria
39.	Helen Roddy	Gloria
40.	Edna Earl Roddy Holden	Gloria
41.	Brenda Bratton	Gloria
42.	Palmer Robinson	Doris
43.	Loreli Bynum	Doris
44.	Hosea Bynum	Doris
45.	Tanya Bynum	Doris

Octavris C. and Leona (Stith) Duffy
Great-Great-Nieces and Nephews (Third-Degree Cousins)

Name		Parents
1.	Terri Ferguson	Dorothy Jean
2.	Sherrie Ferguson	Dorothy Jean
3.	Keith Smith	Dorothy Jean
4.	Johnny Hollis	
5.	Lonnie Hollis	
6.	Doris Ann Hollis	
7.	Marzetta Hollis	
8.	Diane Booker	Polinius
9.	Mack Booker	Polinius

10. Polina Booker   Polinius
11. Joshua Booker   Polinius
12. Scottie Woods   Julia
13. Keanon Woods   Julia
14. Kristen (Goodman) Thomas   Julia
15. Latasha (Barmore) Mellett   Pearl
16. Erica (Phillips) Jackson   Pearl
17. Danyelle Lakita Booker   Demetrius
18. Dana Paulette Booker   Demetrius
19. Dominique Florita Booker   Demetrius
20. Princess Catching   Clifton
21. Yahsha Catching   Clifton
22. Michelle Catching   Clifton
23. Tawana Catching   Clifton

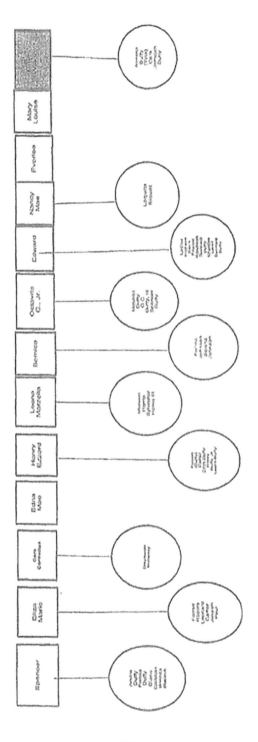

Appendix C

Photographs

Mary Duffy-Lewis, Mayor William Hudnut, and Bernice Duffy Johnson

Last home of the Duffy-Stith family, at 823 Main Street in Augusta, Arkansas. The house burned in 2020.

Cousins
Back Row: Paulette Booker, Doreen Booker, Dominque Booker, Friend, Demetrius Booker, Willow Booker, Dannielle Booker, Friend
Front Row: Isaac Booker and Florita Perryman

Appendix D

The Duffy-Stith Family Children and Where They Live Now

1. Mr. Spencer Lee Duffy, retired research scientist from EPA. Beltsville, Maryland.
2. Reverend Eliza Marie Duffy Bunzy, associate minister MCMBC, LA. Gardena, California.
3. Dr. Cora Cornelius Duffy McHenry, retired president of Shorter College, North Little Rock, Arkansas, and retired president of the Arkansas Education Association. Little Rock, Arkansas.
4. Mrs. Edna Mae Duffy Murphy, director Duffylit Dance Studio, Cleveland, Ohio. Shaker Heights, Ohio.
5. Mr. Henry Ezzard Charles Duffy, painter, carpenter, deceased.
6. Ms. Leona Marzetta Duffy, retired banker and store stock supervisor, Smart Final, LA. Gardena, California.
7. Dr. Bernice Duffy Johnson, retired interim provost and vice chancellor for Academic Affairs, North Carolina Central University. Durham, North Carolina.
8. Mr. Octavris C. Duffy Jr., professor of construction and management and director of the Industrial Technology Center, University of Arkansas at Pine Bluff, Owner and CEO of Tri-State International Building Systems, and director of Duffy's Event Center. Little Rock, Arkansas.
9. Dr. Edward Duffy, retired professor of Psychology, Miami Dade University. Miami, Florida.
10. Mrs. Nancy Mae Duffy Blount, retired Uniserv director for the Arkansas Education Association and former state representative for District 52 in Arkansas. Forrest City, Arkansas.
11. Miss Everlee Duffy, deceased.
12. Mrs. Mary Louise Duffy-Lewis, retired division manager, Division of Family Resources, and retired AFLAC and United Healthcare insurance agent. Indianapolis, Indiana.
13. Mr. James William Duffy, retired senior environmental health specialist, Arkansas Department of Health. Little Rock, Arkansas.

About the Author

Bernice, the seventh and middle child of the Duffy-Stith siblings, was born at the end of WWII. She is a retired professor and interim provost from North Carolina Central University (NCCU) in Durham, North Carolina. While at NCCU, Bernice, along with three colleagues, published a textbook for freshmen: *Dimensions of Learning: Education for Life.*

As the middle child, she was in a unique position to learn from her older siblings and then use that knowledge and disciplined reading to guide and teach her younger siblings. Bernice was the only daughter to be married in the hometown of Augusta, Arkansas; and in 1985, she became the first of the siblings to receive the coveted PhD degree.

This book was inspired by a need to record and document the history and stories of a family that rose from poverty to professional positions and global investments amid formidable odds.

CPSIA information can be obtained
at www.ICGtesting.com
Printed in the USA
LVHW031141081122
732650LV00003B/289